Financial Crisis Containment and Government Guarantees

Edited by

John Raymond LaBrosse

Patterson & LaBrosse Financial Consultants Ltd, Canada and Honorary Visiting Fellow, School of Law, University of Warwick, UK

Rodrigo Olivares-Caminal

Centre for Commercial Law Studies, Queen Mary, University of London, UK

Dalvinder Singh

School of Law, University of Warwick, UK

Edward Elgar

Cheltenham, UK • Northampton, MA, USA

Published by
Edward Elgar Publishing Limited
The Lypiatts
15 Lansdown Road
Cheltenham
Glos GL50 2JA
UK

Edward Elgar Publishing, Inc.
William Pratt House
9 Dewey Court
Northampton
Massachusetts 01060
USA

A catalogue record for this book
is available from the British Library

Library of Congress Control Number: 2012947335

This book is available electronically in the ElgarOnline.com
Law Subject Collection, E-ISBN 978 1 78100 500 2

ISBN 978 1 78100 499 9

Typeset by Servis Filmsetting Ltd, Stockport, Cheshire
Printed by MPG PRINTGROUP, UK

Contents

PART III USING GOVERNMENT GUARANTEES

PART IV SOVEREIGN DEBT ISSUES

Contributors

EDITORS

John Raymond LaBrosse, BA (Economics/Sociology), MA (Economics) both from the University of Calgary (Canada). He is Honorary Visiting Fellow School of Law, University of Warwick, Member of the International Advisory Committee, Centre for Commercial Law and Financial Regulation, University of Reading Law School, Partner, Patterson & LaBrosse Financial Consultants Ltd and a recognized expert on deposit insurance issues. Prior to his appointment as the founding Secretary General of the International Association of Deposit Insurers (IADI) he was Director, International Affairs, Canada Deposit Insurance Corporation and at the same time he was the Executive Director of the Financial Stability Forum's Study and Working Groups on Deposit Insurance which finalized its report in September 2001. He led the reform for two major revisions of the Canadian Bank Act and several other pieces of financial sector legislation (Trust Companies Act, Canadian Payments Association Act, Winding Up Act, Canada Deposit Insurance Corporation Act, Office of the Superintendent of Financial Institutions Act) and has provided policy advice on the design of deposit insurance systems for a number of countries including Malaysia, Hong Kong (SAR), South Africa, Ukraine, Mexico, the Western Balkans, several countries in central Asia, China and the United Kingdom. He is a member of the Editorial Board of the Journal of Banking Regulation and a member of the Advisory Panel of IADI.

Rodrigo Olivares-Caminal, LLB (Bue), LLM (Warwick) and PhD (London). He is a Reader in Banking and Finance Law at the Centre for Commercial Law Studies (CCLS), Queen Mary, University of London. Prior to joining CCLS he was a Senior Lecturer in Financial Law and the Academic Director at the Centre for Financial & Management Studies (SOAS), University of London and has taught undergraduate and postgraduate courses in various Schools of Law and Business in the United Kingdom, Spain, Greece and Argentina as well as delivered professional training courses in Africa, Asia and Europe. Dr Olivares-Caminal acted as a Sovereign Debt Expert for the United Nations Conference on Trade and Development and has consulted with several international institutions in Washington, Europe as well as on several international transactions with Law Firms. He specializes in international finance and insolvency law, is the author/editor of several books, has published extensively in peer-reviewed journals and sits on the editorial/advisory board of several law journals.

Dalvinder Singh, is a Professor of Law at the University of Warwick. He is a Senior Associate Research Fellow, Institute of Advanced Legal Studies, University of London (since 2003); Managing Editor of the Journal of Banking Regulation (Palgrave Macmillan) and Financial Regulation, International (Informa Law); Editorial Advisory Board Member, Journal of Financial Regulation and Compliance (Emerald). He is an External Examiner at the Centre for Commercial Law Studies, Queen Mary, University of London and the Universities of Liverpool and Reading. He is a member of the Advisory Panel of IADI.

CONTRIBUTORS

Lee C. Buchheit, Cleary Gottlieb Steen & Hamilton

Giovanni Calice, University of Southhampton

Jing Chen, Swansea University

Christine M. Cumming, Federal Reserve Bank of New York

Charles Enoch, International Monetary Fund

Arturo Estrella, Rensselaer Polytechnic Institute

Michael Faure, Maastricht University

Gillian G. Garcia, Gillian G.H. Garcia Associates

Charles A.E. Goodhart, Financial Market Group, London School of Economics

Giusèppe Grande, Banca d'Italia

Mitu Gulati, Duke University

Már Guðmundsson, Central Bank of Iceland

Klaus Heine, University of Rotterdam

Eva Hüpkes, Financial Stability Board

John Raymond LaBrosse, Patterson & LaBrosse Financial Consultants Ltd

Rosa M. Lastra, Queen Mary, University of London

Aviram Levy, Banca d'Italia

Jeffrey Manns, George Washington University

David G. Mayes, University of Auckland

James F. McCollum, James F. McCollum and Associates

Maria J. Nieto, Banco de España

Joseph J. Norton, Southern Methodist University

Rodrigo Olivares-Caminal, Queen Mary, University of London

Fabio Panetta, Banca d'Italia

Christopher Pleister, Federal Agency for Financial Market Stability (Germany)

Sebastian Schich, Organization for Economic Cooperation and Development

Dalvinder Singh, University of Warwick

Julian Williams, University of Aberdeen

Arthur E. Wilmarth, Jr., George Washington University Law School

Andrea Zaghini, Banca d'Italia

Foreword

Joseph J. Norton

Do we really need another volume on the current and ongoing global financial crisis (GFC)? As I sit in my home study facing a clutter of GFC-related books, reports, articles, conference materials, and enacted and proposed legislation and rules, my visceral reaction is 'enough is enough'. Yes, it is important to decipher the various 'causes', to sort through the sundry public and private failures, to learn appropriate lessons and to ponder new, appropriate laws, regulations, standards and practices; but, much of this has already been done over the past three years. As aptly pointed out by Professor Lastra, much of the GFC literature and actions are about fighting the last war.

On a personal level, I have developed a large lump of cynicism in my craw as I re-read *Reinhart and Rogoff* (2009) to understand more fully that the GFC, in many (but not all) ways, is really not that different in historical perspective from prior financial crises and that 'all the red lights were blinking in the run-up to the crisis'. Indeed, 'the real problem is that the global economy is badly overleveraged', and that we are probably in for a decade of 'painful deleveraging and slow growth'.

Also, when I reflect upon the value/non-value of my over three decades of comparative study of domestic, regional and international financial law and policy initiatives, I am left with a 'What's it all about, Alfie?' moment. Over the past several decades and on the domestic, regional and international levels, much thought, energy and international collaboration have been generated by well-meaning policy-makers, governmental and intergovernmental bodies, the legal and accounting professions and the Academy in terms of developing and fostering appropriate risk-based and law-based frameworks respecting putting in place and sustaining viable and stable financial sector infrastructures around the world. Yet, we still did not foresee the GFC – the 'Second Great Contraction'.

Further and presently, particularly with the current, polarized political environment in the US Congress and contracting federal budgetary constraints, I have come to harbour increasing doubts whether the 848-page Dodd-Frank Act (with the approximately 400 enacted or contemplated related regulations, 67 studies and 22 periodic reports) and the 298-page proposed 'Volcker Rule' will 'connect all the dots' in any meaningful, enforceable way, particularly as to (i) the resolution of the 'too-big-to-fail' (TBTF) dilemma (which supposedly, in the US, was set to rest in rigorous 1991 federal legislation, which legislation also had provided for a comprehensive 'prompt corrective action' framework) and, as to (ii) the establishment of an effective Financial Stability Oversight Council to oversee excessive macroeconomic risks to the US financial system (that is, a macro-prudential regulator, although its 1988 predecessor, the President's Working Group on Financial Markets, had proved itself wholly ineffective).

Moreover, as I read in the press today (30 May 2012) more about Mr Dimon (supposedly 'the best US banker', a trusted adviser to and Board member of the New York Fed, and the Chairman and CEO of the 'best managed' and recently 'stress-tested' major US bank, JPMorgan Chase (effectively a 'systemically important financial institution' (SIFI), with over 400 bank supervisors embedded throughout this bank on a regular basis) and the unspotted USD2–4 billion loss on derivatives activities out of Chase's Chief Investment Office in London; as I muse again over the incredibly cavalier and uninformed 2010 testimony of former US Treasury Secretary Robert Rubin (whom President Clinton estimated to be the best Treasury Secretary since Alexander Hamilton), former Chairman of Goldman Sachs, and (at 2009), a senior-counsellor to and Board member of Citigroup; and, as I flip through Jon Corzine's (former Chairman of Goldman Sachs, US Senator and New Jersey Governor) clueless 2011 Congressional testimony concerning the financial collapse and bankruptcy of MF Capital, a major global financial derivatives broker he founded and managed and a primary dealer of US Treasuries, my confidence level bottoms-out as to senior financial institutions executives' and to the financial institution regulators' ability to manage risks and otherwise to instil and to maintain prudent governance within complex financial institutions (SIFIs) bottoms-out.

Add to this the high-risk tentacles being generated internally and externally by the current Eurozone crisis (including even possible impact on the November 2012 US presidential elections), and one could easily foresee a bleak global landscape over the next decade (we are already 3–4 years into the GFC). This landscape most probably will portray future domestic, regional and global financial stress and crises, and an absence of the required individual and collective country political-will to redress the fundamental economic disequilibria built up since the 1970s and underpinning our current domestic, regional and global financial systems and economies.

Yet, when I step back and take a deep breath, I see that John Raymond LaBrosse, Rodrigo Olivares-Caminal and Dalvinder Singh, in fact, have assembled another special collection of fresh and thought-provoking insights by leading governmental, intergovernmental, practising and academic experts. This 2013 volume (*Financial Crisis Containment and Government Guarantees*), emanating from a special fall 2011 symposium at the OECD celebrating its 50th anniversary, is most impressive in itself; but, it is even more so when considered in light of their 2009 volume on *Financial Crisis Management and Bank Resolution* and 2011 volume (nearly 30 excellent chapters) on *Managing Risk in the Financial System*.

These three co-editors/contributors represent the very best of the current trend toward considering financial sector reform and crises in a forward-looking context and on an interdisciplinary basis and involving the very best academic, governmental, intergovernmental, financial industry and practitioner minds in the ongoing discussion and debate of the basic and ever-moving question, 'Quo vadis?', as to efforts to assure global financial system stability. These editors and the other stellar contributors are helping to set the policy stage for this coming decade by raising the right questions and by putting forward a provocative range of possible solutions/policy approaches/challenges. I am so impressed with the editors'/contributors' ability to bring together under one roof for an open and candid discussion the following experts: Lee Buchheit (Cleary Gottlieb); Christine Cumming (First Vice President, Federal Reserve Bank of New York); Charles Enoch (International Monetary Fund); Gillian Garcia (Gillian G.H. Garcia Associates); Charles A.E. Goodhart (Financial Market Group, London School of Economics); Már Guðmundsson (Governor, Central Bank of Iceland); Mitu Gulati (Duke University); Eva Hüpkes (Financial Stability Board); Rosa M. Lastra (Queen Mary, University of London); David G. Mayes (University of Auckland), Maria Nieto (Bank of Spain); Fabio Panetta (Banca d'Italia); and Christopher Pleister (German Federal Agency for Financial Market Stability), among others!

Indeed, the GFC has spun-off a high level of pessimism as 'to getting things right this time around'. Real degrees of culpability can be attributed to an incredible array of banking and non-bank financial institutions (and their management), of financial sector regulators/supervisors, and of economic policy-makers (at the domestic, regional and international levels). However, the driving and shifting goal of pursuing global financial stability encompassing 'safe and sound' financial institutions and (at the same time) robust and innovative financial markets is too important a *public good* to give up on.

Financial system stability as a *public good* – in fact, as a *global public good* – has been bandied about in governmental/intergovernmental and academic circles for some time – well before the unfolding of the GFC in 2007–8. In fact, one could well-argue that bank regulators and central banks, while historically placing their primary focus on institutional 'safety and soundness' have long been concerned with systemic stability. For example, the development of the G10, the Basel Committee, IOSCO, IAIS, the Joint Forum, the CPSS, the CGFS, IADI, IASB, the numerous EU/EC financial 'legislation', the Eurozone, IMF enhanced surveillance and efforts to devise Early Warning Systems, the IMF Article IV consultations and ROSC programme, and the IMF-WB FSAP initiative can be seen as being a part of this policy concern. The formation of the Financial Stability Forum in 1999 (now since the GFC, renamed and revamped as the Financial Stability Board) and the G7/8 Finance Ministers since 1994 and also the G20 Finance Ministers since 1999 have focused on directing and coordinating financial stability efforts, albeit (pre-GFC) primarily with emerging and transitioning economies in mind. Yet, all these efforts to create a 'New International Financial Architecture' really did not appreciate the full complexities of, the full set of risks inherent in, and the market interconnections within the so-called global financial system.

Since its creation in the fall of 2008, the G20 (Leaders) has taken upon itself the primary direction of global governmental/intergovernmental strategy on determining, revising, and overseeing the implementation of a comprehensive global 'Work Plan' related to global financial stability. Pursuant to this Plan, the recent work of the FSB and its member institutions (including the OECD, IMF, World Bank, and major domestic bank regulators, finance ministries and central banks) indeed has been most constructive and impressive.

In addition, a key long-term task of the G20 (Leaders) is the establishment over time of a global 'Framework for Strong, Sustainable and Balanced Growth': this Framework is intended to begin to address the fundamental global macroeconomic disequilibria plaguing the global economy since the 1970s. Most recently, as to the US, President Obama has signed an Executive Order directing the relevant bodies with the Executive Branch vigorously to pursue international collaborative efforts respecting implementation of this Framework.

I will be keeping this third volume by the 'dynamic trio' of LaBrosse, Olivares-Caminal and Singh, along with their first two volumes, in the centre of my worktable as I continue to struggle to give a coherent context to the GFC vis-à-vis the US financial system and the related maze of new US laws, regulations and practices. Ray, Rodrigo, and Dal, thank you so very much for 'keeping the faith' and for all you are doing; and, I very much look forward, in due time, to your fourth volume concerning further issues relating to global financial stability.

Foreword

Arthur E. Wilmarth, Jr.

In September 2010, US Federal Reserve Board Chairman Ben Bernanke declared that '[i]f the [financial] crisis has a single lesson, it is that the 'too-big-to-fail' (TBTF) problem must be solved'.[1] Notwithstanding the enactment of reform legislation on both sides of the Atlantic during the past two years, many policy-makers and analysts believe that TBTF banks still pose a major threat to financial stability and fiscal policy. On 9 May 2012, former US Federal Reserve Board Chairman Paul Volcker affirmed that '[t]he greatest structural challenge facing the financial system is how to deal with the wide-spread impression – many would say conviction – that important institutions are deemed "too large or too interconnected" to fail'.[2] The very next day, JPMorgan Chase disclosed a multibillion US dollar loss from a massive 'hedging' strategy that badly misfired. In response to that disclosure, journalist Gillian Tett warned that 'the swelling size of [banking] groups such as JPMorgan is making the [financial] system ever more concentrated, in a dangerous way'.[3]

At the same time, the spreading sovereign debt crisis in Europe revealed the close linkages between government bailouts of banks and fiscal insol-

[1] B.S. Bernanke, 'Causes of the Recent Financial and Economic Crisis: Statement before the Financial Crisis Inquiry Commission' (2 September 2010), available at http://www.federalreserve.gov/newsevents/testimony/bernanke20100902a.htm (last accessed 1 October 2012).

[2] Statement of P.A. Volcker before the Subcommittee on Financial Institutions and Consumer Protection of the Committee on Banking, Housing, and Urban Affairs, United States Senate (9 May 2012), available at http://banking.senate.gov/public/index.cfm?FuseAction=Hearings.Testimony&Hearing_ID=082d377a-5fd9-4e98-892b-26d80120d684&Witness_ID=f4bb09ce-b788-4746-9506-d030eadc62b8 (last accessed 1 October 2012).

[3] G. Tett, 'Size can be deadly in a low-rate world', *FT.com*, 17 May 2012; see also C. Hopkins and C. Sala Gage, 'JPMorgan So-Called Hedge Is Awkward for Fed Knowing Its Meaning', *Bloomberg.com*, 3 June 2012 (questioning whether JPMorgan's strategy, which the bank described as 'portfolio hedging', actually amounted to 'proprietary trading' that Congress intended to prohibit under the Volcker Rule).

vency. On 11 June 2012, EU governments announced that they would lend up to USD125 billion to enable Spain to support its deeply troubled banks.[4] The EU's rescue package for Spain followed similar bailouts totalling more than USD500 billion for Greece, Ireland and Portugal, which the EU and the International Monetary Fund organized after all three nations were overwhelmed by the costs of shoring up their banking systems. At the end of 2011, sovereign debt in the 17 euro-area nations exceeded 87 per cent of gross domestic product, the highest level recorded since the euro was introduced in 1999.[5] The Eurozone's sovereign debt situation has steadily deteriorated since 2008, because most euro-area governments have assumed heavy debt burdens in order to prop up TBTF banks, stabilize their financial systems and cushion the impact of severe economic recessions.[6] As I write this Foreword, the euro's survival is in grave doubt.[7]

This volume includes papers presented at the Banking Law Symposium organized by John Raymond LaBrosse, Rodrigo Olivares-Caminal and Dalvinder Singh and hosted by the Organization for Economic Cooperation and Development (OECD) in October 2011. The organizers of the conference (who also edited this volume) deserve high praise for their prescience in focusing on the issues of (a) containing systemic financial crises, (b) limiting moral hazard and other economic distortions created by government support for financial institutions, and (c) resolving Europe's sovereign debt problems. All three issues dominate today's headlines and preoccupy policy-makers, industry officials and scholars. The conference organizers and editors should also be congratulated for assembling a distinguished group of experts from government, industry and the academy to address these issues. I hope this book will attract a wide readership, because its important research findings and sound policy advice could help us to avoid a recurrence of the global crisis we currently struggle to escape.

---

[4] C. Penty, 'Spain's Bailout Gives Rajoy His Best Chance to Fix Banks', *Bloomberg.com*, 12 June 2012; see also C. Penty, 'Goirigolzarri's Aid Demand Helped Push Spain to Bailout', *Bloomberg.com*, 12 June 2012 (reporting that the EU's support programme was triggered by Spain's admission that it would need USD24 billion to recapitalize Bankia, the nation's third-largest lender).

[5] A. Davis, 'Euro-Region Debt Rises to Highest in Currency's History', *Bloomberg.com*, 23 April 2012.

[6] A. Mody and D. Sandri, 'The Eurozone Crisis; How Banks and Sovereigns Came to be Joined at the Hip', *Economic Policy*, April 2012, at 201–30.

[7] See, for example, P. Boone and S. Johnson, 'The End of the Euro: A Survivor's Guide', *The Baseline Scenario* (blog), 28 May 2012.

Preface

John Raymond LaBrosse, James F. McCollum, Rodrigo Olivares-Caminal and Dalvinder Singh

'Collaboration between financial authorities has never been so testing and yet never has collaboration been so important. We face key coordination challenges in the area of financial regulation, particularly with respect to the consistency of the calculations of risk-weighted assets, the treatment of sovereign exposures, and liquidity standards. Yet, the institutional settings for collaboration are actually improving. Given sufficient commitment from the authorities, these new settings and processes will pave the way for enhanced cooperation'.[1]

I. THE GRAND SLUMP AND SETTING THE SCENE FOR RESTORING PUBLIC CONFIDENCE

At the time that the 2011 Banking Law Symposium[2] took place over 20 books and numerous professional journal articles had been written on the Global Financial Crisis (GFC). Interest in the crisis and its aftermath, including policy responses and corrective measures, continues unabated and the Symposium was one reflection of this. So too is this book and we are pleased to include several of the Symposium's papers in it. The principal objective of this book is to examine the response to the crisis, with particular reference to the extensive use that has been made of government guarantees in private financial markets and the impact that those guarantees have had on sovereign debt.

During the editing process for the book we took the opportunity to look back at what analysts had to say about 2011 before the year began and the policies they felt were needed to restore confidence in governments,

[1] Speech by J. Caruana, General Manager, Bank for International Settlements, at the seminar on 'Long-term growth: organizing the stability and attractiveness of European financial markets', Berlin, 20 January 2012, available at http://www.bis.org/speeches/sp120124.htm (last accessed 1 October 2012).

[2] For a summary of the proceedings please see J.F. McCollum, *Financial Regulation International*, Issue 14.8, pp.4–7, October 2011.

banking systems and, of course, policy-makers and their advisors. At the end of 2010, publications such as *The Economist* were predicting 2011 to be 'a tale of two economies: a rich world struggling with a weak and jobless recovery, and an emerging world growing four times as fast'.[3] One year later, in its outlook for 2012, *The Economist* suggested that national leaders would be pre-occupied with domestic issues and that we should not expect very much out of global gatherings.[4] Leaders will clearly need a new mantra for prospective global gatherings, as there appears to be diminishing interest in committing to necessary initiatives in a co-ordinated way.

It can be suggested that finance 'will be more stable and thus more boring'. In the early days of 2012 and with a focus on the UK, the *Financial Times* released a survey of 83 economists that suggested that '[t]he coming year will rival 2009 for economic weakness as output is hit by the continuing debt crisis in the euro-zone . . .'.[5] It is noteworthy that the survey included '11 former members of the Bank of England's Monetary Policy Committee' and that 'three times more respondents thought the economic outlook would deteriorate rather than would improve in 2012'.[6]

While it is the mission of news organisations to sell their publications, they have no obligation to report on why things did not turn out the way they initially thought; the after-the-fact analysis task is often left to the academy. Accordingly, it is customary for books of this kind to analyse financial issues *ex post* and dissect decisions that were taken by policy-makers. This is a major challenge because so many uncontrollable factors can come into play and materially affect outcomes. Policy-makers concerned with the financial sector often focus on whether there was enough regulation or whether the regulation was of the right kind. In examining a financial crisis questions could be: have laws been adequately designed to smooth the exit of failing banks or to account for situations where sovereigns may not be able to repay bondholders and/or make good on programme entitlements. Answers can be inconsistent, confusing or even biased, as they may reflect less of reality and more of the views of the respondent.

Was the GFC and subsequent recession a result of too much regulation of financial institutions and markets, or not enough? It is still too early to know, but one area that is often overlooked is the impact of demographics on governments and financial markets. While this book focuses on

---

[3] Franklin, D, (ed.), *The Economist*, 'The World in 2011', p. 13.

[4] Franklin, D, (ed.), *The Economist*, 'The World in 2012', p. 15.

[5] C. Giles and S. O'Connor, 'Economists See Bleak Year Ahead', *Financial Times*, (2 January 2012).

[6] *Financial Times*, 3 January 2012.

banking-law type issues, perhaps if we understood more about the impact that demographics can have on financial markets and institutions, we might better understand how to cope with or preferably avoid crises that seem to be recurring all too regularly.[7]

The sub-prime mortgage debacle that emerged in the US is often pointed to as the genesis of the GFC. Why were the accumulating risks to the financial system not recognised and preventive actions not taken? American families were (and still are) encouraged to borrow through tax-deductible mortgage interest. Bets on housing market price appreciation, due partly to demographics, for many years had turned out to be a sure thing. Many Americans acquired more properties than they needed, with a view to flipping houses for a profit. This all worked well until the proverbial music stopped and the chairs were taken away.[8] The glut of houses caused severe price declines and, as underwriting standards had been diluted (or even ignored), builders, homeowners and investors were stuck with huge inventories.

In looking back we could ask: Where were the regulators? Clearly there were some regulatory failures. Another question that could be asked is: Where were the boards of directors since they are 'ultimately responsible for the oversight of management and overall risk governance of financial institutions'?[9] In response we could say that actions or inactions of boards have raised some important governance issues. Clearly, those two critical questions have not been fully addressed and this may explain part of the reason why *Time* magazine determined that the Person of the Year for 2011 was 'The Protestor'. This book does not focus on the Occupy Wall Street Movement and other scenes of protests surrounding the avarice and short-sightedness of certain financial market participants. We do, however, consider several issues surrounding the global financial crisis and many worthwhile suggestions are put forward.

---

7 For a comprehensive look at the history of financial crises, please see C.M. Reinhart and K.S. Rogoff, *This Time Is Different: Eight Centuries of Financial Folly* (Princeton University Press, Princeton, NJ 2009).

8 In an interview with the *Financial Times* one month before the crisis began C. Prince, then Chief Executive Officer of Citigroup, was quoted as saying: 'So long as the music is playing, you've got to get up and dance. We're still dancing'. See *Financial Times* (10 July 2007).

9 Speech by J. Dickson, Superintendent of Financial Institutions (Canada) to the Toronto Board of Trade (4 April 2012).

II. WHAT'S IN THIS BOOK

The book is divided into four parts. We begin with a focus on ways to contain a financial crisis drawing on some lessons learned. Attention then turns to the special problems facing Europe and measures that are being devised and continuously revised to convince financial markets that a corner has been turned. Several scholars consider the role of government guarantees in Part III and in the final section we turn to the sovereign debt problem.

Part I: Containing a Financial Crisis

The primary objectives in containing a financial crisis are first, simply to stop it, and second, to minimize adverse impacts on the real economy.[10] However, pulling out all the stops to contain a crisis can have serious long-term consequences for the ability of a central government to raise finance in the future at rates and levels approaching those prior to the crisis.[11] The GFC has led to considerable costs, which are well documented.[12] Panetta et al. note that:

> The overall amount of resources committed to the various packages by the 11 countries examined totalled around EUR5 trillion or 18.8 per cent of GDP; the outlays have been EUR2 trillion or 7.6 per cent of GDP. The size of the interventions varies greatly across countries: it is higher in countries such as the UK and the Netherlands (where outlays have reached 44.1 per cent and 16.6 per cent of GDP, respectively) where the banking system is large relative to the real economy and is dominated by large institutions that have been severely hit by the crisis.[13]

---

[10] Please see A. Gelpern 'Financial Crisis Containment', (2009) 41 Connecticut Law Review; D.G. Mayes 'Did Recent Experience of a Financial Crisis Help in Coping with the Current Financial Turmoil? The Case of the Nordic Countries', (2009) 47 Journal of Common Market Studies; D.G. Mayes, (2009) 'Resolution Methods For Cross-Border Banks in the Present Crisis' in J.R. LaBrosse, R. Olivares-Caminal and D. Singh (eds) *Financial Crisis Management and Bank Resolution* (Informa, London 2009).

[11] A. Sighvatsson and G. Gunnarsson, 'Iceland's Financial Disaster and its Fiscal Impact', in J.R. LaBrosse, R. Olivares-Caminal and D. Singh, *Managing Risk in the Financial System* (Edward Elgar, Cheltenham, UK and Northampton, MA, USA 2011).

[12] To illustrate, from 2007 to 2011, 430 FDIC-member (insured) institutions failed or received some form of assistance. The FDIC took a number of actions to deal with the losses and stabilize the Deposit Insurance Fund; the measures included increasing assessment rates, imposing a special assessment on member-banks and offering a facility for banks to prepay assessments. For more details on the measures please see www.fdic.gov.

[13] F.T. Panetta, G. Grande, C. Ho, M. King, A. Levy, F.M. Signoretti,

The initial steps are to stabilise market confidence in individual banks and other major financial institutions, thereby reducing the risk of a bank run and to ensure that there is sufficient liquidity in the system. The attempts of depositors to place their money in what are perceived to be healthier banks during a crisis are not a material concern for the authorities if there is a well-publicized and effective deposit protection system. If such a system does not exist then there is a possibility of capital flight and contagion. The attempts to manage the recent crisis included a combination of private as well as public measures to restore confidence in institutions. Examples include moves to recapitalise banks by rights issues, and when this failed recapitalisation by governments. These strategies have been used in efforts to restore liquidity and stave off the insolvency of banks and enable them to continue lending and, in time, return to profitability.

To be sure, government guarantees delivered through the protection of deposits in banks have become an important feature of modern finance. Deposit insurance systems, however, have only a limited role in a systemic crisis, as they are generally designed to deal with small- or medium-sized bank closures, and thereby prevent contagion. What was evident from the GFC was that a poorly designed guarantee system with minimal public information can exacerbate a bank failure and result in a crisis with political implications. Northern Rock in the UK is a case in point.

Is it possible to manage a crisis without government guarantees? That issue is considered in depth by Christine Cumming in her examination of the crisis from the perspective of a senior US policy advisor. She places heavy emphasis on early intervention in resolving banks before technical insolvency. In that regard she underscores that early intervention is essential for resolution if recovery efforts fail. Additionally, the private sector should be readied to play a role. One measure that has been used to accomplish and facilitate action is stress testing of bank balance sheets and, if adjustments are called for but action is not forthcoming, further intervention may be called for.

Is there a handy guidebook to help policy-makers manage a crisis? That question is addressed by John Raymond LaBrosse and Dalvinder Singh as they consider some recent experience and effective practices with a particular focus on Europe. They do so by setting out the main structure of a financial safety net (FSN) and how the mandates, roles and responsibilities of the agencies within it tend to change during the course of a

---

M. Taboga and A. Zaghini, 'An assessment of financial sector rescue programmes', BIS Paper No 48 (2009).

crisis. Recent practices offer many examples of the need for more clarity and coordination in the management of a crisis. As an aid a decision tree is offered and explained as an alternative to a series of *ad hoc* pronouncements that can confuse market participants and undermine the public's confidence in the authorities' effectiveness.

Which member of an FSN should take the lead in tackling a financial crisis or should it be a new agency? Charles A.E. Goodhart notes in Chapter 3 that macro-prudential institutions are springing up, like field mushrooms after a September rain, in a wide range of countries: the Financial Policy Committee in the UK, the Financial Stability Oversight Committee in the US, and the European Systemic Risk Board are but a few examples. Indeed, Professor Goodhart and J-C. Rochet have been separately involved in proposing the adoption of a similar macro-prudential authority in Sweden.[14] If the new macro-prudential authority is to have some bite and ability to provide systemic financial stability, it needs to be given the requisite powers to do so and Goodhart discusses what these powers might be.

Is there a policy framework for resolving systemically important financial institutions? The G20 Leaders asked the Financial Stability Board (FSB) to develop recommendations designed to reduce: moral hazard risks, the potential for contagion and disruptions associated with troubled systemically important financial institutions (SIFIs). Eva Hüpkes notes in Chapter 4 that SIFIs are financial institutions whose distress or disorderly failure, because of their size, complexity and interconnectedness, could cause significant disruptions to the wider financial system and economic activity. Dr Hüpkes explains that to assist policy-makers the FSB has developed a framework that consists of:

- a requirement that SIFIs and initially in particular global SIFIs (G-SIFIs) have additional loss absorption capacity beyond the Basel III standards to reflect the greater risks that these institutions pose to the global financial system;
- improvements to resolution regimes to enable national authorities to resolve financial institutions, whatever their size, without disruptions to the financial system and without taxpayer support;
- more intensive and effective supervision through strengthened supervisory capacity and resources, and raised supervisory expectations

---

14 C.A.E. Goodhart and J-C. Rochet, 'Evaluation of the Riksbank's monetary policy and work with financial stability 2005–2010', Reports from the Riksdag 2010/11:RFR5, The Committee on Finance, Sveriges Riksdag (2011).

for risk management functions, risk data aggregation capabilities, risk governance and internal controls;

- stronger robustness standards for core financial market infrastructures, including central counterparties, central securities depositories and trade repositories; and
- rigorous implementation, monitoring and reviews by an FSB Peer Review Council to evaluate consistency in the implementation of G-SIFI specific requirements.

Part II: The Special Problems of Europe

The second Part of the book focuses on, as its name indicates, the special problems of Europe. The topic, in its entirety, goes beyond the scope of our work, but to make it tractable attention is centred on the banking sector. However, the importance and magnitude of the evolving sovereign debt crisis, which undoubtedly has had an impact on the banking sector and is, for the time being, currently confined to Europe, also receives attention.

We begin with a concise overview of crisis management and the use of government guarantees in Europe with an analysis prepared by Charles Enoch. He starts by outlining the general features of guarantees, why they are attractive, and how they can have both positive and negative effects. He goes on to look at the role of guarantees in the banking sector, in particular for deposits, both in crisis and in more normal times. Enoch then turns to the emerging European deposit guarantee framework in the context of the single European market. To highlight the role of deposit insurance and its use in response to the crisis, a few examples are examined in terms of what can be learnt about deposit guarantees. It is argued that guarantees were extended beyond depositor protection and that they underwent changes during and after the crisis. It is important to emphasise that deposit insurance is only one of several pillars of a financial sector safety net (FSN).

Enoch notes that much progress has been achieved in Europe during recent years in enhancing the FSN. He acknowledges that the idea of permanent deposit guarantee arrangements is on balance on the right track, and that important lessons learned from the crisis are being taken into account. However, gaps remain in the overall safety net. Amongst these he draws attention to the modifications to Basel III in the proposed Capital Regulation Directive noting that: supervisory enhancement has not yet been demonstrated; recapitalization of the European banks is not yet comprehensive (indeed, is far from complete); and that, despite some progress, the bank resolution framework is not yet in place. He concludes by noting that without a resolution framework it is not clear that European authorities would be able to close a large cross-border bank smoothly, and thus bring the deposit guarantee mechanism properly into play.

Rosa Lastra begins her chapter with a quote by Rahm Emmanuel, the former chief of staff to President Barak Obama, in response to the 2007–9 crisis: '[n]ever let a good crisis go to waste'. She provides an account of the most salient regulatory responses to the financial crisis. In particular she analyses the EU, UK and US regulatory frameworks after the 2007–9 crisis. It was noted that while there is consensus regarding the magnitude and the severity of the crisis, there are a range of views when it comes to understanding the causes of the crisis and the regulatory responses that can best tackle the imbalances and fragilities that underlay it. In order not to let a good crisis go to waste, five aspects are considered: (1) what to regulate; (2) who regulates, how to regulate and the intensity of supervision; (3) bankers' behaviour, corporate governance and risk management; (4) fiscal and compensation considerations; and (5) structural reforms.

Her focus is not limited to the EU, which helps build a bridge between the 'global' nature of Part I and the European focus of the chapters in this section of the book. Lastra makes a number of important points. First, that regulators are often fighting a war that already took place, that is, responses to a crisis are by definition *ex post*. Second, that there is a need for international rules due to the global nature of markets and that they need to be supported by much more effective cooperation amongst domestic authorities. Third, she argues that an underlying requirement for optimal results is that both gains and losses need to be internalised.

The chapter by Christopher Pleister outlines the German perspective with an analysis of the role performed by the *Bundesanstalt für Finanzmarktstabilisierung* (Financial Market Stabilisation Agency or FMSA). The collapse of Lehman Brothers had a particularly devastating effect on Germany and as he notes, '[t]he order of the day was to act as fast as possible because the survival of the German banking sector was at stake'. A key element of the response was to establish a new institution to supplement the range of tasks already performed by the Deutsche Bundesbank and the *Bundesanstalt für Finanzdienstleistungsaufsicht* (Germany's Federal Financial Supervisory Authority or BaFin). In the aftermath of the Lehman collapse, neither prudential instruments nor German insolvency laws were adequate to the task of rescuing troubled German banks. The FMSA was established as a temporarily governmental 'lifeline' to help distressed banks.

Pleister highlights that the collaborative efforts between the Bundesbank, BaFin, the Federal Ministry of Finance and the European Commission and FMSA were successful in stabilizing the German banking sector: no

German bank had to be wound up and a second Lehman-type incident may have been averted. He observes that a one-off rescue of a distressed bank may strengthen that particular institution, but at the cost of weakening the overall banking system in the long run. It is noted that since late 2010 Germany has a Restructuring Act and hence an institutionalised legal framework for resolving systemically important banks. Importantly, this means that the tasks of the FMSA have become permanent. The mandate of the FMSA is to rescue only the systemically important parts of a bank while liquidating the others. Emphasis is also put on banks bearing the costs of restructuring themselves by paying a bank levy into a 'restructuring fund', thus relieving taxpayers of bailout costs. This particular aspect of the German system is in line with the policy considerations raised by Lastra in the previous chapter.

The final chapter in this Part analyses the adoption of 'extraordinary measures for extraordinary times' and the need for effective bank resolution laws in Europe. Gillian G. Garcia and Maria J. Nieto argue that a number of EU member states have been struggling to overcome problems with their sovereign debt, whose increase has been attributed to measures adopted during the financial crisis. Those governments committed financial resources equal to 39 per cent and expended 9.3 per cent of 2009 GDP levels in attempts to rescue their banking systems. They also stress that the crisis revealed inadequacies within financial safety nets, including those of Germany and the UK. In that respect they highlight the absence of legal frameworks for resolving failed banks along with limited arrangements for funding failed bank resolutions. Germany and the UK, however, did lead reform efforts by adopting measures designed to better maintain financial stability and protect the public interest, including minimizing costs to taxpayers when banks fail. Consistent with Enoch's remarks, the authors conclude that the financial crisis tested not only the perimeter of safety net policy action but also the inadequacies of traditional safety net mechanisms themselves. In company with Lastra and others, Garcia and Nieto conclude by emphasizing the need for better tools and powers to enable regulators to resolve failed banks. While they acknowledge that a significant improvement has been achieved, the task remains unfinished.

Part III: Using Government Guarantees

The opening chapter by Már Guðmundsson provides an insight into the management of the Icelandic crisis. It highlights how the authorities tried to grapple with the crisis in a way to limit the burden on the state, having recognised that backstopping all the liabilities of the banks would have been catastrophic and would have had little credibility in the international marketplace in any event. The Icelandic authorities introduced the Emergency Act of October 2008 in an effort to protect the domestic payments system and to ring-fence the state, and by extension taxpayers, from the bank failures. The lessons learnt focus on the inadequacy of EU supervision of banks with passport rights; the need for better coordination for crisis containment and management designed to protect both national and regional interests; and, the limited ability of the domestic authorities to cover banks' foreign currency liabilities.

David G. Mayes explores the pressures that can arise for the authorities in a country when a neighbouring state decides to put in place a guarantee to protect the financial system that they simply cannot match. Rather than taking such a step, Mayes argues for better pricing arrangements of guarantees to mitigate spillover effects of such decisions, and thereby limit moral hazard. His chapter explores the range of guarantees employed in a broad sample of countries during the financial crisis, as well as during earlier crises in the Nordic countries. Norway, for example, did not resort to blanket guarantees when Sweden and Finland did. In many cases the alternative to guarantees is that the private sector absorbs the losses, whereas in others it is that the government invests in the troubled institution, thereby taking a stake in the upside gains and not just taking the residual losses.

Guisèppe Grande, Aviram Levy, Fabio Panetta and Andrea Zaghini examine the use of public guarantees of bank bonds to stabilise the ability of banks to access medium-term funding. Their chapter highlights the success of such guarantees and the impact on the creditworthiness and cost of borrowing of the country providing them. It is argued that guarantees need to be more accurately priced to avoid introducing financial market distortions. When the sovereign debt crisis surfaced the markets quickly lost confidence in the guarantees on offer. They suggest that there is a need for a supranational guarantor of last resort so the creditworthiness of national governments would not be impaired by issuing guarantees.

Arturo Estrella and Sebastian Schich offer a framework for pricing sovereign debt guarantees from a contingent claims perspective. The framework would apply to both implicit and explicit government guarantees and their empirical work involves evidence drawn from a sample of 100 large European banks. Their results have implications for pricing sovereign bank debt guarantees, be they provided individually by each sovereign for its domestic banks or by several sovereigns jointly. In the former case, stronger sovereigns should charge higher premiums for their bank debt guarantees for a given level of bank risk to avoid creating distortions to competition. In the latter, the stronger sovereigns should receive greater allotments of premium incomes even where the share of the guarantees provided is identical among countries.

Michael Faure and Klaus Heine offer a different approach to reduce the social costs of future financial crises. They suggest the introduction of insurance along the lines of catastrophe insurance for natural disasters and other risks, such as the costs from the fallout of a terrorist attack. Their multi-layered approach consists of the following features: in the first layer the 'excess' should be borne by the banks, the next layer could be covered by the insurance industry and the third layer absorbed by the state. In order to mitigate the moral hazard created by the insurance instruments the need to accurately price risk has to be built into their model.

Jeffrey Manns provides another view on managing financial crises and bailouts. While bailouts can be a necessary component of dealing with a financial crisis, they have occurred in an *ad hoc* manner and public and political support for them is problematic. He argues that the US government should create an investor-of-last-resort agency to handle bailouts, which he calls the Federal Government Investment Agency (FGIC). Rather than providing short-term financial assistance, the agency could take a medium-term investment position, with the prospect of sharing in upside gains. Such a structure could help depoliticise the bailout process and reduce public criticism of it.

The FGIC would complement the Federal Deposit Insurance Corporation whose functions include not only insuring deposits but also winding up insolvent banks and systemically important financial institutions. As no single government institution is in a position to address bailouts, the FGIC would establish *ex ante* conditions for receiving aid and thereby temper corporate risk taking, protect taxpayers, and establish clear contours for bailouts. Aid would, of course, be contingent on managers, shareholders, and creditors facing upfront reductions in their respective stakes (based on the scale of the FGIC's investment) to deter over-reliance on the new agency and excessive risk taking. Second, the FGIC would assume a proportional stake in beneficiaries and seek longer term returns. Third, beneficiaries would be required to implement corporate governance reforms, including the appointment of independent directors in proportion to the government's stake, and to adopt substantive reforms to target the roots of systemic risk.

Part IV: Sovereign Debt Issues

The global financial crisis and ensuing economic downturn has resulted in the deterioration of budget deficits and caused an overall increase of sovereign debt levels. According to the IMF's data for 2010, advanced countries averaged budget deficits of 8.3 per cent of GDP while emerging economies averaged just 3.3 per cent.[15] In that same year the public debt relative to gross domestic product in advanced economies reached a level of 97 per cent (rising from below 75 per cent in 2006) while in emerging economies that ratio reached 37 per cent (about equal to the 2006 level).

In advanced economies the fiscal deterioration has been associated with revaluations of risk and less willingness to take it on. Turmoil within the banking sector was linked to large infusions of government financial aid, which in turn resulted in a considerable increase in the amount of sovereign debt. That development has undermined the fundamentals of sovereign sustainability and produced a severe deterioration in their borrowing prospects as sovereign debt markets have become more fragile. The euro-area member states (EAMS) are of particular interest since they are at the epicentre of the sovereign debt crisis. Greece, Ireland and Portugal have had to procure financial assistance from the EU, other EAMS, the IMF, the ECB and other non-EAMS sovereigns in an attempt to reduce their sovereign debt burden in an orderly manner. As an added complication this all followed the earlier crisis in Iceland.

Due to the seriousness and magnitude of the sovereign debt crisis, which is ongoing and could involve other countries, they highlight some key aspects of the interrelationships of sovereign debt and government guarantees. The three main areas identified are: (1) the treatment of contingent liabilities in the context of sovereign debt, particularly due to the possibility of grossing up the total amount which potentially could be owed under a guarantee; (2) what has been the EU response to the crisis and the development of a new regional architecture; and, (3) what has happened within the credit default swaps arena, including the (in)experience with these hedging instruments in the sovereign context.

Lee Buchheit and Mitu Gulati played a critical role in the Greek debt exchange offer and were instrumental on the political and legal sides of the deal. Their remarks are contained in 'The treatment of contingent liabilities in a sovereign debt restructuring', the first chapter in this Part. At the outset, they pose the question of how to best treat contingent liabilities. They identify the central problem with contingent guarantees as being that neither the beneficiary of the guarantee (the creditor) nor the sovereign guarantor can know at the outset whether the primary obligor (the borrower) will be able to repay the debt on its own. Thus, it is difficult to place a value on them. If the beneficiary is forced to call on the sovereign guarantee as a means of bringing the liability into a restructuring in order

15 IMF, *World Economic Outlook* (2010).

to treat it in a manner identical to other debts, the sovereign may have to explicitly recognize the guarantee as a liability on its balance sheet and as a component of public debt. However, if on the contrary, contingent liabilities are not included in a sovereign debt restructuring, this may result in a 'land mine on the road to debt sustainability once the restructuring closes'.[16]

Buchheit and Gulati identified different options and highlight their respective problems. They draw on some historical examples from the 1980s and 1990s plus the more recent experience with Grenada in 2006. From those experiences they put forward the following view: the preservation of the economics of 'two-name paper'. By this they mean that when a beneficiary joins a sovereign's debt restructuring, if the exercise of any subrogation rights against the primary obligor produces a recovery after the restructuring closes, the proceeds of that recovery will be paid first to the beneficiary up to the amount of the financial loss it realized by joining the restructuring. After that point funds are paid to the sovereign.

In Chapter 16, Rodrigo Olivares-Caminal analyses the EU institutional reaction to the sovereign debt crisis and, in particular, focuses on the new architecture designed to avert similar events. This chapter considers the impact that global conditions have had on Greece and the need for financial assistance. It is noted that this modern 'Greek tragedy' provided the basis for the development of new arrangements mainly based on: (1) the European Financial Stabilisation Mechanism (EFSM), a financial assistance scheme available to all 27 member states; (2) the European Financial Stability Facility (EFSF), a temporary credit-enhanced special purpose vehicle with minimal capitalization created to raise funds from the capital markets (via an investment grade rating) and provide financial assistance to distressed EAMS at comparatively lower interest rates; and, (3) the European Stability Mechanism (ESM), an intergovernmental organization created under public international law.

Considerable attention is given by Rodrigo Olivares-Caminal to the ESM since by the time of publication of this book the role of the EFSF is likely to have been overshadowed by the ESM, which was scheduled to be put in place by mid-2012. He notes that the ESM should be welcomed as the latest pillar of the international architecture to prevent and/or minimise the effects of a European financial crisis. However, the work of the architects remains far from complete.

---

[16] Please see L.C. Buchheit and M. Gulati, 'The Treatment of Contingent Liabilities in a Sovereign Debt Restructuring', Chapter 15 in this volume.

The final chapter addresses the problems related to liquidity spillovers in credit markets in the EAMS. Giovanni Calice, Jing Chen and Julian Williams note that the theory of complete markets suggests that sovereign debt and credit default swap (CDS) spreads should track each other very closely. In addition, liquidity risk should be priced into both instruments in such a way that buying exposure to the same default risk is identically priced, given appropriate collateral requirements for the hedging instruments and the payout structure in the CDS providing the desired recovery on the defaulting cash flow instrument. In this regard, the authors developed an empirical model of the co-evolution of credit and liquidity spreads in sovereign bond and CDS markets to study the liquidity and credit interactions for euro-zone countries over a period of time. They observed that a sudden loss of confidence in sovereign debt markets revealed itself in the form of a widening of credit spreads between several EAMSs and Germany.

In addition, Calice and his colleagues investigate the potential spillover effects between the credit and liquidity spreads among EAMS sovereign bonds and sovereign credit default swaps (CDS) during 2010. They found that: (1) explosive trends appeared during the 2010 sovereign debt crisis and the CDS market appears to have been a driver in most cases; (2) a positive and significant lagged transmission from the liquidity spread of the CDS market (using the bid-ask spread as a proxy) to the credit spread in the bond market; and (3) there have been several variance breaks in the time varying models indicating that the noise structure inundating the VAR models has changed markedly over the 2007–10 period. To conclude, they suggest that future research focus on an analysis of potential spillover effects between countries, rather than simply the CDS versus the bond market for individual countries.

III. A DEBATE ON THE USE OF GOVERNMENT GUARANTEES AND FINANCIAL CRISIS MANAGEMENT

The chapters included in this book were discussed at the Third Banking Law Symposium held on 3 and 4 October 2011 at the OECD in Paris. The participants reviewed recent and prospective measures (both national and international) as well as further changes needed to contain and prevent financial crises. *Inter alia*, they focused on:

- the role of sovereign guarantees, particularly in relation to the newly established European Financial Stability Fund;

- an assessment of public guarantees on bank assets in the light of the recent experience in several countries;
- the valuation and hedging of contingent fiscal liabilities associated with government guarantees and the linkage between guarantees and European sovereign debt issues;
- the pricing of government guarantees and the implications for financial sector competition; and
- the containment of moral hazard and taxpayer exposure.

The Symposium was organized by John Raymond LaBrosse, Rodrigo Olivares-Caminal, and Dalvinder Singh with the assistance of Sebastian Schich from the Secretariat for the Committee on Financial Markets (CMF). The event was part of the OECD's 50th anniversary special events and took place just prior to a regular meeting of the CMF of the OECD, serving as an input to it. This very timely symposium, in light of concurrent European financial developments, was part of the OECD's ongoing work on the fallout of the global financial crisis and major financial sector issues, of which the role of government guarantees is a significant component.

Keynote speakers included: Christine Cumming, First Vice President, Federal Reserve Bank of New York; Charles A.E. Goodhart, Professor Emeritus, London School of Economics, Már Guðmundsson, Governor, Central Bank of Iceland; Lee Buchheit, Partner, Cleary Gottlieb Steen & Hamilton, Mitu Gulati, Professor, Duke University, and Charles Enoch, Deputy Director, Monetary and Capital Markets Department of the IMF. Additionally, some 20 presentations were made by academics, as well as private and public financial sector specialists.

When problems began to appear in the US sub-prime mortgage-backed securities market in 2007, it was largely felt that, despite some strains, the banking system, or the financial system more generally, could absorb them within a relatively short time frame and that the world would go on as before. Underlying this was the experience of other financial shocks during the past 25 years or so, when financial safety nets, despite some country specific exceptions, proved equal to the task.

As it has turned out, problems quickly revealed other fragilities and that systemic risk in the financial system more broadly had been building up for some time. As the situation evolved the various problems began to feed on each other, resulting in a virulent global financial crisis. It can be argued that one type of financial crisis can quickly morph into another, with 2008–09 clearly being a case in point. It seems fair to say, with the benefit of hindsight, to be sure, that there was a lack of awareness and understanding of accumulating systemic risks, both by the private sector as well as by the authorities, and that safety nets in most cases were inadequate and/or incomplete and risked being overwhelmed. Financial innovation, globalisation and the introduction of the Euro all had implications for risk containment that were not fully recognized at the time.

The Symposium, however, was a clear example of the international community's commitment to forging enhanced, well thought-out, mechanisms for containing systemic risks in the context of a highly interconnected global financial framework with ongoing financial innovation.

While the use of government guarantees was a central theme, the Symposium also analysed the roles played by prudential regulators, central banks, deposit insurers and treasuries in dealing with the crisis. These included traditional measures such as the central banks' lender of last resort role (including its lack of availability, particularly in some European countries), some extraordinary measures, such as recapitalisation, asset purchase and guarantee schemes, as well as more inclusive guarantees on the liability and asset sides of bank balance sheets. Even by traditional standards a number of countries had a less than complete financial safety net and deposit insurance had to be quickly introduced and/or substantially enhanced. Under the circumstances, and the need to act quickly, mistakes – often very expensive ones – were made at public, that is, taxpayers', expense, and they will shoulder a burden for many years. A central message is that the midst of a global financial crisis is not the best time to start thinking about creating a safety net and those guarantors should have some idea of potential exposure beforehand. Insufficient financial institution supervision coupled with blanket guarantees can jeopardise the financial viability of the state.

Acknowledgments

This book would not have been possible without the effort of a number of people and the financial support of several organizations. The editors would like to thank Sebastian Schich and Angelique Servin from the Secretariat for the Committee on Financial Markets (CMF) at the OECD. Financial support for the Symposium was provided by the Warwick Legal Research Institute; the Centre for Commercial Law and Financial Regulation, University of Reading Law School; the Centre for Financial & Management Studies and the School of Oriental and African Studies (SOAS), University of London; and, Patterson & LaBrosse Financial Consultants Ltd.

The chapters were drawn from papers delivered at the Third Banking Law Symposium. We are grateful and thank all of the speakers, presenters and discussants for their contributions and participation. The moderators did a superb job and the observations and questions from the attendees at the Symposium helped to improve the focus of our work.

We also acknowledge the efforts of Ben Booth, our commissioning editor, from Edward Elgar Law and the administrative team behind our institutions who helped us in the organisation and development of the event, including among others Anna Denby, Anne Perkins, Rahima Begun and Jane Savory.

John Raymond LaBrosse would like to thank his mother, Frances, and Gail, Scott, Kendra and Conrad for their patience, love and support. He would also like to thank his long-time friend and colleague Jim McCollum for his help beyond the call of duty in acting as the Rapporteur to the Third Banking Law Symposium and for his assistance in preparing the preface and several chapters of this book. Thanks as well to my fellow members of the Great Beaver Society of New York who helped me throughout my career in learning more about the functioning of Wall Street

Rodrigo Olivares-Caminal would like to thank Teresa and Felipe for their love and support; his co-organisers for their help and collaboration in making another Symposium possible; Lee Buchheit, Mitu Gulati and Joseph J. Norton for their support; and, Rosa Lastra for her friendship.

Dalvinder Singh would like to thank Sarbjit, Amaryn and Arvind for their love and support.

PART I

Managing the financial crisis

1. Managing crises without government guarantees: How do we get there?

Christine M. Cumming

The times are extraordinary. The years of financial turbulence that we have experienced and continue to experience have illuminated both the power and the limitations of government intervention in managing financial crises. These years have illustrated how much more we need to understand about good design principles for intervention and sound strategies for the restoration of financial and banking market functions following a crisis. And these years have highlighted the interaction between the fiscal condition and capacity of countries and the size and health of the domestic financial system.

I speak of government intervention broadly, because the answer to the provocative question I am to discuss – how can we conduct crisis management without financial guarantees – depends a great deal on which types of government intervention we hope to avert. Certain guarantee or contingent arrangements can short-circuit incipient instability or stabilize already roiled financial institutions and markets; we do not want to end them. Other interventions are more intrusive and involve more socialization of loss; we want to reduce their necessity.

Guarantee has a legal meaning – for example, the Federal Reserve is not authorized to issue a guarantee – but I will use the word more broadly to describe contingent arrangements. Definitions of guarantee are variations of: 'a warrant, pledge, or formal assurance given as security that another's debt or obligation will be fulfilled'; in the financial sector that primarily means credit risk protection.

Guarantees, insurance and options have similar structures. They are contingent, they have prices and triggers, and the payout is meant to cover a specific risk. Because guarantees, like insurance, change the risks to the guaranteed party and its creditors, both third-party guarantees and insurance can change the affected parties' behaviour in an adverse way, and therefore create moral hazard. Thus, the provision of a guarantee also involves various control activities – underwriting, monitoring, imposing penalties for deviation from terms – intended to correct those incentives. The cost of the guarantee therefore is not only the cost of hedging and absorbing credit risk, but also the costs of control activities and an adjustment for any social efficiency gains or losses.

One reason that I draw the connection between guarantees, insurance and options is that the theory and techniques for valuing insurance and options have advanced substantially in the last three decades. Thus, guarantees can in concept be valued. I stress 'in concept' because those valuation efforts are still approximate. But the measures show promise. For example, Lucas and McDonald in a 2006 *Journal of Monetary Economics* paper used a 'stress value at risk' measure to capture the risk in the implicit government guarantee to Fannie Mae and Freddie Mac and obtained values that indicated the large and growing risk of those institutions.[1] The value of a guarantee, even an approximation of its value, provides a potentially powerful signal of risk to the financial authorities.

Let me now turn to the US experience during the recent financial crisis to describe an approach that characterizes the spectrum of government interventions.

I. THE US EXPERIENCE WITH INTERVENTION DURING THE 2008–09 FINANCIAL CRISIS

Of course, no one can do justice in a few words to the unprecedented central bank and government interventions during the 2008–09 financial crisis. Fortunately, much information is available on the internet; for example, www.federalreserve.gov contains a section called 'Credit and Liquidity Programmes' with a wealth of detail on the Fed's actions during the crisis.

The US deployed four major types of interventions in the financial crisis. The first interventions were expanded programmes providing liability insurance. The Federal Deposit Insurance Corporation (FDIC) raised the standard deposit insurance coverage limit and it established a Temporary Liquidity Guarantee Programme with two arms – a transaction-type (checking) account programme that effectively covered corporate deposits and a debt guarantee programme that covered unsecured short- and

---

[1] D. Lucas and R. McDonald, 'An options-based approach to evaluating the risk of Fannie Mae and Freddie Mac', Journal of Monetary Economics, 53(1), 2006.

medium-term financial company debt. In addition, the US Department of the Treasury offered insurance for money market mutual funds to curb 'run risk' in those funds.

The second interventions were the market liquidity facilities provided by the Federal Reserve. While the Federal Reserve has authority to lend on a collateralized basis to banks, a large proportion of US short- and medium-term funding for financial and non-financial firms now occurs in markets. The tri-party repo market finances securities holdings for broker-dealers; the commercial paper market provides working capital for corporations; and the asset-backed commercial paper and securities markets fund receivables and loans arising in business activities.

Under section 13(3) of the US Federal Reserve Act, in unusual and exigent circumstances, the Federal Reserve can make loans to non-bank borrowers. As funding markets came under duress in 2008 and 2009, the Federal Reserve acted in a series of these markets. The common problem in each market was concern that an obligation would not be repaid at maturity because the obligor might experience either credit problems or liquidity constraints.

The interesting 'contingent' aspect of these liquidity facilities was the pricing. The price, expressed as a borrowing rate, was set to stand well above the interest rates that prevailed prior to the crisis, but well below the rates then posted in strained markets. The pricing created a dynamic in which the availability of the facility eased funding pressures, borrowing rates in that market began to fall, and as markets gradually normalized, the market rate eventually fell below the rate charged by the Federal Reserve. With that fall in the market rate, borrowing tailed off and the facility was gradually wound down. The volume of transactions in the facility and the market pricing gave the Federal Reserve – and market participants – insight into the programme's impact and the market's recovery.

The third interventions were more firm specific: loans and other support to AIG, assistance to the Bear Stearns merger and an asset guarantee programme announced for two financial institutions and implemented for one. The fourth and most well-known interventions were the capital injections in financial firms using funds from TARP, the US government's Troubled Asset Relief Programme.

These various interventions can be arrayed along two dimensions. The first is the nature and extent of loss absorption inherent in the design of the intervention – just how much 'tail' or catastrophe risk the government is taking on. For deposit insurance arrangements, long experience suggests that the cost of the 'tail' of losses during even a very distressed period is low relative to the benefits of prevention of runs and contagion. Similarly, the Federal Reserve's market liquidity facilities were meant to provide a backstop for market funding, predicated on the soundness of the underlying collateral assets and their margining. Moreover, both types of programmes required little upfront investment of cash. In contrast, the direct loan to AIG, while collateralized, and the TARP investments themselves involved substantial risk-taking and massive funding.

The second dimension is the economic cost of the intervention – just how intrusive the intervention is. All forms of intervention require some kind of underwriting, monitoring and enforcement, and many distort private market incentives and function, as I noted earlier. Ideally, I would include measures of both administrative costs and economic distortion in total cost.

Each intervention involved administrative burdens of varying extent. The FDIC's and Treasury's liability insurance programmes rested largely on the existing licensing and supervision of regulated financial companies. The Federal Reserve's liquidity facilities rested on eligibility standards for borrowers and collateral, with a heavy reliance on the existing market infrastructure and processes for controls. By contrast, the firm-specific interventions required significant firm and examiner resources and extensive new financial controls. The TARP capital injections involved not only statutory constraints, most notably on executive compensation, but also a high level of scrutiny through public reports by the US Congressional Oversight Panel and the Special Inspector General for TARP.

There are actual and potential programmes that fall between the poles on both dimensions. The Term Asset-Backed Securities Loan Facility (TALF) created by the Federal Reserve to restart asset securitization markets lent to investors against asset-backed securities for terms of three and five years. Arguably, the Federal Reserve took on more risk of loss with the term of the loan, its non-recourse nature, and the type of collateral than it did in its other facilities. For that reason, TALF was complemented by arrangements for any workout of defaulted collateral and was supported by TARP funding. On the administrative side, both borrowers and collateral had to meet eligibility requirements; the Federal Reserve Bank of New York extensively reviewed potential collateral and conducted compliance reviews at dealers arranging TALF borrowing.

The types of interventions for any given country will reflect its financial system structure and its institutional setting. The US approach reflected the heavy reliance on markets and non-banks for financing specific to our financial system. In addition, judgments about how much government loss absorption and intrusion are appropriate in central bank and government interventions will reflect country-specific circumstances and preferences.

As a final note, what did not work well in the US experience were implicit guarantees – that is, assumptions that the government would protect holders of certain liability and equity instruments that had no explicit guarantee. Official actions that laid bare the absence of the explicit guarantee – the imposition of losses on equity and subordinated debt investors when Fannie Mae and Freddie Mac were taken into conservatorship and on senior unsecured bondholders in the resolution of Washington Mutual – contributed to the dynamic of an escalating panic in the fall of 2008. Each action was one more shock at the time, but the investors' shock also pointed to the lack of hoped-for monitoring and market discipline by debt and equity investors in the run up to the crisis.

II. CONTINGENT ARRANGEMENTS AND FINANCIAL INSTITUTION FAILURE

Guarantees as I described them earlier are about protection against failure to meet financial obligations, that is, against default and insolvency. The alternative to escalating government intervention during the crisis was accepting a higher rate of financial institution insolvencies. The consequences of multiple failures of large, complex and international organizations were largely unknowable. They included the likelihood of disruption of systemically important financial activities (such as payment services, where the customer need is immediate and customers cannot quickly switch to another provider) and the almost certain contagion to other institutions. The September 2008 bankruptcy of Lehman Brothers Holdings, Inc., underscored the difficulty of controlling the ramifications of the failure of just one large cross-border institution and the cost, complexity and extreme inefficiency of the existing cross-border insolvency process.

The 'too-big-to-fail' (TBTF) problem – the expectation that a large financial institution insolvency would be too disorderly and too destructive of wealth to risk – has frustrated financial authorities, legislators, and academics since at least the failure of Continental Illinois Bank in 1984. In the wake of the crisis, the frustration is now shared by the public. Having intervened so forcefully in the crisis, financial authorities and others also worry that moral hazard has increased as a result.

An important avenue to tackle the TBTF problem is to improve the feasibility of cross-border resolution of large financial firms. The Financial Stability Board (FSB) in 2009 commissioned work on improving the process for cross-border resolution of systemically important financial institutions. The work since then is reflected in a set of proposed principles published in 2011, *Key Attributes of Effective Resolution Regimes*.[2]

The *Key Attributes* paper is more than a set of principles or emerging standards; the paper also maps out a series of actions to be taken in order to improve the feasibility of resolving a systemically important financial firm. The goal is to take actions that ease and speed the resolution of the largest firms while preserving critical functions and reducing the contagion and the destruction of value that occurs in liquidation and most important to do so without recourse to public funds that exposes taxpayers to risk of loss.

The FSB proposes that all jurisdictions have a set of resolution powers, among them, the ability to create a bridge or similar institution, into which the healthy parts of a financial firm, including its critical activities, can be placed. In addition, the resolution authority needs the power to transfer, sell and restructure all or part of the firm. These powers have been used successfully by the FDIC in the US, and a number of jurisdictions have adopted or have plans to adopt similar powers. The increased international use of bridge institutions is likely to require jurisdictions to recognize bridge banks from other countries, in order that some business functions, such as payment activities, can seamlessly transition to the successor bridge institution.

The bridge institution concept is quite powerful. The FDIC recently published a paper in its *Quarterly* that described how it could have handled the Lehman bankruptcy using its new powers under the Dodd-Frank Act to resolve systemically important non-bank financial institutions.[3] The FDIC outlines how it could have created a bridge institution for the Lehman holding company, how it could have transferred to the bridge Lehman's equity holdings in its key subsidiaries, including its major broker/dealers, potentially avoiding their insolvency, and how it could have funded the London broker/dealer, a key problem following Lehman Holding's bankruptcy in New York. Selling the broker/dealer subsidiaries as going concerns would preserve far more of their value and continuity of operations, as illustrated by the sale of most of Lehman's US broker/dealer, which did not immediately enter into insolvency.

The FDIC's article offers a promising path toward a workable cross-border insolvency process, a potential solution to a daunting problem,

---

2 Financial Stability Board, 'Key Attributes of Effective Resolution Regimes for Financial Institutions', October 2011, available at www.financialstabilityboard.org/publications/r_111104cc.pdf

3 FDIC, 'The orderly liquidation of Lehman Brothers Holdings Inc. under the Dodd-Frank Act', FDIC Quarterly, 5(2), 2011.

especially when viewed against the meaningful, but small progress made in the efforts of the past two decades. To build out the FDIC's proposed path to a workable cross-border insolvency process requires conforming changes to laws and rules across most jurisdictions. I do not want to minimize the challenges in developing the approach further, but simply highlight its potential to ameliorate a problem we would all like solved.

The FSB also proposes to make the process of recovery planning by firms and resolution planning by financial authorities an important principle. This planning, already underway for many systemically important financial firms, is being carried out by firm-specific crisis management groups, made up of regulators and resolution authorities from the jurisdictions where a given firm has its principal operations. The FSB also sets a broad direction for involving and communicating with host country jurisdictions where the host authorities view the financial firm to be of local systemic importance.

The FSB further proposes that the home country authorities, collaborating and coordinating with the crisis management group, produce an annual resolvability assessment. This assessment would identify a set of impediments to resolution and provide a list of follow-up actions, potentially some for the firm, but also some for the jurisdiction. Progress on the follow-up actions would be assessed in the following year.

The stated goal of the FSB's work is to make possible the resolution of systemically important financial institutions without exposing taxpayers to risk of loss. That will not happen overnight. In my view, we should be striving year-by-year to improve the feasibility and possibility of cross-border resolutions. That means a dynamic assessment process that seeks improvement against the current baseline and addresses key changes in the firm and in the industry that either facilitate or complicate resolution. A stronger, more common resolution framework, a meaningful resolution planning process, and an annual resolvability assessment to ensure progress should make resolution a stronger alternative to government intervention.

III. FINAL THOUGHTS ON CRISIS MANAGEMENT WITHOUT GOVERNMENT GUARANTEES

Financial authorities are never really out of the crisis management business. The recent US experience with the crisis has illuminated vulnerabilities in the US financial system, such as the role and structure of the government sponsored enterprises (GSEs), Fannie Mae and Freddie Mac, and the need for reform in the tri-party repo market and money market mutual fund sector.

The systematic search for such points of vulnerability and new ones should be an important and permanent part of the work at the domestic and the international levels by financial authorities. What we need in the financial system is defence in depth, a series of actions both macro- and micro-prudential, that both help prevent crises and help us manage them more effectively when they occur. The preventive measures include the new proposed Basel rules on capital and liquidity, intended to make financial institutions more resilient, especially systemically important firms; the international effort to strengthen the market infrastructure and supervisory oversight of financial derivatives; in the US, the extension of comprehensive supervision to systemically important non-bank financial firms; and our ongoing efforts to reform the GSEs, the tri-party repo market and the structure of money market mutual funds.

So let me conclude with some thoughts on the question of how close we might get to crisis management without government guarantees. For me, the paradigm of managing crises was the US response in the early 1990s to its real-estate and leveraged buyout problems; while smaller than the more recent problems, the potential losses then threatened to engulf some of our largest banks. The paradigm consisted of three interconnected elements: identifying and isolating the problem assets for dedicated work-out management; replenishing the capital and liquidity of the firm; and drawing up new and credible business plans demonstrating the future profitability of the firm. The supervisors sought to be pre-emptive and proactive – propelling firms to acknowledge problems and take actions earlier than they might otherwise have done.

Where this paradigm was applied, we avoided failure. That experience illustrates that there is no substitute for early intervention in preserving value in the firm and in limiting externalities and other spillovers. Early intervention calls for strong supervisory oversight, as envisioned by the Basel Committee on Banking Supervision. It is significant that the FSB's *Key Attributes* paper on resolution highlights the important role of recovery planning by firms. Recovery planning and the dialogue with and among supervisors that accompanies it should facilitate early intervention. The recovery plan will already be on paper and the supervisory dialogue begun even before the firm starts to experience difficulty.

Early intervention will also be essential in resolution if recovery efforts fail. The *Key Attributes* paper highlights the need for resolution authorities to be able to act before technical insolvency. Resolution planning should once again facilitate that difficult decision to place a firm into an insolvency proceeding when it is necessary.

Second, government intervention measures such as those I described at the onset cannot substitute for the hard work that goes on in a private restructuring or in a resolution. For example, even after the passage of a massive TARP fund and the injection of capital into the largest banks, market pressures continued for some banks, and those pressures only eased with more intervention and the thorough Supervisory Capital Assessment Programme, also called the stress tests, for which results were disclosed, and a plan for specific capital actions by some firms. Problems need to be identified, capital and liquidity raised, new business plans put in place and old ones abandoned. Delays in taking and executing these hard, for the firm often life-changing, decisions contribute to the necessity for further intervention.

Third, I believe that having some types of contingent arrangements in reserve will continue to be necessary, even with a much stronger cross-border resolution process. The role of deposit insurance in stemming financial crises is well-documented. A period of multiple financial institution failures, even with a strong resolution process, might trigger the same risk aversion in funding markets that we saw in 2008 and 2009. The ability to backstop key funding markets could prove valuable, and the Dodd-Frank Act preserved for the Fed authority under section 13(3) to provide market liquidity facilities even while eliminating other aspects. But in designing these interventions, an exit strategy needs to be clear. Leaving those arrangements in place too long distorts incentives and erodes private market functions.

And for those contingent arrangements that are ongoing, such as deposit insurance, measuring the value of the guarantee could be an important test of overall design of the guarantee and the accompanying monitoring regime. Continuing to refine our ability to value guarantees would provide a useful measure for supervisory authorities and for the deposit insurers, especially when they consider changes to deposit insurance. The value of guarantees also would complement other measures being developed for financial stability monitoring. Further, I suggest that all guarantees should not only be measured, but documented and reported, not left as implicit.

Fourth, it will still be important to have a set of progressive actions that government can turn to if human judgement or the tools available at a time of incipient financial crisis prevent financial authorities from defusing the crisis. While such measures buy time and cannot substitute for more permanent solutions, sometimes time *is* the scarce resource. Deterioration in financial conditions – at individual financial institutions and in the economy – is inevitable as a crisis wears on in a financial system, given its leverage. Understanding that, financial authorities should feel great urgency both to apply the progressive measures when they are needed, doing so with the force and size that truly arrests the crisis forces, and to entertain the usually difficult measures needed to resolve the fundamental problems behind the crisis.

2. Improving the decision-making framework for financial crisis management

John Raymond LaBrosse and Dalvinder Singh

'The Greatest pleasure in life is doing what people say you cannot do'

Walter Bagehot, English economist and journalist (1826–1877)

INTRODUCTION

Public confidence plays an important role in sustaining financial system stability. In normal times prudential regulation and supervision of banks, the promotion and use of standards of sound business and financial practice, central bank actions, explicit deposit protection and an effective bank closure mechanism all help to reduce the adverse consequences of a financial crisis emanating from bank failures. It is understood that banks, like other firms, will fail[1] and the likelihood of this happening is higher when risks in a particular banking concern are not managed appropriately, bubbles in certain markets burst, or financial markets are very fragile due to either domestic or foreign reasons.

In an astonishing chronicle of eight centuries of financial crisis Reinhart and Rogoff explored the question as to whether the current one is really any different.[2] What is becoming quite clear is that very little attention is given as to how best to manage them. One explanation could be that one crisis seems to lead to another and so it is difficult to determine the endpoints. Another explanation might be that

[1] Bank failures in the US are quite common. There were only two years (2005 and 2006) since 1934 where there were no bank failures. For a full list see http://www.fdic.gov/bank/historical/bank/ (last accessed 17 September 2012).

[2] C. Reinhart and K.S. Rogoff, *This Time is Different: Eight Centuries of Financial Folly* (Princeton, NJ, USA: Princeton University Press 2009).

crisis management needs more attention so that lessons learned can be incorporated into improved techniques to minimize the effects of catastrophic events.

Notwithstanding the fact that a considerable amount has been learnt about crisis management, lessons from the past seem to be amiss in terms of guiding future directions, so the risk of repeating mistakes continues.

This chapter sets out the main structure of a financial system safety net (FSN) and how the mandates, roles and responsibilities of the agencies within it tend to change during the course of a crisis. Attention is also given to the interests and impact that stakeholders in the marketplace outside the FSN can have during a bank failure or financial disaster. The chapter then sets out why careful attention to the FSN and the market stakeholders is now quite important. To help policy-makers a decision-making tree is offered and explained as an alternative to the spurt of *ad hoc* pronouncements that have done little more than confuse markets and undermine the public's confidence in policy-makers. The role and functions of a financial stability committee (FSC) are explored in the context of coordinating actions and some conclusions are offered in the final section of the chapter.

I. ROLES AND RESPONSIBILITIES OF FSN PLAYERS

The financial crisis that began in 2008 demonstrated severe weaknesses in FSNs.[3] While the deficiencies were evident almost worldwide, the most severe problems were found in European markets, largely due to the lack of coordination, consultation and development of coherent strategies to deal with the crisis.[4] For those reasons it is important to know at the outset what organizations should be included in a FSN, including their roles and responsibilities, and why the interests of other stakeholders are also quite important. In basic terms the question becomes: who should be included

---

[3] International Monetary Fund, 'Financial Sector Assessment Program, United States of America, Crisis Management Arrangements, Technical Note', May 2010; J.R. LaBrosse and J.F. McCollum, 'An Evaluation of the Canadian Financial Safety Net During the Global Financial Crisis' in J.R. LaBrosse, R.Olivares-Caminal and D. Singh, (eds), *Managing Risk in the Financial System* (Edward Elgar, Cheltenham, UK and Northampton, MA, USA 2011).

[4] European Commission, 'An EU Framework for Crisis Management in the Financial Sector – Frequently Asked Questions', MEMO/10/506, Brussels, 20 October 2010; European Commission, 'Commission Sets Out its Plans for a New EU Framework for Crisis Management in the Financial Sector', IP/10/1353, Brussels, 20 October 2010.

in the official safety net and deemed the core stakeholders in the financial system? The answer is important because during a crisis there needs be a high level of consultation, coordination and cooperation between the various interested parties.

A. The Official Safety Net Players

The FSN has traditionally been defined to include a lender of last resort (central bank), prudential regulation (by a bank supervisor), a government department (Ministry of Finance or Treasury) and explicit deposit protection (insurance or other form of a limited guarantee).[5] But the financial crisis has underscored that the group of players that can influence outcomes is now quite elastic. There is a need to consider the roles of the legislative body, non-bank regulators such as securities commissions, housing agencies and insurance company regulators, as decisions that they take can have an important impact and threaten financial system stability. Moreover, there are compelling reasons to consider other stakeholders and bring them into the dialogue so that financial system stability can be addressed more effectively and efficiently.

The roles of shareholders, external auditors, the courts and credit-rating agencies need to be appreciated and understood better in the pursuit of financial system stability as external decisions by those parties can have a direct impact on the official safety net players' response to safeguard system stability. This is not to suggest that they reside in the FSN, but to ensure the FSN is able to respond proactively rather than reactively to instil a better degree of confidence in the financial system.

The Ministries of Finance, or Treasuries, take a particular interest in the efficient functioning of FSNs. During relatively stable times the Treasury sets tax policy, manages a country's finances, is the steward of the government's accounts, and provides advice on financial sector policy issues. In light of these tasks it has oversight responsibility for monetary and economic policy. The role of the Treasury inevitably brings it under the surveillance of the IMF and into OECD forums, where its performance is assessed on a regular basis. Broadly speaking the Treasury will act in good faith in terms of how it manages a country's finances. The exercise of its

---

[5] Financial Stability Forum, 'Working Group on Deposit Insurance', BIS, Basel, Switzerland, September 2001; S. Schich, 'Expanded Government Guarantees for Bank Liabilities: Selected Issues' (2009) OECD Journal: Financial Market Trends 1.

discretion can and may well be directed by the government with limited autonomy or, as in the case of Germany, the right to veto government decisions on public finances.

In terms of financial sector policy development the Treasury's role is broadly speaking one of oversight, with responsibility for monetary policy and financial regulation and supervision delegated to other organisations within the FSN. In the context of the euro-area the European Central Bank (ECB) has the mandate for setting monetary policy. In other countries monetary policy is delegated to the central bank and the functions of regulation and supervision to a different department of the central bank or a separate authority. International forums for policy discussions on financial matters are technically the responsibility of the Treasury, but it may have the central bank, the prudential supervisor and the deposit insurer by its side.

In most instances the prudential supervisor has direct responsibility for day-to-day oversight of the financial system, and may be able to initiate changes in regulatory policy with relative independence once the regulatory architecture is agreed by the government and a country's legislative body. The gaps in financial regulation could reasonably be laid at the door of the Treasury since it is its role to initiate reform in this area, which in practical terms leads it to rely on its central bank and prudential supervisor and perhaps other regulators for advice. Moreover, the move towards macro- and micro-prudential regulation highlights a need for a holistic approach to the management of financial sectors.

Central banks are responsible for safeguarding the payments system and providing liquidity against security to the financial system and, at times, to individual but still solvent banks. The primary forums for dialogue between central banks is the BIS, and in the euro context the ECB. Such activities are often called lender of last resort (LOLR) facilities or emergency liquidity assistance.[6] The facility of LOLR is used with an eye to avoiding a liquidity problem that might otherwise turn into a panic in the banking and financial system. The central bank could exercise the LOLR function either through open-market operations or by providing loans to individual banks.

Interventions by central banks are designed to promote and if needed stabilise market confidence and avoid unnecessary bank failures that result from temporary liquidity problems. In Bagehot's view it should be made available provided that it is used to avoid panics when banks

---

[6] G. Wood, 'The Lender of Last Resort Reconsidered' (2000) 18 Journal of Financial Services Research 203.

experience such problems.[7] It is given at a rate to ensure repayment is made expeditiously once the event is over; and it should also only be given against good forms of collateral. Moreover, during a crisis LOLR can be provided to solvent institutions with collateral. Another important ingredient in providing liquidity is that the central bank must act decisively and quickly without hesitation, otherwise a panic could be prolonged and spread into other parts of the financial system which were unaffected by the original problem.

The LOLR facility is traditionally considered the preserve of the banking system, but it can be and has been used to avoid liquidity problems more widely. However, the existence of the LOLR does give rise to a number of concerns that require central banks and prudential supervisors to gauge carefully when support is given, namely moral hazard and 'too-big-to-fail' (TBTF) connotations.[8] The concern over moral hazard is exacerbated by the policy of intervening with financial support if the institution is considered TBTF.

The primary member of the FSN tasked with day-to-day responsibilities for the financial system is most likely to be the prudential supervisor. It must protect the perimeter in terms of both entry to and exit from the financial system. This is notwithstanding the fact that the resolution of a problem bank may be located in another part of the official safety net. A focus on adherence to prudential requirements and compliance is a way to influence and, in the extreme, change the behaviour of banking institutions either collectively or individually. The supervisor needs to be equipped with appropriate enforcement tools to ensure compliance with laws, regulations and guidelines. In relation to enforcement a problematic issue is supervisory forbearance, as it can lead to accommodations rather than formal actions, and questions about what the regulator knew about a bank that is subsequently closed or fails.[9]

It is generally asserted to be a best practice that the tasks of supervision should be conducted independently of political interference. However, the extent to which this can be accomplished during a crisis is questionable, considering the political response during the recent crisis to bailout depositors and individual banks. Decisions to protect depositors or even banks when formal systems of explicit deposit insurance and a bank

---

[7] W. Bagehot, *Lombard Street: A Description of the Money Market* (Kegan Paul, Trench, Trubner & Co. Ltd, 1915 reprint).

[8] A.E. Wilmarth, 'Reforming Financial Regulation to Address the Too-Big-To-Fail Problem' (2010) 35 Brooklyn Journal of International Law 707.

[9] G.G.H. Garcia, 'Failing Prompt Corrective Action' (2010) 11 Journal of Banking Regulation 171.

resolution regime are in place are primarily political rather than regulatory. Obviously, during a systemic crisis the policy rationale of letting a bank fail or providing full coverage for depositors must address the loss of confidence in financial markets. Again, it is evident that the FSN can also forbear from closing non-viable banks because they are perceived to be TBTF.[10]

Deposit protection has become an important feature of modern banking systems. Its role in a systemic crisis is limited, as it is generally designed to deal with either a few small bank closures or the failure of one medium-sized bank. What is evident from the current financial crisis is that a poorly designed system of deposit protection can escalate a bank failure into a crisis, as experienced in the UK with Northern Rock.

Implicit deposit protection exists when depositors will be fully reimbursed if a bank fails and in regimes where taxpayers rescue banks that might otherwise fail. The belief that depositors will be fully compensated is usually linked to past statements by government officials. Governments may also believe that the failure of one bank will precipitate a run on deposits in otherwise healthy banks. It is important to note that implicit arrangements do not have an administrative mechanism to repay depositors, which may mean using the courts to settle claims. The uncertainty that is created as to whether a government will actually step in to reimburse depositors in a failed bank encourages customers to place their savings in larger banks and banking markets tend to become less competitive. Trust in an implicit guarantee could be misjudged in light of the fact that the guarantee may mean only a partial rather than a full payout. As well, the pressure on governments that results from depositors having reduced or no access to their funds can create instability in financial systems. These problems, coupled with the instability and uncertainty inherent in implicit systems, lead governments to consider adopting explicit deposit protection.[11]

Interestingly, the number of explicit deposit protection systems has increased significantly to over 100 countries.[12] Explicit arrangements can

---

[10] G.G.H. Garcia, 'The Troubled Asset Relief Program: Has Forbearance As Far As the Eye Can See Saved the US Economy' in J.R. LaBrosse, R. Olivares-Caminal and D. Singh (eds) *Managing Risk in the Financial System* (Edward Elgar, Cheltenham, UK and Northampton, MA, USA 2011).

[11] While we note that there are several deposit protection systems in existence, some of which like the FDIC in the US for over 75 years, surprising little attention has been paid to pricing of the guarantees.

[12] For a full list of deposit protection agencies either established or in the process of being developed please see www.iadi.org.

take the form of a formalized insurance system (sometimes referred to as the 'North American model') or a guarantee system (the 'European approach').[13] While both kinds of arrangements have many features in common (such as setting defined coverage limits and compulsory membership), the system funding facilities can be quite different. It is evident that guarantee systems often are not well funded and tend to rely on *ex post* industry levies to repay depositor claims on the estate of a failed bank. Also, many features of guarantee systems are not well understood by the public (very few such systems spend any time or money on public awareness activities). While the insurance aspects of both approaches may increase moral hazard, the North American-type systems, if used properly, can address the hazard created in a much more direct way: they use differentiated *ex ante* premiums, which instils greater market discipline and discourages excessive risk taking, and have proactive prudential supervisors that undertake mutually reinforcing actions.

Legislative bodies obviously play a crucial role in the development of laws and holding incumbent governments and their agencies accountable. Legislative bodies principally safeguard the constitutional and public interest by calling officials to testify in open forums. The legislative body will also be the primary port-of-call for holding the FSN players accountable for their decisions,[14] and may consider the interests and activities of various stakeholders. While legislative scrutiny is a continuous process, its intensity is much more marked during times like these: the level of public finances used to bail out or prop up the financial markets and the extent and depth of crisis make it vital.[15] The principle of the right to protect one's private property is certainly controversial when the state intervenes and takes some interest in or takes control over or interferes with those property rights.[16] Only through legislative means could such steps be taken.

---

[13] D. Singh and D. Walker, 'The European Deposit Guarantee Directive: An Appraisal of the Reforms', in J.R. LaBrosse, R. Olivares-Caminal and D. Singh (eds) *Financial Crisis Management and Bank Resolution* (Informa, London 2009); More recently, M. Gerhardt and K. Lannoo, 'Options for Reforming Deposit Protection Schemes in the EU' (2011) March ECRI Policy Brief No. 4.

[14] The usual three questions asked of officials during *post mortems* by Parliamentary-type committees are: What did they know about the situation, when did they find out and what did they do about the problem? Attention then focuses on who was responsible and, of course, what were the costs.

[15] BBC (2011), 'German court rejects challenge to Eurozone bailouts', BBC online news (7 September 2011), available at: http://www.bbc.co.uk/news/business-14818978 (last accessed 14 September 2012).

[16] K.J. Hopt, C. Kumpin and F. Steffek 'Preventing Bank Insolvencies in

The response to the 2008 financial crisis has meant that the mandates of FSN players have been extended, either by legislative means or through delegation by the Ministry of Finance or Treasury. It is therefore important to assess what likely role the legislative body will play in any given crisis. It is clear that the approach to initiating responses to the crisis varied quite significantly. The level of *ex ante* and or *ex post* accountability of the decisions is also evident. However, one principal ingredient in the majority of responses was the need for the legislative body to enable the FSN to use the tools necessary to contain the crisis.[17] Appropriate discussion and influence on the mandates certainly needs formal consideration.

B. Stakeholders in the Financial Markets

Intervention by the authorities during the crisis was partly a result of financial intermediaries' inability to raise funds in the markets. It is suggested that in normal times the principal focus of managements is the interests of shareholders and shareholder value. The reaction of the various stakeholders will also vary because of the asymmetry of information the principals and agents have about one another; and how distress has an impact on their interests in the institution. Interlinked is the role of the external auditor, as the party which is required to provide an opinion on the performance of the institution to the shareholders, but is also relied upon by FSN players when they conduct supervisory responsibilities for the regulator.

The interests of depositors in such periods are not necessarily at the forefront of the minds of the banks, albeit there is a general duty on the FSN to protect depositors and to a lesser extent investors rather than owing a duty to the shareholders as a whole. The responsibility to exercise enforcement of regulation and supervision requirements to protect the interests of depositors and investors is an illustration.

In times of crisis the priority placed on the interests of stakeholders changes. During the crisis the interests of depositors were very much at

the Financial Crisis: The German Financial Market Stabilisation Act' (2009) 10 European Business Organization Law Review 515.

[17] This is in contrast to the UK position as explained by Alistair Darling: 'I was also struck by the fact that the US president . . . cannot automatically get what he wants at home. He has to horse-trade. In contrast, when I effectively wrote a cheque to buy £50 billion of bank shares in the UK, I did not even have to get specific parliamentary authority to do so.' A. Darling, *Back from the Brink: 1,000 days at Number 11* (Atlantic Books, London 2011).

the forefront of the FSN players' minds because of concerns of a bank run or panic selling.[18] Once risks at a bank are publicised the prospect of a run is very real and sustaining confidence in the retail deposit market is paramount. It is normatively argued that stakeholders in the equity and debt markets can also affect the decisions of the FSN players in the course of containing a crisis. The response is likely to be coordinated rather than reactive given the speed at which these markets operate and their size and transnational nature. It is useful, however, to try to put these stakeholders into any decision-making process to reflect on their importance. A principal point of the containment process is the need to get the markets to orchestrate a response which is considered acceptable without setting off a panic. In many instances the steps to recapitalise a bank are initiated by the prudential supervisor. But the success of the rights issue offered by the institution will essentially be dependent on the market's confidence in the institution.[19] If it is not evident, the FSN players may intervene with public funds to recapitalise the institution. In such cases the interests of shareholders and other creditors are first in line to be wiped out. The bondholders of distressed banks will also be concerned about any risk to the credit rating of the institution and haircuts that may need to be made.

Credit-rating agencies and external auditors should be viewed as 'information intermediaries', and also play an important role: a decision to downgrade or qualify the accounts will likely result in a panic in the markets.[20] In light of these decisions the FSN players have to respond to restore confidence. However, the ability of the official safety net to assist with public support can burden the state and place pressure on its own credit rating. How these information intermediaries work with the official FSN players does vary when it comes to external auditors, with some governments relying heavily on undertaking day-to-day monitoring

---

18 D.G. Mayes, 'Moral Hazard, Bank Governance and the Protection of Depositors', *Finance and Corporate Governance Conference*, 30 November 2010.

19 E. Ferran, 'Limits of Private Sector Solutions for Banks: Recent UK Rights Issues', (2009) University of Cambridge Working Paper, No. 115/2008; E. Hüpkes, 'Special Bank Resolution and Shareholders' Rights: Balancing Competing Interests' (2009) 17 Journal of Financial Regulation and Compliance 277.

20 EFinancialNews, 'EU says need for a European rating agency' (EFinancialNews, 8 July 2011), available at http://www.efinancialnews.com/story/2011-07-08/eu-says-need-for-european-rating-agency (last accessed 14 September 2012); Evans-Pritchard, 'Europe declares war on ratings agencies', *The Telegraph*, 6 July 2011 available at http://www.telegraph.co.uk/finance/economics/8621520/Europe-declares-war-on-rating-agencies.html (last accessed 14 September 2012).

including on-site inspections.[21] However, how credit-rating agencies are to be brought under the broad regulatory umbrella has not been given as much attention as how external auditors are used in bank supervision.[22]

To avoid coordination problems between the regulator and the credit-rating agencies it may be an idea to devise a memorandum of understanding to assist in this matter in the first instance. It is suggested lessons learnt from how external auditors are used could provide valuable insights. This would mean both the external auditor and the credit-rating agency would become 'supervisory gatekeepers' in one form or another.[23] The opportunity for dialogue between the information intermediaries enables the authorities to orchestrate a response to information disclosed to the markets in a coordinated fashion rather than reacting without prior knowledge.

II. IMPROVING THE DECISION-MAKING PROCESS

Dealing with a failing financial institution or indeed a crisis is a complex matter and can involve numerous FSN players and stakeholders. In Figure 2.1 we present a decision-making guide that should be used in financial crisis management. When a crisis occurs (stage 1), particularly if it involves a bank failure that becomes the focus of media attention, it is important to determine if it is a material event (stage 2). If it is not, then no action may need to be taken. On the other hand, a large bank failure or several small or medium-sized banks failing in a short period could be problematic and lead to a systemic event which could trigger a number of subsequent steps.

Once a material event is identified the prudential regulator will be required to initiate even more intensive supervision and surveillance continuously until the matter is resolved (stage 7). It would also be hoped that the issues arising are identified soon through a formal system of early intervention which could reduce the social and economic costs of any subsequent action.[24] In addition to these steps officials need to initiate

21 House of Lords (2011), *Auditors: Market Concentration and their Role*, Volume I: Report, 30 March 2011.

22 Basel Committee on Banking Supervision, *External audit quality and banking supervision*, 2 December 2008.

23 J.C. Coffee, Jr., *Gatekeepers: The Profession and Corporate Governance* (Oxford University Press, Oxford 2006); D. Singh, 'Banking and the Role of the External Auditor: A Supervisory Gate Keeper?' Unpublished paper, 2011.

24 M. Krimminger, and R. Lastra, 'Early Intervention', in R. Lastra (ed.)

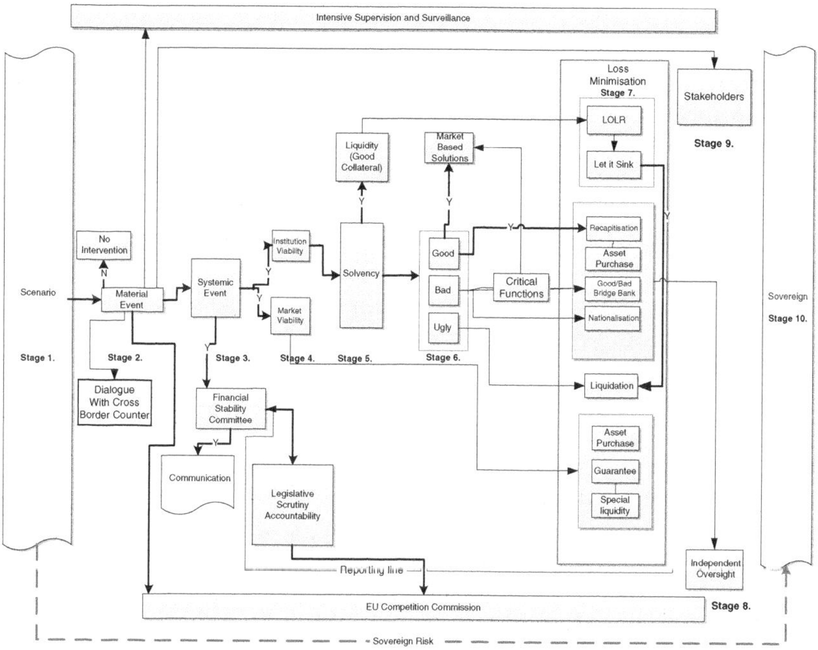

Figure 2.1 Improving decision making during a financial crisis

dialogue with overseas counterparts where the institution has a material presence to coordinate any subsequent actions.[25] One of the first initiatives should be the creation of a steering group, possibly around the financial stability committee that will oversee the management of subsequent events (stage 3).

The steering group will find value in establishing two specific committees: one charged with generating a communications plan and the other asked to develop legislative reforms that may need to be deployed at a

Cross Border Bank Insolvency, (Oxford University Press, Oxford 2011). D. Singh, 'The UK Banking Act 2009, Pre-Insolvency and Early Intervention: Policy and Practice' (2011) 1 Journal of Business Law 20.

[25] D.G. Mayes, 'Banking Crisis Resolution Policy – Lessons from Recent Experience – Which Elements are Needed for Robust and Efficient Crisis Resolution?' (2009) CESifo Working Paper Series No. 2823; R.R. Bliss and G. Kaufman, 'Resolving Large Complex Financial Institutions Within and Across Jurisdictions', in R. Herring (ed.) *Cross Border Issues in Resolving Systemically Important Financial Institutions* (Wharton Financial Institutions Center, Philadelphia 2011).

later stage of the crisis. During stage 3 the legislative body should be continuously informed and required, when necessary, to empower the FSN players with the tools to contain the crisis through legislative means, so that the public interest can be safeguarded.

When a bank is failing policy-makers are often faced with the challenge of determining whether the bank is viable (stage 4). We believe that using a test of viability is important, as it is generally considered to be a point at a higher capital level than insolvency – the latter is the stage where there is no capital left to support the bank (stages 5–6). There is always an interest in trying to 'ring-fence' a failing bank (stage 6), as failure to do so may precipitate a run on other banks and thus deepen the crisis. Policy responses could include measures such as increasing a bank's capital ratio, strengthening the quality and sources of bank capital, evaluating a bank's liquidity plans based on future cash flows, increasing credit monitoring, undertaking special examinations that could be necessary in the event of a depositor payout and expediting asset recovery.

We have introduced another dimension to this discussion: market viability, which requires a different set of containment measures. In this context we argue the tools that are utilised are market-wide facilities. Compounding the problem could be a lack of liquidity, which may require closer monitoring by the prudential regulator and possibly an extension of a government guarantee. A good example of this would be the OTC derivatives market and the concentration of risk in a relatively small number of broker dealers. If the institution is viable there might be a number of options available – the 'good' (collateral) could be sold as part of a market-based solution and the 'bad' (non-performing loans) part of the bank could be recapitalised through public funds. In that regard a bridge bank could be created to assist in a transition of parts of a bank's business to save certain critical functions.[26]

Some parts of a bank's assets book might simply be 'ugly' (non-performing after three months, severely impaired or simply ready to be written off), but with the careful attention of a bank resolution agency could be rehabilitated. For example, if a bank has taken security on a property that would have little or no value in liquidation, a bank resolution agency might be able to minimise its exposure to loss by injecting funds or taking an equity interest in the completion of the property. Guidance respect-

---

26 D.G. Mayes, 'Bridge Banks and Too Big to Fail: Systemic Risk Exemption', in D.G. Evanoff, G. Kaufman and J.R. LaBrosse *International Financial Instability: Global Banking and National Regulation*, (World Scientific, Hackensack 2007); J.R. LaBrosse, 'Save banking, not banks: formulating a standard for the use of bridge banks' (2011) Journal of International Banking and Financial Law 344.

ing bank resolutions is now more widely available and some of the more important aspects have been developed based on a survey of good and effective practices and lessons learned. Research by the Financial Stability Forum (2001), encapsulated in stages 7–9, found there are many ways to resolve a failing bank, and the techniques can generally be grouped under three headings: liquidation and reimbursement of depositors' claims; purchase-and-assumption transactions (sales); and open-bank financial assistance. Clearly, the more recent attention to 'living wills' can be helpful to regulators in evaluating options.[27] Existing bankruptcy/insolvency and other laws regulating things such as depositor priority may influence heavily the choice of resolution methods, and in some cases may make a particular resolution method difficult to implement.

The potential failure of a number of banks in a short period can threaten the stability of markets, so we have provided a separate category within the concept of viability to include market viability. We argue normatively that the need to maintain market viability may not necessarily be minimised by the introduction of innovative restructuring and resolution powers. So in a market where liquidity is scarce the FSN players may still be required to step in with additional liquidity support or other schemes, namely asset purchase or liability guarantee schemes. When the market as a whole becomes too fragile, the option of closing several banks or non-banks may not be available.

In stage 7 we address various options and strategies for loss minimisation. The first group surrounds the role of LOLR for institutions that are experiencing short-term liquidity problems. The next set of options is for institutions that are primarily experiencing insolvency issues of various degrees. The subsections provide options either to recapitalise or restructure the bank and ring-fence the good parts from the bad. In circumstances where the bank is possibly too big to rescue, as a last resort the FSN may decide the best option is to nationalise it. A primary task with those options is to ensure that the critical functions are safeguarded.[28] The last set of options, the provision of guarantees to the market, gives rise to contingent liabilities that require careful monitoring. Finally, we have set out a stage 9: the FSN needs to consider the various stakeholders, as they can have a significant impact on decisions.

---

27 E. Avgouleas, C. Goodhart and D. Schoenmaker, 'Living Wills as a Catalyst for Action' (2010) DSF Policy Paper, No. 4, 1.

28 E. Hüpkes, 'Too Big to Save – Towards a Functional Approach to Resolving Crises in Global Financial Institutions', in D. Evanoff, and G. Kaufman, *Systemic Financial Crises: Resolving Large Bank Insolvencies* (World Scientific, Hackensack 2005).

The 2008 financial crisis provoked extensive use of techniques such as loan guarantees, capital injections and sales of assets, banks or parts thereof (stage 7).[29] The exercise of these additional tools requires the setting up of an independent body (stage 8) to oversee the public interest in government assistance to private banks. As we show below, a number of countries introduced various types of independent oversight bodies, such as asset management companies or simply an entity to manage the relationship between the government and the publicly recapitalised banks. It is suggested that some kind of reporting line needs to be put in place between the newly established body and the legislative body so there is additional oversight of what they are doing. We have set out the need for the FSN players to have in mind the decisions taken by key stakeholders, namely credit-rating agencies and external auditors, referred to here as 'supervisory gatekeepers' (stage 9).[30]

The power of shareholders needs to be considered, as they can potentially block any negotiated takeover during such periods. It is clear that some countries experienced difficulties in accessing international financial markets which led to a position where they needed either to seek assistance from the IMF (Hungary) or assistance from key regional players (Iceland, which was helped by certain Nordic countries). Later, as the problem with Ireland worsened, the UK provided assistance and both Iceland and Ireland subsequently received IMF assistance.

At the bottom of the decision tree we have placed the EU Competition Commission. It is evident that the Competition Commission has been crucial to monitor the moral hazard implications of the bailout operations.

As we have shown, the agencies within the FSN all have mandates and roles, and benefits can be achieved through the creation of an FSC: it would bring those discrete roles together so that if a change in supervision needs to take place it can be initiated from a broader vantage point.[31] If certain stress points are detected, it would be a good platform to direct change or hold those responsible for regulation and supervision to account. The stress points in the financial markets were certainly discussed in the financial stability reports, but how the information trickled down into day-to-day regulation and supervision is not so clear.

---

[29] D. Singh, 'UK Approach to Financial Crisis Management', Transnational Law and Contemporary Problems, Winter 2011, 872; R. Lastra and G. Wood, 'Bank Insolvency in the Context of Crisis Management', in R. Lastra (ed.) *Cross Border Bank Insolvency* (Oxford University Press, Oxford 2011).

[30] Singh (2011) supra n. 24.

[31] E.W. Nier, J. Osiński, L.I. Jácome and P. Madrid (2011), 'Towards Effective Macroprudential Policy Frameworks: An Assessment of Stylized Institutional Models' (2011) IMF Working Paper, WP/11/250.

The FSC therefore needs to have a surveillance role linking macro-oversight with micro-regulation, distinguishing it from any regulatory or supervisory role. One thing which does seem inevitable with the introduction of the new generation of financial stability oversight is that the 'conversation' about financial stability could flow into a range of financial and economic policy affairs. The FSC will need to have a mandate to act and initiate actions to prevent a financial and economic system overheating. This will obviously pose considerable political tensions, but as we have seen the risk to financial stability can arise from a variety of sources and bank and non-bank institutions, and the following of certain social and economic policy objectives. Nor is it likely that the FSC will extend or be allowed to extend its reach beyond concerns about the financial system, hence the political expectations will not mirror the actual reality.

The role of crisis management needs to be clearly given to one of the FSN players. But to whom is quite possibly a contentious issue. Crisis management does raise a variety of concerns about conflicts of interests over whether or not banks and markets should be assisted. One option would be to allocate crisis management and bank resolution to an independent FSC. This would be sensible on two counts: firstly, no agent responsible for the day-to-day oversight of a firm or a market will ultimately have the power to decide to use public finances for a bailout; and secondly, there would be a degree of independence over crisis management separate from the political body. This is obviously controversial but it would build on the principle of independent regulators under the Basel core principles 2006, with an extension to include independent crisis management. It could also be desirable to have a voting system on such decisions to reduce supervisory and political capture.

The creation of an FSC is well established. However, recent experience has highlighted the need for better coordination and cooperation between the official safety net players when considering stability. The preliminary research in this section suggests there is no real specific model on structuring financial stability oversight. What seems to be important is what powers it should be given. Certainly an expectation gap will grow with the introduction of a new generation of financial stability committees. At first glance it seems EU members that experienced some sort of crisis do have some responsibility for crisis management. In other jurisdictions it is implicit that maintaining financial stability will inherently mean restoring it, if and when a crisis occurs. One point that must be highlighted is the need for a separate budget and resources to enable the FSC to fulfil its mandate. It is suggested that it should be separately funded to safeguard its independent position.

CONCLUSIONS

The chapter examined a decision-making process associated with containing a financial crisis and the possible policy options. It first highlighted the importance of having access to a range of options. It suggests a ten-step process to dealing with a crisis and the possible issues associated with the decision making. However, as we have explained, many of these options are not within the traditional toolkit of the narrow set of FSN players, and gaining those powers during a crisis could delay matters.

It is suggested that elaborating on the specific roles of the various interested parties helps policy-makers better understand how the FSN should work during times of crisis. Moreover, it will assist with a better understanding of what tools are actually required to contain a crisis and whether the legislative body needs to provide those tools. A key lesson learnt during the crisis has been the need to understand the roles of the different FSN players and how they work together as a crisis intensifies. The chapter has also tried to bring in the importance of the key stakeholders and the influence they can have on the decision making associated with a systemic crisis. While the countries at the epicentre of the crisis may now recognise the importance of the FSN, those not quite gripped by the crisis can certainly learn lessons: the importance of timely decision making and the expectations associated with the FSN players and the wider stakeholders.

Another facet is how to bring the key themes of the crisis together. The perimeter of the macro-prudential and micro-prudential dialogue highlights the complexity of managing a financial crisis and the difficulty of trying to build a coherent decision-making process. The move to a separate oversight body like an FSC is certainly a useful one to try and should be given appropriate attention. However, the powers and responsibilities it will have need further reflection. One issue that needs to be addressed is with whom the ultimate responsibility for crisis management should reside. It is suggested that the new generation of financial stability committees should have the responsibility in order to improve the level of independence of decision making and quite possibly the speed with which decisions can be made. Had policy-makers better understood the roles and responsibilities of the agencies within and outside the FSN and had they adopted a better decision-making process, then perhaps the crisis might have turned out just a bit different this time.

3. Powers and scope of the macro-prudential authority

Charles A.E. Goodhart

INTRODUCTION

The onset of the financial crisis, which began in mid-2007 and is still with us, led to a general realisation that there had been a missing link in the overall structure of financial regulation. Monetary policy had focused (successfully) on price stability and general macroeconomic stability. But this was not enough to ensure financial stability; indeed it might even be inimical to it, as Minsky had warned in 1977, 1982 and 1986.[1] Micro-prudential regulation, as promulgated internationally by the Basel Committee on Banking Supervision[2] and operated nationally by a variety of official organisations, some within and mostly without their national Central Banks, had focused unduly on the conditions and prospects of the *individual* financial intermediary, in particular the individual bank. Far too much weight was attached to the achievement and implementation of the Basel II Capital Accord for individual banks (and in the US for the large investment houses). Particularly in conjunction with the increasing application of mark-to-market accounting, the regulatory apparatus had allowed the financial system as a whole to become dangerously procyclical. Leverage increased in many countries and in many guises. Not only did regulators fail to appreciate the lurking dangers, but so did markets, as illustrated by the decline in major bank CDS rates to their low point in early 2007.

---

1 H.P. Minsky, 'A Theory of Systemic Fragility', in E.I. Altman and A.W. Sametz (eds), *Financial Crises* (Wiley, New York 1977); H.P. Minsky, *Can 'It' Happen Again? Essays on Instability and Finance*, (M.E. Sharpe, Inc., Armonk, NY 1982); H.P. Minsky, *Stabilizing an Unstable Economy* (Yale University Press, New Haven 1986).

2 See C.A.E Goodhart, *The Basel Committee on Banking Supervision: A History of the Early Years, 1974–1997*, (Cambridge University Press, Cambridge 2011).

Following shortly after the onset of the financial crisis in 2007, this theme has been argued and has been now widely accepted.[3] A new approach, macro-prudential, is to be adopted by the authorities, with the relevant macro-prudential organisation bridging the (now revealed) gap between the Central Bank (CB), in its role as monetary policy authority, and the micro-prudential authority. Such macro-prudential institutions are springing up, like field mushrooms after a September rain, in a wide range of countries; the Financial Policy Committee in the UK, the Financial Stability Oversight Committee in the US, the European Systemic Risk Board; J-C. Rochet and I have separately been involved in proposing the adoption of a similar macro-prudential authority in Sweden.[4]

If the new macro-prudential authority is to have some bite and ability to provide systemic financial stability, it needs to be given the requisite powers to do so. We discuss what these powers might be.

I. THE POWERS OF THE MACRO-PRUDENTIAL AUTHORITY

A. The Central Bank's Balance Sheet

In a crisis money is 'king'. In modern economies the CB is the monopoly issuer of 'high-powered' money, notably to the financial system. A macro-prudential authority by itself has no money. So, it has to have access to the CB's balance sheet. Buiter has argued that such an authority could be separate from the CB,[5] but yet have an independent ability to draw on the CB's balance sheet without getting prior permission from the CB. In my view that would diminish the independence and powers of the CB, so much so that the macro-prudential authority (M-PA) would become itself

---

3 M.K Brunnermeier, A. Crockett, C.A. Goodhart, A.D. Persaud and Hyun Song Shin, 'The Fundamental Principles of Financial Regulation', (2010) July, Center for Economic Policy Research 1.

4 C.A.E Goodhart and J.-C. Rochet, 'Evaluation of the Riksbank's monetary policy and work with financial stability 2005–2010', (2011) Reports from the Riksdag 2010/11:RFR5, The Committee on Finance, Sveriges Riksdag.

5 W. Buiter, 'Central banks and financial crises', paper presented at the Federal Reserve Bank of Kansas City's symposium on 'Maintaining Stability in a Changing Financial System', Jackson Hole, Wyoming, 21–23 August 2008 and W. Buiter, 'Reversing unconventional monetary policy', lecture given at the 28th SUERF Colloquium in Utrecht, the Netherlands, 3 September 2009.

a second CB. This would be constitutionally and institutionally difficult, and could build conflict into the heart of the regulatory system. In my view this is the central argument why the M-PA has to be located within the CB.

But such a location does not, of itself, resolve the potential conflict between the price stability and the financial stability objectives of policy. Both in some large part depend upon the manipulation and control of the CB's balance sheet. Yet there is a (quite neat) potential separation between the (balance sheet) requirements for the two objectives. The official short-term interest rate requires – that is, is the 'dual' of – a certain quantum of (bank) high-powered money balances. Thus the overall size (quantum) of the CB's balance sheet must be controlled by the Monetary Policy Committee (MPC). When such official rates hit the zero bound, further quantitative easing (QE) is again a function of the MPC. Since World War II, the greater bulk of most CBs' assets have been held in government debt. Insofar as the CB wants, and feels able, to affect the yield curve of interest rates on government debt by varying the maturity/duration of public sector debt that it holds, then that also should be within the province of the MPC.

While the achievement of a chosen official interest rate requires a given quantum of CB liabilities, the nature and form of the counterpart assets in the CB's portfolio is, as a generality, irrelevant to that end. Such CB assets can take the form of claims on the public sector, claims on the private sector and claims on the rest of the world (ROW). CB claims on the ROW, part of the official reserves of each country, are in most countries determined strategically by the government, with the CB acting as agent in the tactical management of such reserves. By the same token the Financial Policy Committee (FPC) should decide on the main outlines, and quantum, of CB lending to the private sector. Such lending could take several forms: Lender of Last Resort (LOLR) loans and/or Emergency Liquidity Assistance (ELA) lending to individual, or sets of, financial intermediaries is the main traditional form of such lending, but credit easing (CE), as practised recently by the Fed in the US, in order to restore the proper activity of dysfunctional markets, is another example. Moreover, in previous centuries the main staple of CB balance sheets had been commercial bills of exchange, rather than government debt. The purchase of such 'real bills' was then thought to be less inherently inflationary and more conducive to financial stability than that of government debt. Prior to 1914 claims on the private sector, rather than claims on the public sector, formed the main part of CB balance sheets.

Currently, however, there is a strong contention, mostly emanating from the US (for example, Goodfriend[6] but also see Buiter[7]) that such purchases of claims on the private sector should be minimized, or even avoided altogether. This assertion rests on a number of arguments. Some of them are better founded than others. Let me start with those that I regard as least well founded.

1. Purchasing private sector claims is 'quasi-fiscal'

In one sense this is a ridiculous assertion. What could be more fiscal than a purchase of public sector assets, thereby changing the interest rate burden that the taxpayer has to meet. Assuming that the return is identical, the seignorage transferred to the Treasury is the same whether the CB holds public or private sector debt.

So what is presumably meant by this assertion is that the pattern of purchases of assets by the CB alters the distribution of relative yields/returns, and so benefits one sector of the private sector relative to another; in other words, that the composition of the CB's balance sheet can have a distributional effect, and that such allocative/distributional effects are properly a function of the Treasury/legislature.

There are problems with this argument. Insofar as the financial system is perfectly efficient, the yield/return on all such assets should be a function of fundamentals, for example, prospective future cash flows. So shifting the balance sheet of one (relatively small) player in the financial market should have zero effect on relative prices (and Operation Twist should fail). So, in order for the composition of the CB's balance sheet, including LOLR or ELA loans, to matter there must be frictions, asymmetric information, inefficiencies in the financial systems, as of course there are. Indeed, it is exactly those frictions, inefficiencies and so on, that require the ministration of an M-PA in the first place. It follows, therefore, that those who believe that macro-prudential policy is needed should also believe that this might properly be undertaken, at least in part, via CB operations in private sector assets.

2. Purchasing private sector assets is too risky

In view of the recent travails of the sovereign debt of peripheral euro-zone countries, it is not obvious that longer-duration public sector debt is less

---

6 M. Goodfriend, 'Central Banking in the Credit Turmoil: An Assessment of Federal Reserve Practice' presented at the Conference on 'Monetary-Fiscal Policy Interactions, Expectations, and Dynamics in the Current Economic Crisis', 22–23 May 2009, Princeton University, Princeton, NJ.

7 Buiter above (n. 5) and W. Buiter, 'Accountability of the Bank of England' Global Economics View, Citigroup Global Markets, 1 June 2011.

risky than shorter-dated private sector debt. But there is an additional consideration. The CB is within the public sector. Thus a loss (gain) to the CB from valuation changes on holding its *own* government's debt is, more or less, exactly counterbalanced by an offsetting change in the net present value of the Exchequer's debt.[8] The taxpayer is not affected directly, though the associated change in interest rates will of course have an impact.

In contrast, when a CB holds claims on the private sector, then changes in the value of such claims feed through directly into changes in the net debt of the public sector; though the net wealth of the country remains unchanged, it does shift the balance between taxpayers and others. Even so, the scale of CB claims on the private sector is usually minute, relative to overall public sector indebtedness. Moreover, so long as the financial system is efficient, with prices/yields dependent on fundamentals only, purchases/sales by the CB should have minimal impact on relative prices. It is only if/when financial frictions/inefficiencies occur, that CB market intervention could have a major effect on such relative prices. But it is in exactly such conditions that macro-prudential actions can be effective and would be desirable if done appropriately.

That said, CBs can be, and are, often blamed for interventions that subsequently lose money. The recent attacks on the Swiss National Bank for their intervention in the foreign exchange market provide an illustration. The desire by the CB to obtain some prior Treasury indemnity against losses on its purchases of assets, other than its own government debt, is more a function of institutional self-protection then of economic validity. Nevertheless concerns for self-protection are deeply felt, and ground rules for CB interventions in private sector markets might need to be spelt out in advance.

3. Private sector markets are relatively efficient

In some senses this argument is the reverse of the previous two, to wit that private sector markets are so efficient that CB intervention will, on balance, drive prices/yields further away from, rather than closer to, their fundamental equilibrium. If so, the intervention of a relatively small investor should not have much effect. Once again, it is the existence of financial frictions, of asymmetric information, of externalities and systemic effects that justifies such intervention.

Thus the first macro-prudential instrument that should be used by CBs is the ability to intervene in order to purchase (or sell) claims on the private

---

8 When a CB, such as the ECB, holds the debt of subsidiary states, there will then of course be differential effects on the taxpayers of each relevant state.

sector, including of course loans to banks or other systemically important financial institutions (SIFIs).

This division of the responsibilities for the MPC, on the quantum of the CB's balance sheet, and for the FPC, for the private sector component of that balance sheet, has the further connotation that policy conflicts between the two bodies (MPC and FPC) should not be a serious issue. Of course, actions by each affect the context in which the other works, though tightening by the FPC on ratio controls can either raise, or lower, interest rates, depending on whether the strengthened ratio falls on a lender or a borrower (for example, loan-to-value (LTV)). Nevertheless coordination problems between the MPC and FPC need be no more severe, probably much less, than coordination between the fiscal and the monetary authorities. While this latter could become more problematical, as public sector debts and deficits rise, they have not, as yet, prevented the successful operation of an independent MPC. On this view the potentiality for conflict between the FPC and the MPC is a non-issue, especially given the overlap of Committee members.

B. Constraints on the Process of Financial Intermediation

Constraints on the exercise of financial intermediation can take the form of applying various kinds of controls over the capital adequacy and liquid asset holdings of financial intermediaries. In a sense they can be viewed as margin requirements with respect to financial intermediation. They can, moreover, be accompanied by controls over the payment of dividends and certain forms of remuneration (for example, bonuses), in some cases as sanctions should the intermediaries violate their margin (capital/liquidity) requirements (see for example the current proposals for the European Commission's (EC) Capital Requirements Directive, Fourth Version (CRD4)).

If such constraints are to bite, they presumably put those on whom the requirements fall in a less preferred position. In this sense direct constraints are somewhat similar to a tax, (as will be discussed later in I.C below). In a global financial system, without exchange controls, how far can any single M-PA impose penalties/taxes on its own financial intermediaries/markets without losing a large proportion of its financial business abroad? The 'level-playing-field' argument has always been the most potent argument against individual authorities' attempts to tighten regulation in its own jurisdiction, and this specifically does include the US. Consequently almost all effective attempts to impose common ratio requirements, especially on capital, have been taken at the global, international level, for example, by the Basel Committee on Banking Supervision (BCBS) and/or by the Financial Stability Board (FSB), previously the Financial Stability Forum (FSF).

In theory margin controls, for example, in the form of capital adequacy ratios (CARs), ought to be tightened during periods of credit/asset price expansion, and lowered during recessions, in a counter-cyclical manner.[9] But such financial cycles are not uniform across countries, as was exemplified during the build-up to the current crisis, with the US, the UK, Spain, Ireland, and Iceland having much stronger financial cycles than Germany, France, Italy and Japan. So, if there is to be some counter-cyclical element in the application of ratio requirements, this would seem to push responsibility for such actions back to national authorities and raise again the 'level-playing-field' issue.

In this latter respect there has been one, potentially major, step forward, offset by a partial step backwards. The advance was achieved in a recent BCBS agreement on Countercyclical Capital Buffers[10] that lending into a host country, whether by an intermediary located inside, or outside, that country, should bear the capital ratio applicable within that host country. So, should Canada, for example, raise the CAR on loans to commercial property in Canada by an additional X per cent, then a Japanese bank making such loans out of its Tokyo office would have to apply the same extra X per cent CAR on them. While this complicates somewhat the administrative calculation of CARs, this does provide much more scope for individual countries to apply counter-cyclical (time and state varying) ratios, freer from the 'level-playing-field' critique.

The partial step backwards is to be found in the current proposals by the EC that the regulatory requirements in the EU should involve a rule-book which not only provided minimum harmonisation (no member state could apply lower ratios unilaterally), but also maximum harmonisation (no country allowed to impose tougher requirements unilaterally). This would prevent any member state introducing additional requirements independently. There is no necessary barrier that would prevent the option of more granular (member state/sectoral) counter-cyclical, time-varying, ratios being built into EU-wide rules, to be put in place by agreement *between* the EU regulator and the member state M-PA, but such general enthusiasm for a single,

---

9 See C. Borio, 'Implementing the Macroprudential Approach to Financial Regulation and Supervision', (2009) 13 Banque de France Financial Stability Review 31–41; M. Drehmann, C. Borio, L. Gambacorta, G. Jiménez, and C. Trucharte, 'Countercyclical Capital Buffers: Exploring Options', 298 BIS Working Papers (2010).

10 2010, pp. 3–9, available at http://www.bis.org/publ/bcbs172.htm (last accessed 14 September 2012).

common EU-wide application of rules will, on this view, lead to a strong bias towards 'one regulation fits all'. This is another illustration of the tension between differing national conditions, for example in fiscal, legal and institutional arrangements, leading to differing economic and financial conditions, and the desire for monetary and financial harmonization within the EU.

It will be interesting to see how far the European Systemic Risk Board (ESRB) focuses on particular national danger spots, or confines itself, as does the ECB in its pursuit of price stability, to examining some EU average. If tiny Greece is at risk of financial explosion, but mighty Germany is robust, would the ESRB declare the average to be sound, with no worries? In view of the contagion, observed both with the ERM collapses in 1991–92 and with the current sovereign debt crisis, such a concentration on the EU average would be hard to justify. If the ESRB, then, is going to explore potential fragilities market by market, country by country, it must then endorse individual country M-PAs' and FSAs' ability to take independent countervailing action. So might the ESRB and the EC find themselves in some conflict over the ability of the member states to vary such required ratios?

Because of the 'level-playing-field' concern, the minimum level of CARs and liquidity ratios will need to be set internationally, at Basel. One perennial problem is that the BCBS/FSB has always shied away from proposing how such ratios might be enforced, regarding the application of sanctions as a national prerogative in a Westphalian system. While understandable, this stance has been most regrettable.[11] The more that regulations are now tightened, to represent desirable conditions rather than irreducible minima, the more the question of designing ladders of sanctions (slight initially, toughened steadily, and ultimately involving intervention by the state to take over the weakening institution), needs to be urgently addressed. If the international bodies continue to refuse to do this, it will have to be tackled by the national macro- and micro-prudential authorities. Penalties for violation of CARs have now apparently been built into the current proposals for CRD4; the details will need to be examined to consider how appropriate these may be.

Thus, on this front, the proposal is that national M-PAs should be given the power to impose additional ratio requirements on capital and liquidity, within their own domain, above those agreed internationally. These should be capable of counter-cyclical time variation and also be as sectorally granular as the M-PA thinks appropriate. Beyond this, the

---

[11] C.A.E Goodhart, *The Basel Committee on Banking Supervision: A History of the Early Years, 1974–1997*, (Cambridge University Press, Cambridge 2011).

M-PA should think carefully about sanctions for intermediaries falling below the desired ratios, the more so the less willing are the international bodies to grasp this nettle.

Ratios applied to banks (and to insurance companies) alone may penalise intermediation through this particular channel, and encourage disintermediation via other shadowy sub-systems. By the same token margins on derivative transactions (to be encouraged to be undertaken *via* centralised counter-parties (CCPs) or even on more formalised exchanges), may induce substitution into over-the-counter (OTC) transactions. As Kashyap, Berner and Goodhart[12] argue, there needs to be a degree of harmonisation of margin controls, between banks and non-banks, and between markets, whether formal exchanges or OTC. There is a 'level-playing-field' argument between institutional arrangements within countries, as well as between countries. The imposition of (asymmetric) penalties (taxes) on the most visible, largest and probably the most efficient intermediaries (that is, the banks) may have an increasing effect in diverting such intermediation towards less visible, and possibly less efficient, channels.

There is also a question as to whether margin controls should be imposed primarily on the lender, for example the bank, or on the borrower. Since money is fungible, imposing such controls on A rather than B just encourages a diversion whereby B borrows and then lends to A; and there are other ways of avoiding such controls. Nevertheless, if lending is much cheaper if it can be collateralised, as in the case of a mortgage, then restricting the extent of such securitisation *via* a loan-to-value ratio, or a loan-to-income ratio can be (partially) effective.

To date margin controls in the shape of CARs and liquidity ratios for banks (and insurance companies) have been at the centre of regulators' attention. Particularly if such ratio controls are now to be considerably tightened (as can well be justified), much more thought needs to be given to a ladder of sanctions for transgression, and to the possible application of somewhat similar ratios to other channels of intermediation and to some sets of borrowers (for example, households borrowing on mortgages for house purchase).

C. Taxation

In I.B above, the correspondence between direct regulatory controls, for example, in the form of required ratios, and taxation applied to banks was

---

12 A.K. Kashyap, R. Berner and C.A.E. Goodhart, 'The Macroprudential Toolkit', (2011) 59 IMF Economic Review 145.

noted. For any regulatory requirement, supported by some set of sanctions for violation, there is a tax regime (or regimes) applied to the same base that would achieve the same objective. Thus, if the authorities want banks, say, on average to hold 10 per cent of core tier 1 equity capital, they can either impose a minimum requirement of, say, eight per cent, and sufficient penalties on violation that banks on average hold a two per cent buffer margin, or they can impose a graduated tax on capital ratios below, say, 15 per cent, such that banks choose to hold the 10 per cent desired ratio. In that sense a requirement can be regarded as the dual of the tax.

Controlling banks, and their risk taking, by taxation rather than by direct requirements has both advantages and disadvantages. Amongst the advantages is that it gives the individual institution (bank) more chance to optimise its position, subject to its own particular preferences/conditions/constraints. Requirements tend to be one-size-fits-all; and when varied between institutions this is usually based on broad-brush, somewhat arbitrary characteristics (for example, size). Another advantage, of course, is that this approach provides revenue to the relevant fiscal authorities, whereas direct requirements generally do not do so (apart from pecuniary violation penalties, if any).

This latter is, however, also a disadvantage from the point of view of the macro-prudential authorities, whether national or international, since the imposition of taxes is clearly a fiscal exercise, and such M-PAs have no fiscal competence, whereas they have been accorded the ability to recommend, indeed now to require, the application of ratio (and other margin requirements). Another drawback of taxes, as a means of limiting risk-taking, is that, without considerable experience and experimentation, one does not know quite what average results one may get from a tax, whereas a minimum requirement, supported by appropriate sanctions, will deliver outcomes slightly above that minimum. Moreover, those institutions keenest to take on risk, to gamble for resurrection, will choose to absorb most tax and hold the lowest ratios, whereas ideally one would want the greatest risk-lovers to be forced to hold the highest ratios. Against this it can be argued that at least those imposing most risk on the community at least pay more for doing so (and the tax need not be linear in application).

Whatever the balance of advantages and disadvantages, what is somewhat remarkable is how little attention was given to the possibility of using taxation on intermediaries (or on housing transactions) as a potential macro-prudential and counter-cyclical instrument, at least prior to the last couple of years. This was partly due to a mind-set whereby financial regulation was supposed to be done by direct imposition of (ratio) controls, whereas taxation was a separate fiscal exercise. The point that financial regulation was primarily justified by the existence of, socially adverse, externalities and that (Pigovian) taxes represented a feasible remedy for such externalities was simply not taken on board.

Once, however, President Obama raised the issue of potentially imposing taxes on banks, in early 2010, the floodgates opened, and bank taxation has since remained a common topic of policy discussion. From the macro-prudential viewpoint, however, a disadvantage of bank tax proposals is that there are many other motives for taxing banks besides influencing their risk-taking. Such taxes raise revenue for the public sector at a time of high public sector deficit/debt. Part of such deficit/debt was due to taxpayer support for a fragile banking system, so taxing the perpetrators of the need for such support seems 'appropriate'. Furthermore, banks are castigated not only for their behaviour but also for their excessive remuneration, so bank taxes can be seen as 'pay-back' time; bank taxation is politically popular. Some large part of bank activity is (loosely) described as a 'casino', 'speculative' or 'socially useless'. Insofar as such activity can be separately identified, it would seem ripe for taxation.

In the midst of this emotional cauldron the fact that any such taxation is likely to change the behaviour of banks towards risk-taking, and alter the wider financial stability of the banking system as a whole can potentially get lost. An example was the (soon abandoned) proposal (dated 21 July 2011) to tax euro-zone banks to provide some private sector support for Greek sovereign debt; since much of the problem of the euro-zone periphery comes from the interaction between bank and sovereign debt, it is not immediately obvious why extra bank taxes, for example, on Irish and Spanish banks, would be a sensible response.

In view of the many potential purposes of bank taxation, the fact that such taxation should be constitutionally introduced by the relevant legislature, and that any proposals for such taxation may get hijacked by special interest groups, what, if any, should be the role of M-PAs in relation to such taxation? In my view they should have a right and a duty in this respect. Their right should be to advocate to the executive and to the legislature proposals for the adoption of a bank tax that would in their view improve the country's financial stability. In view of the above considerations I would not expect such a right to be exercised often. Moreover, any citizen has a right to propose a tax change, so this right is not particularly valuable. However, insofar as a Financial Policy Committee, or an ESRB, gains credibility, its authority would mean that any specific proposal by them would be taken seriously.

The duty, suggested here, is likely to be far more important. This is that the FPC should have the obligation of assessing the implications for the stability of the financial system of any proposal to tax financial intermediaries or financial transactions undertaken within the country, and to present such assessment in the shape of a public document before the (relevant Committee of the) legislature. We should not allow any such legislation to be adopted without a careful, professional assessment of its effects on financial stability by the M-PA.

By the same token the FPC should have the right to propose legislation that would alter the structural features of the financial system, such as limits on the size or functions of banks, and the duty to comment on legislative proposals with these same effects emanating from other entities. The Independent Commission on Banking (Vickers Commission) is just such an instance. The FPC should report to the House of Commons in the UK its own view on the implications of their recommendations for the financial stability of this country.

Such structural measures should also include those that would affect the relative rights of creditors and debtors in the event of the failure of a financial intermediary, such as (changes in) deposit insurance arrangements, government guarantees to be offered to various classes of creditors, netting procedures, revisions to bankruptcy laws applicable to financial intermediaries, once again an MP-A should have the right to make proposals, and the duty to comment, in public, on proposals put forward by others.

These latter measures concern legal and structural circumstances relating to crisis resolution, whereas all the prior discussion had been about the role of the M-PA in crisis prevention. This brings us neatly to the next general topic of what role, if any, an M-PA should have in crisis resolution.

D. Crisis Resolution

Although some aspects of crisis prevention have fiscal aspects, notably taxes that influence bank behaviour, most do not. Nevertheless CB independence in this respect (crisis prevention) is just as cogent and desirable as in the case of the MPC and price stability, and for similar reasons. Amongst these are that counter-cyclical measures to dampen (asset price) booms are widely and politically unpopular. But crisis resolution generally requires the allocation of losses, and these often fall on taxpayers. So, the control and governance of crisis resolution organisations should come under the direct control of the relevant Minister of Finance. The UK Chancellor of the Exchequer, George Osborne, was reported in the Press as having emphasised the need to distinguish between the governance of crisis prevention and of crisis management. He is right to do so.

Moreover, the professional skills in instances of crisis resolution will be primarily legal and accounting, and related to micro-issues such as asset managing and running-off portfolios of impaired loans, rather than the economic and analytical expertise of an M-PA. In those countries with specialised resolution agencies, such as the FDIC in the US or the Swedish National Debt Office, there is no suggestion, nor enthusiasm, for merging these into an M-PA or an expanded CB.

Nevertheless many countries have not previously had a Special Resolution Regime for banks, or SIFIs, and many of these will not have an organisation ready on hand to undertake the resultant requirements for handling such crisis situations. The options would seem to be three. First, to create a new stand-alone body; second, to imbed it in the existing micro-prudential FSA; and third, to place it in the CB/M-PA.

The first option is the least attractive; it would be wasteful of scarce resources, especially since crises should be rare events. A stand-alone organisation would have too little to do normally, but would be overwhelmed at times of crisis. On this view the second option, to imbed the resolution organisation in the FSA is preferable to the third option. The skill profiles required match more closely; and the need for the CB/M-PA to be (mostly) independent of government, whereas the resolution authority should work closely with the Ministry of Finance, are reasons for incorporating the resolution authority with the FSA, not with the CB/M-PA.

Yet the opposite was chosen in the UK. Under the Banking Act of 2009, establishing a Special Resolution Regime, the Bank of England was made responsible for carrying out resolutions of intermediaries subject to that Act. There was relatively little discussion whether this latter was appropriate. Now that the FSA has been disbanded, and the legacy Prudential Regulation Authority (PRA) brought under the aegis of the FPC and of the Bank of England, there is perhaps an opportunity for reconsideration, and reallocation of the organisation responsible for resolution back to the PRA, rather than having it in the Bank of England.

SUMMARY

In this Chapter we have established a rather neat taxonomy of macro-prudential powers and functions. These are:

(a) the power to alter the composition of Central Bank assets, for liquidity and market interventions;
(b) the power to adjust margins (CARs, liquidity ratios, LTVs and so on) to influence the conduct of financial intermediation;
(c) the power to propose fiscal and structural amendments affecting financial intermediation, and the duty to comment on such proposals emanating from other sources;
(d) the power to undertake financial resolutions.

Partly because of the difference in the appropriate governance (and accountability) mechanisms, we have argued that potential power D should *not* be assigned to an M-PA, but should either go to a specialist entity, such as the FDIC, or be imbedded in the micro-prudential FSA.

4. Resolving systemically important financial institutions (SIFIs): The Financial Stability Board key attributes of effective resolution regimes

Eva Hüpkes[1]

INTRODUCTION

At a recent Summit, G20 Leaders asked the Financial Stability Board (FSB) to develop a policy framework to reduce the risks of moral hazard and the potential for contagion and systemic disruption associated with systemically important financial institutions (SIFIs). SIFIs are financial institutions whose distress or disorderly failure, because of their size, complexity and systemic interconnectedness, would cause significant disruption to the wider financial system and economic activity.

In 2010 in Seoul, the G20 endorsed the broad policy framework which is set out in a report to the G20 entitled 'Reducing the moral hazard posed by systemically important financial institutions'.[2] This framework consists of:

- a requirement that SIFIs and initially in particular global SIFIs (G-SIFIs) have additional loss absorption capacity beyond the Basel III standards to reflect the greater risks that these institutions pose to the global financial system;
- improvements to resolution regimes to enable national authorities to resolve financial institutions whatever their size without disruptions to the financial system and without taxpayer support;

[1] The views expressed in this chapter are those of the author in her personal capacity and do not necessarily reflect the views of the FSB or any of its members.

[2] 'Reducing the moral hazard posed by systemically important financial institutions', 20 October 2010, available at http://www.financialstabilityboard.org/publications/r_101111a.pdf (last accessed 17 September 2012).

- more intensive and effective supervision through strengthened supervisory capacity and resources, and raised supervisory expectations for risk management functions, risk data aggregation capabilities, risk governance and internal controls;
- stronger robustness standards for core financial market infrastructures, including central counterparties (CCPs), central securities depositories (CSDs) and trade repositories; and
- rigorous implementation monitoring and reviews by an FSB Peer Review Council (PRC) to evaluate consistency in the implementation of G-SIFI specific requirements.

At the Cannes Summit in November 2011, the G20 endorsed the critical elements of this framework. A core element is a new international standard for resolution – the 'FSB Key Attributes of Effective Resolution Regimes'[3] (FSB Key Attributes).[4] This chapter reviews the key elements of effective resolution regimes as articulated by the FSB.

I. THE FSB KEY ATTRIBUTES OF EFFECTIVE RESOLUTION REGIMES

The Key Attributes set out 12 essential features that should be part of resolution regimes in all jurisdictions. Their implementation should improve authorities' capacity to resolve failing SIFIs. The Preamble to the Key Attributes defines the public policy objectives and key functions of effective resolution regimes: in particular, effective resolution regimes should make feasible the resolution of failing or problem financial institutions without severe systemic disruption and without exposing taxpayers to loss while preserving the vital economic functions.

A. Scope

Key Attribute 1 sets out the scope of the new standard: any financial institution that could be systemically significant or critical if it fails should be subject to a resolution regime that has the attributes set out by the FSB. The scope is not limited to banks, but also covers finan-

---

[3] 'Key Attributes of Effective Resolution Regimes for Financial Institutions', October 2011, available at http://www.financialstabilityboard.org/publications/r_111104cc.pdf (last accessed 17 September 2012).

[4] Ibid.

cial market infrastructures (FMIs), including central counterparties, and other non-bank financial institutions. To facilitate comprehensive group-wide solutions, the resolution authority should extend to holding companies of the failing financial institution that are located within the same jurisdiction as well as non-regulated operational entities within a financial group that are significant to the regulated business of the financial group.

B. Resolution Authority

Key Attribute 2 provides that the resolution regime should be administered by a designated administrative authority or authorities with the expertise, resources and the operational capacity and independence to effectively apply the resolution measures. The resolution authority (or authorities in jurisdictions where more than one authority is charged with the exercise of resolution powers) should have unimpeded access to firms as necessary for the purposes of resolution planning, and the preparation and implementation of resolution measures. The resolution authority and its staff should be protected against liability for actions taken and omissions made while discharging their duties in the exercise of resolution powers in good faith, including when taking actions in support of foreign resolution proceedings. Where different resolution authorities are in charge of resolving entities of the same group within a single jurisdiction, the resolution regime of that jurisdiction should identify a lead authority ('group resolution authority') that coordinates the resolution of the legal entities within that jurisdiction.

Consistent with the overall objectives of resolution as set out in the Preamble of the Key Attributes, the resolution authority should in the exercise of its resolution powers and as part of its statutory mandate promote financial stability and the continued performance of critical functions and at the same time duly consider the potential impact of their resolution actions on financial stability in other jurisdictions. Such a statutory mandate sets the resolution authorities apart from bankruptcy authorities under general corporate insolvency law. This is needed because ordinary bankruptcy courts have a mandate to protect the interests of individual creditors but they do not generally have a mandate to consider the financial stability implication of bankruptcy measures.

C. Resolution Powers

Key Attribute 3 sets out the range of powers that resolution authorities should have at their disposal to include a broad range of resolution powers. These include powers to achieve a sale or transfer of the shares in the failing firm or of all or parts of the firm's business to a third party, either directly or through a bridge institution without such transactions requiring consent from shareholders or counterparties, and powers to achieve the orderly closure and wind-down of all or parts of the firm's business with timely payout or the transfer of insured deposits.

The Key Attributes also recommend that authorities have the requisite tools to convert debt instruments into equity and achieve a creditor-financed recapitalisation ('bail-in') by way of recapitalising the entity that is no longer viable, or, alternatively, by capitalising a newly established entity or bridge institution to which the distressed firm's critical functions have been transferred following closure of the non-viable firm (the residual business of which would then be wound up and the firm liquidated). The concept of bail-in is important as it seeks to minimize the frictions and non-linearities associated with closure and liquidation. It also presents an alternative to temporary government ownership and to solutions, such as a sale or merger with an existing institution, which can increase concentration, thereby exacerbating the 'too-big-to-fail' problem. The Key Attributes stipulate that bail-in powers should be exercised in a manner that respects the hierarchy of claims in liquidation. The extent to which banks maintain a sufficient level of bail-in debt so that bail-in may be a suitable resolution option may be reviewed as part of resolvability assessments (see I.J below).

The Key Attributes also recognize the need for special tools to resolve insurance companies. These include powers to undertake a portfolio transfer of all or part of the insurance business to another insurer without the consent of each and every policyholder and to discontinue the writing of new business by an insurance firm in resolution while continuing to administer existing contractual policy obligations for in-force business.

In applying resolution powers to individual components of a financial group located in its jurisdiction, the resolution authority should be required to take into account the impact on the group as a whole and on financial stability in other affected jurisdictions, and undertake best efforts to avoid taking actions that could reasonably be expected to trigger instability elsewhere in the group or in the financial system.

Resolution by means of application of one or a combination of resolution tools should be initiated when a firm is no longer viable or likely to be no longer viable, and has no reasonable prospect of becoming so. This means that resolution should be possible before the total equity value of a firm has been extinguished.

D. Set-off, Netting, Collateralization, and Segregation of Client Assets

Key Attribute 4 recognizes the importance of legal certainty and enforceability of financial contracts, which include netting and collateralisation agreements. Entry into resolution and the exercise of any resolution powers should not in principle constitute an event that entitles any counterparty of the firm in resolution to exercise acceleration or early termination rights under such agreements provided the substantive obligations under the contract continue to be performed.[5] Should acceleration or termination rights nevertheless be exercisable, resolution authorities should have the power to stay such rights temporarily. If a temporary stay is imposed, counterparties of the firm will not be able to terminate and close-out the contract based solely upon the entry into resolution or the exercise of resolution powers. They would have such a right if the firm in resolution or the resolution authority failed to meet any margin, collateral or settlement obligations that arise under a financial contract or as a result of membership or participation in an FMI. The objective is to avoid the unnecessary termination of large volumes of financial contracts and resulting fire sales where the contracts can be continued, for instance by way of transfer to a sound financial market participant or bridge bank, in a manner that does not interfere with payment or delivery obligations under the contract.

E. Safeguards

Key Attribute 5 stresses the need for legal certainty and predictability with regard to the exercise of resolution powers and stipulates that resolution powers should be exercised in a way that respects the hierarchy of claims. Authorities should have some flexibility to depart from the general principle of equal (*pari passu*) treatment of creditors of the same class if necessary to contain the potential systemic impact of a firm's failure or to maximise the value for the benefit of all creditors as a whole, provided that all creditors receive at a minimum what they would have received in a liquidation of the firm ('no creditor worse off than in liquidation' safeguard). Judicial review mechanisms should not constrain the implementation of, or result in a reversal of, measures taken by resolution authorities acting within their legal powers and in good faith. Instead, they should provide for redress by awarding compensation, if justified.

---

[5] See n. 3 and in particular its Annex IV.

F. Funding of Firms in Resolution

Key Attribute 6 requires jurisdictions to put in place privately-financed funding mechanisms that can provide temporary financing to facilitate the resolution of a firm. Such funding mechanism may consist of resolution funds financed by levies or mechanisms that rely on *ex post* recovery from the industry. They also include deposit insurance funds which can be used to facilitate the resolution of a firm's deposit-taking activities, for example, by funding the transfer of insured deposits to a sound institution or bridge bank. The resolution authority or authority extending the temporary funding should make a provision to recover any losses incurred from shareholders and unsecured creditors or, if necessary, from the financial system more widely.

G. Legal Framework Conditions for Cross-Border Cooperation

Key Attribute 7 sets out legal framework conditions that should facilitate the resolution of cross-border institutions. Recognizing that cross-border firms remain governed by national laws administered by national authorities, it provides that the statutory mandate of a resolution authority should empower and strongly encourage the authority wherever possible to act to achieve a cooperative solution with foreign resolution authorities.

Legislation and regulations in jurisdictions should not contain provisions that trigger an automatic action in that jurisdiction as a result of official intervention or the initiation of resolution or insolvency proceedings in another jurisdiction. Jurisdictions should provide for transparent and expedited processes to give effect to foreign resolution measures, either by way of a mutual recognition process or by taking measures under the domestic resolution regime that support implementation and are consistent with the resolution measures taken by the foreign home resolution authority.

H. Crisis Management Groups (CMGs)

Key Attribute 8 requires home and key host authorities of all G-SIFIs to maintain Crisis Management Groups with the objective of enhancing preparedness for, and facilitating the management and resolution of a failing cross-border firm. CMGs should include as necessary the supervisory authorities, central banks, resolution authorities, finance ministries and the public authorities responsible for guarantee schemes of jurisdictions that are home or host to entities of the group that are material to its resolution, and should cooperate closely with authorities in other jurisdictions where firms have a systemic presence. At the Summit in Pittsburgh in September 2009 the G20 called for the establishment of CMGs for all major firms.[6] The FSB now requires CMGs to be in place at least for all those firms that have been designated as globally systemically significant.[7]

I. Institution-Specific Cross-Border Cooperation Agreements

Key Attribute 9 calls for institution-specific cooperation agreements to be in place between the home and relevant host authorities that need to be involved in the preparation and management of a crisis affecting a firm that has been designated as globally systemically significant.

Effective resolution in a cross-border context requires an understanding among the relevant home and host authorities on how they will cooperate over the resolution of individual firms, both in the planning phase and during a crisis. Annex I to the Key Attributes 'Essential elements of institution-specific cooperation agreements' sets out the necessary core elements of such agreements. These agreements should, *inter alia*, establish the objectives and processes for cooperation through CMGs; define the roles and responsibilities of the authorities pre-crisis (that is, in the recovery and resolution planning phase) and during a crisis; set out the processes for information sharing, including sharing with any host authorities that are not represented in the CMG, and for coordination in the development of the RRPs. They should also provide for meetings to be held at least annually, involving top officials of the home and relevant host authorities, to review the robustness of the overall resolution strategy for G-SIFIs; and provide for regular (at least annual) reviews by appropriate senior officials of the operational plans implementing the resolution strategies.

J. Resolvability Assessments

FSB Key Attribute 10 calls for regular resolvability assessments of at least those firms that have been designated as globally systemically significant.[8] Resolvability assessments should constitute a continuous and iterative process aimed at identifying and addressing material obstacles to

---

6 Leaders' Statement: The Pittsburgh Summit, 24–25 September 2009 ('Our authorities should establish crisis management groups for the major cross-border firms . . .')

7 See n. 3 above.

8 Ibid.

resolvability until the required level of resolvability is reached. They should be led by the home authority and coordinated with key host authorities.

Annex II to the Key Attributes document elaborates on the elements of such assessments and the process for carrying them out. In undertaking resolvability assessments, resolution authorities should in coordination with other relevant authorities assess, in particular: the extent to which critical financial services, and payment, clearing and settlement functions can continue to be performed; the nature and extent of intra-group exposures and their impact on resolution if they need to be unwound; the extent to which the institution holds sufficient 'bail-inable' debt to allow for a creditor-financed recapitalization of the firm in distress or of a newly established firm by way of conversion of the debt into equity; the capacity of the firm to deliver sufficiently detailed accurate and timely information to support resolution; and the robustness of cross-border cooperation and information sharing arrangements.

Resolvability assessments should extend to the group as a whole and be conducted by the home authority of the G-SIFI and coordinated within the firm's CMG taking into account national assessments by host authorities. Host resolution authorities that conduct resolvability assessments of subsidiaries located in their jurisdiction should coordinate as far as possible with the home authority that conducts resolvability assessment for the group as a whole.

The Key Attributes do not express any preference for a particular group structure or business model. However, given that structural factors may limit authorities' choices of resolution options, the Key Attributes require that authorities have powers to address such factors where financial and legal operational structures render a firm unresolvable.

K. Recovery and Resolution Planning

Key Attribute 11 sets out a requirement for an adequate and credible recovery and resolution plan (RRP) for all G-SIFIs[9] and any firm the failure of which is assessed by its home authority to have a potential impact on financial stability. The RRPs should contain the essential elements set out in Annex III. It should be informed by resolvability assessments and take account of the specific circumstances of the firm and reflect its nature, complexity, interconnectedness, level of substitutability and size. It consists of a recovery plan and a resolution plan:

---

[9] Echoing the SIFI Recommendations, supra n. 2, which calls for RRPs to be put in place for all G-SIFIs.

- The recovery plan should be prepared by the firms themselves and identify options to restore financial strength and viability when the firm comes under severe stress.
- The resolution plan should be prepared by the authorities and is intended to facilitate the effective use of resolution powers to protect systemically important functions, with the aim of making the resolution of any firm feasible without severe disruption and without exposing taxpayers to loss. It should identify, in particular, financial and economic functions for which continuity is critical; suitable resolution options to preserve those functions or wind them down in an orderly manner; data requirements on the firm's business operations, structures, and systemically important functions; potential barriers to effective resolution and actions to mitigate those barriers; actions to protect insured depositors and insurance policyholders and ensure the rapid return of segregated client assets; and clear options or principles for the exit from the resolution process.

For G-SIFIs, the home resolution authority should lead the development of the group resolution plan in coordination with all members of the firm's CMG. Host resolution authorities may maintain their own resolution plans for the firm's operations in their jurisdictions cooperating with the home authority to ensure that the plan is as consistent as possible with the group plan.

RRPs are expected to be regularly updated and evolve over time. They should be subject to at least annual reviews by the relevant CMG. To ensure that key decision makers are sufficiently informed and involved in the process, the adequacy of RRPs of G-SIFIs should also be subject to, at least annual, formal review by top officials of home and relevant host supervisory and resolution authorities.

L. Access to Information and Information Sharing

Key Attribute 12 requires jurisdictions to remove legal, regulatory or policy impediments that hinder the appropriate exchange of information, including firm-specific information, between supervisory authorities, central banks, resolution authorities, finance ministries and the public authorities responsible for guarantee schemes. In particular, the sharing of all information relevant for recovery and resolution should be possible in normal times and during a crisis at a domestic and a cross-border level. Firms should be required, in particular, to be able to demonstrate, as part of the recovery and resolution planning process, that they are able to produce the essential information needed to implement RRPs within a short period of time.

II. RESOLUTION PLANNING REQUIREMENTS FOR GLOBAL SIFIs (G-SIFIs)

In November 2011, the FSB released a list of 29 institutions which have been identified as globally systemically important banks based on a methodology developed by the Basel Committee.[10] These firms (G-SIFIs) are subject to specific resolution planning requirements which include mandatory recovery and resolution plans, regular resolvability assessments and institution-specific cross-border cooperation agreements. National authorities may decide to extend these recovery and resolution planning requirements to other institutions in their jurisdictions. By the end of 2012, the home authorities of all 29 G-SIFIs should have entered into institution-specific cooperation agreements with the key host authorities and completed first resolvability assessments and recovery and resolution plans.

To promote the effective and consistent implementation of these requirements across all G-SIFIs, the FSB announced the establishment of a Peer Review Council (PRC). The function of the PRC will be to assess whether the standards and policy measures for the G-SIFIs are being implemented and applied consistently and in a manner commensurate with the risk posed by each G-SIFI. The PRC will initiate an evaluation of the resolution planning requirements in early 2013.[11]

CONCLUSION

Agreement on the Key Attributes is a significant step towards putting in place a cooperative framework that can achieve an orderly resolution of failing cross-border firms. To effectively implement the Key Attributes in their national legal and regulatory frameworks and to remove remaining obstacles to cooperation, authorities and firms will have considerable work to do. Challenges arise from remaining differences among national

---

[10] Financial Stability Board, 'Policy Measures to Address Systemically Important Financial Institutions', 4 November 2011, available at http://www.financialstabilityboard.org/publications/r_111104bb.pdf (last accessed 17 September 2012).

[11] Ibid.

resolution regimes. For instance, the differing treatment or ranking of creditor claims may affect incentives of authorities to agree to cooperative solution if as a result of deference to a foreign authority, local creditors would be treated less favourably.

Impediments to information sharing between members of a CMG can pose obstacles to joint resolution planning work and hamper effective cooperation in a crisis. Different funding arrangements across jurisdictions can complicate cross-border coordination, for instance, if in some jurisdictions a resolution fund can be used only once an institution has been closed and placed in receivership whereas in others resolution funding is available prior to closure in the context of a 'going concern' bank restructuring. Resolution planning will need to be stepped up significantly to address these and other issues so that cross-border cooperation will materialize in times of crisis.

Finally, the scope of resolution regimes matters. Institutions that engage in 'shadow banking activities'[12] not only operate outside of the safety net and regulatory perimeter; they also tend to be outside of the special resolution regime perimeter. It is therefore important to ensure that they do not trigger systemic problems and that there are effective resolution arrangements in place for them when they fail.

---

12 The FSB describes the 'shadow banking system' as 'credit intermediation involving entities and activities outside the regular banking system'. See 'Shadow Banking: Strengthening Oversight and Regulation', Recommendations of the Financial Stability Board, 27 October 2011, available at http://www.financialstabilityboard.org/publications/r_111027a.pdf (last accessed 17 September 2012).

PART II

The special problems of Europe

5. Crisis management and guarantees in Europe

Charles Enoch[1]

INTRODUCTION

This chapter explores the use of government guarantees during the recent financial crisis. First, it looks at some guarantees that have nothing to do with the banking sector, why they are attractive, and how they can have both positive and negative effects. Then the theme of this book is addressed more specifically, and the banking sector, and the role of guarantees in the banking sector, in particular on deposits, both in crisis and in other times are looked at. There follows a very brief history of deposit guarantees, and a look at the emerging European deposit guarantees in the context of the single European market. A few examples of banking sector problems during the crisis, and what they taught us about deposit guarantees are covered. Guarantees were extended beyond depositor protection but only some of these are examined briefly. The changes to the European deposit guarantees in the crisis are surveyed, and finally some areas where this work is not yet complete are identified.

I. WHY GUARANTEES IN A CRISIS?

Guarantees in a crisis are often designed to calm a situation, to avoid behaviour that might otherwise be rational from an individual's point of view but that would lead to outcomes that are not beneficial for society as a whole. In that regard the objective is that the guarantee is so effective in changing individuals' behaviour that the guarantee does not have to be invoked at all. It therefore becomes costless *ex post* as well as *ex ante*.

[1] The views expressed in this chapter are those of the author and they should not be attributed to the International Monetary Fund, its Management or its Executive Directors.

Another purpose of the guarantee in a crisis may be 'consumer protection', to ensure that those perceived to be innocent victims are not seen to be suffering. In a crisis the public sector comes in because the private sector would not: no company would insure a house once it is already on fire. But this then leads to a question: why was the guarantee or the insurance not put in place before the fire started? Perhaps the fire was unforeseeable. Perhaps the prospect of fire was being denied, because someone with a vested interest, such as the builder, would otherwise have had to undertake expensive preventative action. Or perhaps the individual just wished to take the risk: if the house is not burning, why spend money to insure?

So we come quickly to the policy dilemma. If the government comes in during the fire, or other crisis, perhaps moved by pictures of people losing their houses, this will indeed give an impression of activism and empathy; but, on the other hand, it may tell the person who had decided not to insure that they were right not to do so, and – worse – may encourage them to go back and build their house in the same place with the same structure until the government comes back and pays for the next burn out. The government too may learn this lesson: it may make it mandatory to insure one's house against fire from the start, so the state is not on the hook in the event of a fire. And ideally, even if insured, the owner should be left with a small co-payment, so that he realizes that he will share in the cost if his house does burn.

II. GUARANTEES: A RESPONSE TO A DANGEROUS WORLD

In the US, flooding, especially in Florida and the Gulf States, has been a perennial issue. In 1968 Congress passed the National Flood Insurance Act, and in 1973 the Disaster Prevention Act. But the world is becoming an increasingly dangerous place. Hurricane Andrew, a category 5 hurricane, hit Florida in 1992 and caused a minimum of USD26 billion damage and probably the loss of hundreds of lives. Pictures of devastation filled television screens, as well as stories of uninsured families who had lost their homes and their businesses and now faced ruin.

After recriminations and denials, and further hurricane devastation, the protection framework was enhanced. Evidence was mounting that Florida was becoming increasingly subject to meteorological catastrophe. Insurance was made compulsory on all properties in particular areas. After several further catastrophes, November 2007 saw the creation of the Federal Disaster Insurance Program. The government at present is insuring USD764 billion of housing through 4.7 million policies; in addition, the states are underwriting USD400 billion through 1.9 million policies.

There has been considerable support for the enhanced protection that these measures provide, but they are not without their critics. Sebastian Mallaby, in 'Flood Insurance for Dummies',[2] argued that the pan-state pricing imposed for flood insurance meant that 'workers in Orlando subsidize millionaires in beachfront homes'. On the other hand, *The Washington Post* has argued that state-based coverage has underwritten coastal development that has been vital to regional growth. Indeed, until the recent global financial crisis, the growth of coastal areas was spectacular. Meanwhile, the guarantees had in principle been pre-funded, within an overall debt ceiling, based on estimates from experience of earlier years, but these had not taken account of increasing severity of storms, general increases in building costs, or the requirements of tighter building standards, thus putting the funding ceilings under repeated stress.

III. GUARANTEES: A RESPONSE TO DANGERS IN BANKING

Guarantees also have a long history in the banking sector. Deposit guarantees were introduced as a calming and protective measure in the 1930s, to protect the 'uninformed' individual and enhance financial stability. In 1959 Milton Friedman called these amongst the most important measures to safeguard the banking sector and the economy. For many years individuals were reassured by knowing that deposits up to USD100 000 would be fully insured. And since the Federal Deposit Insurance Corporation (FDIC) was in charge of resolution as well as deposit guarantee, in most cases depositors would be aware of the failure of their bank only when they were informed that a new bank had taken over their previous bank's business.

Guarantees in the US have not been just on the liabilities side. As part of the objective of encouraging home ownership, two parastatal organizations, Freddie Mac and Fannie Mae, guaranteed a large part of the mortgage market, fostering the objective that as many people as possible should own their own homes. Participating in the securitization of these mortgage obligations they also fostered the development of a range of capital markets.

---

2 Sebastian Mallaby, 'Flood Insurance for Dummies', *Washington Post*, 9 October 2006.

While moral hazard effects are evident in deposit insurance they are even more pervasive with guarantees on the assets side. If the loan is guaranteed, there is rarely any incentive to assess the soundness of the loan; there may also be limited incentives to collect payments. In any case, Europeans have long been more leery than the Americans as to the desirability of such guarantees, and recent experience will only have served to increase this leeriness.

The rest of this chapter therefore focuses on deposit guarantees.

IV. THE ASIAN CRISIS

In 1997 much of east and south East Asia fell into an economic crisis. A central element was the collapse of confidence in the banking sector; liquidity pressures made evident the widespread lack of soundness. In Thailand the IMF-supported programme was accompanied by the introduction of a blanket guarantee. In Indonesia in November 1997 the authorities first put in place, and sought to enforce, a limited guarantee. But although this covered in full over 90 per cent of depositors (although a commensurately smaller share of total deposits) many of those not covered were angry, and also powerful, and continued to press for full payout of deposits from the banks that had been closed. By January 1998 the authorities reversed policy and introduced a blanket guarantee, explicitly for at least five years. The guarantee was not of itself instantly credible, and bank runs continued, but when the next set of banks were closed, in April 2008, depositors were rapidly paid out in full through designated state banks; the bank runs rapidly declined and through the various ups and downs of the remainder of the crisis there were no further runs on the system as a whole.

While the system had not stabilized sufficiently by the end of five years to lift the blanket guarantee on its earliest possible date, soon thereafter a progressive limitation to the guarantee was introduced, so that deposits would be guaranteed only up to a specific maximum. Similar moves had taken place in the other countries where the blanket guarantee had been in place. Meanwhile, in most of the Asian crisis countries, the banking system was restructured and strengthened. During the recent global economic crisis these countries' banking systems proved resilient.

V. BANK DEPOSIT GUARANTEES; CONSIDERATIONS AND PRACTICES

Deposit guarantees have very different characteristics in different circumstances. In 'normal' times, traditional 'best practices' are called for:

deposit insurance is limited, and there may be a 'small' co-payment. In crisis, the authorities may impose a 'blanket' guarantee. This is often subject to criticism, since it can be expensive, and protects those who arguably do not 'deserve' to be protected, but it is arguably cheaper than any alternative, and it 'buys' time for the authorities to take more fundamental action to sort out the banking difficulties: the patient is anaesthetized, so that the doctors can do their work properly.

Experience has shown that the mere announcement of the guarantee may have only a limited impact on the populace. Its credibility will depend on the perceived ability of the government to finance the guarantee (its fiscal capacity), the expectation that any payout would be carried out quickly and fairly (its organizational capacity), and in the credibility of the government more generally. In Bulgaria in 1995, for instance, the government failed on all these scores, and the announcement of the blanket guarantee in the crisis had no discernible effect.

The Asian crisis demonstrated the importance of depositor guarantees, as well as the range of existing practices, and how some of the choices with respect to these practices could be significant in determining the efficacy of the guarantees. The Financial Stability Forum (FSF) established a working group on deposit insurance, under the leadership of Canada Deposit Insurance Corporation. This group identified a number of desirable characteristics. It also led to the formation of a more permanent body, the International Association of Deposit Insurers, now located in Basel at the Bank for International Settlements. And this group in turn has, since the recent global economic crisis, commissioned a study of deposit insurance practices, with a view to developing a glossary of best practices, and an approved standard to measure to what extent existing deposit insurance schemes comply with these best practices. The IMF has long looked at deposit insurance schemes as part of its Financial Sector Assessment Programme (FSAP) reports on member countries, and sought to foster practices in line with these emerging best practices.

VI. DEPOSIT GUARANTEES IN EUROPE BEFORE THE CRISIS

As a result of this earlier experience, as well as smaller banking failures in Europe, in 1994 a European Commission (EC) Directive made deposit insurance mandatory, requiring that in each member state there would be an explicit scheme, providing at least 90 per cent coverage for a minimum of EUR20 000. This was a significant step towards enhancing consumer protection in banking in the European Union (EU), as well as towards harmonizing deposit insurance practices. Nevertheless, significant differences remained over the following years, from near-universal coverage in Germany, to much lower levels that were protected by transition arrangements in some of the new members. The IMF conducted a regional FSAP of the Nordic countries in 2005. It identified significant differences, even in countries with apparently very similar economies and institutional structures, as regards the levels of coverage, the types of deposit covered, the pricing mechanism and the institutional governance. For instance, Denmark, alone in the region, included pension payments within the guarantee. And Norway (European Economic Association (EEA) countries have to follow the Directives of the EU) had coverage many times that of the mandated minimum.

The Nordic FSAP highlighted in this connection the differing costs to the banks across countries of the various national deposit insurance schemes, and thus the concern that there might be relocations by the large cross-border Nordic banks. In that regard issues also arose as to what would happen to the paid-in premia if a bank did relocate: should the deposit insurance agency in the country from which the bank was leaving pay the premia the bank had deposited into the agency in the country where the bank was arriving? The consensus was that it should not, so as not to encourage such migration, but these issues flagged the point that there could be a strong case for further harmonization in this area.

Guarantees in the European system thus raise not just the issues associated with deposit guarantees and indeed guarantees more generally, but also those specifically connected to the progressive integration of the European economies. The 'European passport' means that a bank can locate anywhere in Europe if it has a licence in any member state. Banking supervision meanwhile remains a national responsibility, with defined distribution of powers and authority between home and host supervisors. A national supervisor has limited powers over the branches of a foreign bank. The risk of regulatory arbitrage across jurisdictions is significant. Although differences in deposit insurance may not be the principal factor prompting such arbitrage, they may contribute to it. This is significant, as depositors in host countries may have deposit insurance protection from banks headquartered outside that country and over which the host authorities have few oversight powers. While one can argue that they should be aware of such qualification to their protection, these depositors are unlikely to simply accept this as bad luck if things go wrong.

VII. DEPOSIT GUARANTEES: SOME EXAMPLES FROM THE CRISIS

The recent global financial crisis highlighted a number of deficiencies in the existing deposit insurance arrangements and prompted changes as well as arguments over further changes. Below are three of the best-known examples.

First, in 2009 there was a loss of confidence in the Irish banks, as weaknesses became apparent, initially in Anglo-Irish, the third largest Irish bank. In order to restore confidence, the Irish government announced a blanket guarantee on all deposits of Irish banks. This did indeed avert bank runs and the risk of disorderly withdrawals from the banking system. At the same time, however, the move caused consternation in other European capitals. With deposits so mobile in Europe, and sentiment already fragile, there was a concern that the Irish moves might prompt deposit flight out of other banks and into Irish banks.

The UK and other EU countries felt compelled also to raise the limits for their deposit protection, albeit not to the extent offered to their banks by the Irish authorities. This demonstrated the interconnectedness of infrastructural changes across Europe. Such examples have led the European Commission (EC) to press for 'maximum harmonization', a subject discussed in section IX.A, below. It also showed that second-tier banks could have systemic importance: the stress tests conducted a short time previously by the Committee of European Bank Supervisors had not included Anglo-Irish. And thirdly, it showed the interconnectedness between banking and fiscal problems. Although initially fiscally sound, the blanket guarantee and subsequent realization of losses across the Irish banking sector put the country's fiscal position under substantial strain, and led the country to have to request financial support from the EU and the IMF.

Second, a significant precursor to the global financial crisis had been the failure of Northern Rock, a UK bank that had – in line with most of its peers – converted from a building society some years before. With substantial losses emerging due to the aggressive build-up of its housing loan portfolio, depositors lost confidence, and the UK experienced its first significant bank runs since the middle of the 19th century. The government announced a full guarantee for depositors, but this did little initially to stem the withdrawals. With the length of time before the payouts would take place uncertain, people preferred to have their cash in hand. The government at first sought to avoid a full takeover of the bank, but as the scale of the losses became evident, and no private sector interest in acquiring it was found, the government was forced to take it over. The guarantee had not served to protect the bank: first, uncertainty of payout timing provided sufficient incentive to withdraw liquidity; and secondly, guarantees can do little to help an institution if ultimately it is the case that the institution is insolvent.

Third, perhaps the most acrimonious example was that of Icesave – the internet branch bank of a major Icelandic bank, with a significant customer base in the UK and the Netherlands. When the bank failed, the Icelandic authorities initially said that they would pay out in full only to Icelandic depositors. The UK and Netherlands objected, with the UK taking the unprecedented step of invoking the country's anti-terrorism laws in order to prevent assets being taken out of the country. Eventually an agreement was reached, with the UK and the Netherlands lending the Icelandic government part of the resources in order for it to carry out its obligations under the guarantee to the citizens of those countries. Again, a number of lessons can be drawn.

There are dangers in having a bank that is large relative to the size of the country. Landsbanki, Icesave's parent, together with the two other principal banks that failed, had deposits equivalent in size to 900 per cent of the Icelandic GDP. This was a textbook case of a bank so systemically important that it was perversely 'too big to save', in a system whose failure was by some measures, relative to the country's GDP, the largest ever. Another issue is that the European 'single passport' can threaten financial stability as well as enhance it. With Icesave a branch of a bank of a fellow-EEA member, the UK and the Netherlands had little option other than to allow it to operate, and they had limited supervisory oversight. A solution put forward in this regard, but criticized on the grounds that it may be inconsistent with the idea of a single European market, is to require that banks operate cross-border through subsidiaries rather than branches. Lastly, as regards guarantees, it shows that deposit guarantees can be burdensome to a country whose banks operate overseas; it demonstrates the need for high quality cross-border supervision, and more generally recognition that having large cross-border banks brings a country responsibilities and costs as well as benefits.

VIII. DEPOSIT GUARANTEES: ONLY PART OF THE FINANCIAL SAFETY NET

So, how has the global financial crisis impacted on the system of guarantees in Europe? In this connection one has to stress that guarantees are only one part of the financial system safety net. Just as flood damage management is not ended with the introduction of mandatory flood insurance, so the financial system is of itself not protected just by guarantees on deposit insurance. Flood-prone environments need strong building codes, and regulations as to where to build. Financial systems similarly need a strong underpinning to ensure that the vicissitudes of the modern global economy do not lead to them being washed away.

IX. THE NEW EU FINANCIAL STABILITY INFRASTRUCTURE

The EC has been very busy seeking to create a new financial stability infrastructure. The extraordinary difficulty of this endeavour lies in large part because of the need to create an infrastructure to maintain financial stability while still having a major ongoing crisis to address.

As of the beginning of 2011 a system of European Supervisory Authorities (ESAs) was established: this comprises the European Banking Authority (EBA), the European Insurance and Occupational Pensions Authority (EIOPA); and the European Securities Market Authority (ESMA). Each derives from an earlier agency, but has been accorded enhanced responsibilities, and each has been faced with immediate challenges. The EBA has run stress tests on European banks that have been subject to intense scrutiny, and the credibility of which will rest in large part as to whether the stress test results are seen to be borne out by events; EIOPA has to contend with the paradigm shift in business model in the insurance industry as the industry copes with low interest rates and enhanced longevity, while simultaneously having oversight of Solvency 2, a thoroughgoing revision to the regulatory framework. And ESMA has oversight of a wide range of more or less opaque market innovations: it also is the first EU agency to have direct oversight of a set of EU institutions without depending on the national agencies as intermediaries, as it assumes responsibility over the credit-rating agencies.

Finally, the European Systemic Risk Board (ESRB) has been established, to provide macro-prudential oversight. This brings potentially a fundamental enhancement to Europe's management of financial stability, but a number of apparent weaknesses in its construction have been identified, and its effectiveness is yet to be established: the ESRB's council is extremely large, with over 60 participants, and the ESRB has no decision-making powers, it issues warnings – public or private – and the country being warned has to 'comply or explain'. That said, voting formulae have been established, the organization has so far not proved unwieldy, and the first warning has reportedly been issued.

All these institutions start with dual roles. They are designed with the long-term objective of maintaining stability in normal times, while immediately needing to achieve financial stability in the highly unstable present times. This may lead to dilemmas on a daily basis, with policies designed for one state of the world being different from those for the other. Deposit guarantees are an obvious example of this. Even the time frame under which decisions have to be made is bifurcated. In a crisis one operates in real time, as delays are costly and potentially disastrous. When setting up a structure for the longer term, however, one may wish to act in a more deliberative manner. Thus, with a focus particularly on this second aspect, the EC regards what has been already established in the financial stability framework as a complete initial phase, and plans to review this initial phase only in 2014.

A. The 'European Project'

A further challenge arises from the 'European project' aspect of these innovations. A critical objective of the EC is the fostering of the single market. Regarding the banking sector, this implies the development of a 'single rulebook', which may be interpreted as financial institutions throughout the EU having to operate under similar regulations. This in turn implies that, where regulations differ across countries, the EC should work to harmonize them. There are two aspects to this: to harmonize the instruments and to harmonize the levels. And in both regards there is the contentious issue: minimum harmonization or maximum harmonization.

Minimum harmonization of instruments would involve setting out an expansive set of instruments that may be used, possibly with provisions so that additional instruments can also be considered for use if they meet certain criteria; minimum harmonization of calibration would mean that the EU agencies could specify a particular level of the instrument but individual countries would be empowered to go further. Few would disagree with minimum harmonization; the arguments for maximum harmonization have been subject to more disputes, and rest in large part on having achievement of the single market as a dominant objective. But the Irish experience discussed earlier shows the cross-border impact of a country calibrating its instrument above the common level; the impact on other countries demonstrates that other countries do have a legitimate interest in limiting the discretion of an individual country in setting its instrument.

B. The Other Parts of the Financial Safety Net

So, what is the role of deposit guarantees within this infrastructure, and how have they been affected by the ongoing work since the crisis? As noted before, deposit guarantees are only one part of a comprehensive financial sector safety net. The main elements are:

- strong regulations (EU responsibility);
- strong supervision (national responsibility);
- strong supportive macroeconomic policies (largely national responsibility) and macro safety net (EU/IMF responsibilities);
- strong resolution (national responsibility); and
- strong depositor protection (EU/national responsibilities).

All these elements are necessary for financial stability.

1. Regulation

As regards the first of these, regulation, the Basel Committee has developed a new set of minimum requirements (Basel III). The EU is amongst the most advanced areas in the world in carrying forward the implementation of these proposals. A revised Capital Regulation Directive (CRDIV) will make it mandatory for EU members to implement the EU version of the new capital standard. To a large extent CRDIV follows Basel III, but there are a few areas where it is perceived to be weaker: some forms of non-common equities are to be allowed as tier one capital, unlike in the Basel III framework, and some additional deductions are to be permitted. While these differences possibly have some merit and are not of themselves substantial, it would be unfortunate to give the impression that countries can pick and choose from amongst the elements of Basel III, since that might give cover for others to make more significant adaptations.

An additional issue, superimposed on the need to balance creating a new financial regulatory infrastructure and exiting from the financial crisis, is the objective of fostering the single market. To some extent this complements the other objectives, in particular insofar as the creation of the single market aids the creation of a strong European banking system that can underpin economic growth. On the regulatory side however the single market objective may lead to a policy of 'maximum harmonization'. But given that Europe's economic cycle is far from aligned it is not clear that, at this stage, it is optimal to have the same levels of, for instance, capital adequacy, required in all parts of the Union. Rather, there is a risk that such a policy may lead to regulatory levels in some member states below those that particular national supervisors would think appropriate. This dilemma seems to be recognized: ongoing work in the relevant bodies looks likely to lead to a workable arrangement under which the single market objective is balanced by recognition of cyclical divergences, perhaps through explicitly allowing for counter-cyclical capital buffers or by endorsing a range of macro-prudential instruments that can be applied at a sub-Union level.

2. Supervision

Second, on the supervision side, the single European passport leaves national authorities with limited powers over branches of foreign banks, although they do now have some powers over liquidity issues. This gap may, however, remain a risk. For cross-border collaboration the main instrument is to be the colleges of supervisors, under which all banks with significant cross-border operations are forming colleges of supervisors comprising representatives of all the countries in which the bank has a significant presence. In the case of large banks present in many countries, much of the work is to be delegated to a core college.

On the surface this looks good. Some productive meetings of these colleges have already taken place. However, there is a risk that they may just become talking shops. It is not clear what the incentives are to be fully open to one's colleagues in revealing emerging problems. Especially if a bank is in difficulty and is seeking to retrench, national supervisors may seek to conceal emerging problems so as to avoid the possibility that the head office might ring fence against it. And in some areas it is simply a zero sum game whether resources go to one or another national jurisdiction: for instance, whether enhanced capital should go to a capital-poor parent or its capital-poor subsidiary. There have been open arguments at meetings of the colleges that have not served to enhance confidence in the process.

In that connection it is worth noting that nearly all the discussion on the supervisory response to the crisis has been in terms of offsite innovations. But a major culprit in the crisis was inadequacy in onsite supervision. The emphasis on offsite may indeed serve to reduce onsite resources, thus even impeding development of onsite supervision. For cross-border institutions, an onsite counterpart to the colleges of supervisors could be that there should be joint inspections for those banks where a representative participates in the core college, so that countries participating in a college (or core college) in some way participate also in the onsite inspection.

3. The macroeconomy

Third, turning to the macro side, until recently there was an assumed guarantee that the authorities would have available a range of appropriate macroeconomic policies, and would 'do what it takes' to support financial and economic stability. The rapid cuts in interest rates at the start of the crisis were an example of this. Similarly, so was the initial fiscal stimulus. Nowadays, however, there seems to be less ability to maintain the guarantee. The perceived increasing ineffectiveness of a possible QE3 in the US, inflation fears in Europe, concern at rising fiscal burdens and general policy paralysis suggest that the arsenal of measures to support financial stability may be nearing exhaustion. In that regard, the focus on macro-prudential policies and instruments looks to be particularly timely. These could be a key part of the overall toolkit going forward. The IMF, in consultation with its members and many others are devoting considerable resources into identifying and specifying appropriate macro-prudential policies, as well as the governance of operating these policies.

The ESRB, as noted above, was specifically created to handle these policies from a European perspective. In all these endeavours there is great promise. But so far there is limited experience: there is neither full agreement as to how such instruments should be operated: nor what the appropriate level of calibration should be; and many of these instruments – for instance a loan-to-value ratio – are likely to be politically contentious.

4. Bank resolution

The fourth component of the financial stability safety net is bank resolution, which remains a national responsibility in Europe, although this has proven to be particularly awkward in the case of cross-border banks. Fortis bank is a clear case of failure at cross-border resolution during the crisis. Although the Dutch and Belgian authorities had worked together for many years, and had similar frameworks and aspirations, it proved impossible to handle Fortis bank jointly, and the Dutch and Belgian components were broken into their respective national components.

It is not clear how much has been achieved in this area since the onset of the crisis. Resolution is a topic that it is envisaged will be handled during the reviews in 2014. The IMF's recently conducted European Financial Stability Framework Exercise (EFFE) identified the lack of a European resolution agency as a major gap in the emerging European financial stability infrastructure, but there seems insufficient political support to move far in the direction of centralization at the moment, given that it might involve treaty change as well as some form of fiscal pooling. Nevertheless, while bank resolution remains a national responsibility, there need to be enhancements in the handling of the resolution of cross-border banks. In particular, firm *ex ante* agreement is needed, at least of the principles, for resolving a bank with a significant presence in more than one EU member. And, as with all parts of the infrastructure, it will be important that once rules are established they are actually followed (the history of memorandums of understanding (MOUs) in the past does not provide grounds for much confidence). Mere announcement of an agreement as to how cross-border resolution will be accomplished will not of itself provide much assurance; this assurance will only be generated once the rules are seen to be carried out (in practice) in full.

5. Guarantees in the post-crisis infrastructure: revision of the Directive on Deposit Guarantee Schemes

Fifthly and finally, we come to the role of deposit guarantees in the post-crisis European infrastructure. In 2010 the EC announced the revision of the 1994 Directive on Depositor Guarantee Schemes. Under its new proposals the higher limit introduced as a temporary measure in many countries was made permanent at EUR100 000, or the rough equivalent in non-Euro currency countries. Co-insurance, which had been up to 10 per cent in a number of countries, was abandoned, so 100 per cent of deposits are to be guaranteed up to the agreed maximum. The coverage of the guarantees is harmonized, excluding the deposits of financial institutions, public authorities, and structured investment products. There are to be speedier payouts – within seven days, not up to several months, as before. There is to be enhanced consumer information about the guarantee; all currencies are to be covered; and the logistics are being improved, through cross-border banks paying out locally and head office responsibilities sorted out with the host agencies afterwards.

Much of this is commendable, and it certainly marks a significant step forward, although the elements of compromise between a system designed for a crisis and one for other times may leave some residual awkwardness. For instance, if one were still in a crisis, and worried about systemic runs, would one wish to exclude any large deposits from the guarantee?

Beyond this, issues can be considered within four broad topics: technical issues; credibility issues; deposit insurance within the overall financial sector safety net; and deposit insurance within the European project.

(a) Technical issues As noted above, there are many positive elements in the proposals, but some technical issues remain. First, is the issue of governance: how are the funds to be managed? Best practice would probably indicate an independent agency, or at least an autonomous department within the agency, to manage the funds and the payouts. Second, there is the issue of *ex ante* funding. At the moment most EU members do not try to finance their deposit guarantee in advance, but operate on the basis of collecting payments when needed. The directive does not aim to harmonize in this regard, which leads to the possibility of pro-cyclical imposts on the banking sector. It would be preferable to aim to build up a fund in advance as, for instance, Sweden does. A target figure of 4 per cent of GDP has been suggested for the medium term. *Ex ante* funding

would mean that the money will be visibly there when needed. The banks themselves should make the payments, so this approach minimizes the cost to the public purse. Also, any bank that fails will have paid into the fund, thus at least sharing in the financing of its depositors. Preferably also the premia will be risk-based, so banks will be rewarded for prudent practices and those banks most likely to fall into difficulty will have paid most heavily. And, to minimize the possible cost to the taxpayers, the directive should propose 'depositor preference', that is that depositors and their guarantee funds get paid out from the assets of the failing bank before other creditors.

At the moment the EC proposals envisage that the depositor guarantee funds can be used only for the purpose of paying out depositors when a bank has failed. This may, however, not be the most effective use of these funds. There would seem to be scope to permit the guarantee to pursue a 'least cost solution' option, even where this does not result in the failure of the bank and the payout to depositors: the classic alternative is 'a purchase and assumption' agreement under which another institution is prepared to take on (some of) the liabilities and assets of the failing institution. In some other countries the deposit guarantor works with the resolution agency to identify and execute a least cost solution; in some countries the two functions are undertaken by the same agency, thus facilitating a consistent and efficient approach to handling the bank failure.

(b) Credibility issues The prospective deposit guarantee arrangements will also face credibility issues. The agencies will need to demonstrate that they can deliver in line with their commitments. There have already been rumblings, for instance, that a seven-day payout is too ambitious a target. There are, however, important reasons for having such an ambitious target; as we saw for instance with Northern Rock, uncertainty over timing of payouts may make the whole deposit protection exercise a waste of time and money. In any case, once seven days has been adopted as the commitment, the deposit insurance agencies will need to ensure that their processes are in place so that they can deliver in line with this commitment. In this regard, it will be appropriate to conduct a thorough analysis to ensure that only legitimately guaranteed deposits are paid out; but such surveillance will need to be carried out expeditiously, since delays beyond the commitment period could have devastating effects on the credibility of the entire arrangements.

The agencies need also to ensure credibility from the other side – that is, that they do not compensate more than is mandated. Past history of crises is that governments fearing a systemic threat move to guarantee everything – they announce a 'blanket guarantee'. Behaviour in the recent crisis will have strongly supported that perception. If once again there is payout above the specified EUR100000 maximum it will at once be assumed that we are back in the world of the blanket guarantee, with all the moral hazard and other issues that arise, and it will be even more difficult in the future to try to persuade the public that the guarantee really is limited.

(c) Deposit insurance within the financial stability framework So, to conclude, how can one assess the 2010 Directive within the overall financial stability framework? Much progress has been achieved, and the deposit guarantee proposals will ultimately be an important element within this overall financial stability infrastructure. Nevertheless, gaps remain. The regulatory framework, while much enhanced, still has a few issues, in particular that CRDIV in some ways can be seen as a modification of Basel III. Also, the needed supervisory enhancements have so far not been demonstrated. Some central banks, such as the Netherlands Central Bank, have published booklets showing how supervision has been subject to a 'change in culture' but such demonstrations are relatively rare. Also importantly, the recapitalization of European banks is not yet complete; undercapitalized banks may not be effective in playing their part in intermediating funds to revive growth; and on the other side, they may be particularly vulnerable to adverse shocks and ultimately to the government needing to invoke the deposit guarantee. And finally in this regard, a European resolution framework is not yet in place: without such a framework it is not clear that European authorities will be able to close a bank with significant cross-border activities and thus bring the deposit guarantee mechanism into play. The proposed SIFI capital surcharge may be seen as a lack of assurance as to the possibility of efficient closure of large banks and the extra costs that the authorities may incur in having to keep them open.

(d) Deposit insurance within the European project How do the deposit guarantee arrangements fit within the European project as it was applied to the financial sector in the crisis? On the one side, one can argue that the crisis management has had 'too much Europe'. Banks receiving state aid were subjected to requirements from the competition authority that may not have been fully in line with expediting the return to financial stability. Also, proposals for 'maximum harmonization' envisage that once an appropriate level is determined for banks' capital or other regulatory norms, each bank in the EEA will not only have to regard this as a minimum but also a maximum. There is admittedly some merit in this

argument as regards deposit insurance. Giving higher levels of guarantee may serve to create an uneven playing field, and attract depositors to place their funds in the location with the highest level of the guarantee; especially where the guarantee reflects distress in a country's banking system, such as was the case when Ireland offered its blanket guarantee, such movement may even be perverse. In any case, it is questionable whether setting higher levels of deposit insurance is a legitimate form of intra-union banking competition.

This comes to the argument on the other side that there is indeed 'too little Europe' in this area. National jurisdictions looking at national conditions are bound to come to differing conclusions about the appropriate levels of deposit insurance. Since most large European banks have significant cross-border activities there could potentially be a range of levels of coverage within a single institution. As already noted, there would be incentives for banks to locate to jurisdictions with lower levels of deposit insurance and depositors to place their deposits in locations where insurance is higher.

One possibility therefore is that the EU should set up a complementary EU-administered deposit insurance scheme, perhaps one specifically designed for cross-border banks. This would give assurance that there would be no distortionary incentives for banks or depositors to locate their activities in particular member states. Pricing and other conditions would need to be carefully calibrated if one did not wish the European scheme quickly to drive national schemes out of business, unless the European scheme would be exclusively available just to the biggest banks – the so-called E-SIFIs, who may, under Basel proposals, be subject to higher capital adequacy requirements than will other banks.

Beyond this, over time, perhaps deposit insurance could be provided within the EU by a single European agency. A particular strength of such an initiative would be that the new agency could mesh with a single European resolution agency. Deposit insurance and resolution are flip sides of how one handles a single topic. As argued above, there is a good case for a single European resolution agency, at least as a medium-term objective. By the same measure, there would be a good case to have deposit insurance handled on an EU basis. Although an EDIC, a European Deposit Insurance Agency, with responsibilities for both insurance and resolution may take such a movement further than one might wish, nevertheless the synergies in such an arrangement, or an arrangement where two European agencies collaborated closely on the handling of any failing European banks, would be a major step forward in securing the European financial sector safety net.

CONCLUSIONS

To conclude, much progress has been achieved in Europe in the last three years in enhancing the financial sector safety net. The proposals for the permanent deposit guarantee arrangements are overall very much on the right track, and they bring to bear important lessons learned from the crisis. However, gaps remain in the overall safety net. Amongst these one may draw attention to the modifications to Basel III in the proposed CRDIV; that supervisory enhancement has not yet been demonstrated; recapitalization of the European banks is not yet complete; and the bank resolution framework is not yet in place. Without a resolution framework it is not clear that European authorities would be able to close a large cross-border bank smoothly, and thus bring the deposit guarantee mechanism properly into play. A comprehensive approach to address all these remaining issues would stand Europe's financial sector in good stead for the period ahead.

6. Regulatory responses to the financial crisis

Rosa M. Lastra

INTRODUCTION

'Never let a good crisis go to waste'

That phrase was coined by Rahm Emmanuel, the former chief of staff of US President Barak Obama, in response to the crisis, and since then it has been used in a variety of contexts. It encapsulates the policy, regulatory and political need to do something, to respond to the popular (or populist) demand for regulation. 'Never again' is a slogan that policy-makers and politicians have often uttered in response to the worst global financial crisis since the Great Depression.

While there is a consensus regarding the magnitude and severity of the crisis, there are contrasting – even opposing – views, when it comes to understanding the causes of the crisis and the regulatory responses that can best tackle the imbalances and fragilities that were at its root and thus fix the problems of the financial system.

In a 2010 article Geoffrey Wood and I[1] looked at the multiple causes of the crisis and organised the regulatory proposals and responses under five headings:

(1) What to regulate
(2) Who regulates, how to regulate and the intensity of supervision
(3) Bankers' behaviour, corporate governance and risk management
(4) Fiscal and compensation considerations
(5) Structural reforms.

[1] Rosa Lastra and Geoffrey Wood, 'The Crisis of 2007–2009: Nature, Causes and Reactions', (2010) 13(3) Journal of International Economic Law 531–50.

This chapter focuses on some of the regulatory responses following the above classification (in particular categories 1 and 2) and examines developments in the US, UK, EU and elsewhere.

At the outset, I would like to make three points. The first is that regulators are often seen as fighting the last war; responses to crises are by definition *ex post*. This, in combination with a degree of 'regulatory fatigue', is a useful reminder of the limits of regulation. The second is that we need international rules for global markets and much more effective cooperation amongst national authorities. Inconsistent or uncoordinated national responses are inadequate in the presence of internationally integrated financial markets. The *modus operandi* of central bankers is an example, for politicians and treasury officials, of a model of effective international cooperation. The third point is a wider philosophical reflection that concerns capitalism and its critics. An underlying requirement for optimal results under capitalism is that both gains and losses be privatised (that is, that market failure due to externalities be minimal). The idea embedded in the too-big-to-fail doctrine (TBTF) (and its variants) that losses should somehow be socialised runs against this.

I. WHAT TO REGULATE

The question of 'what to regulate' has triggered a multiplicity of rules (or proposed rules) for capital, liquidity and other indicators of banking and financial soundness. Banking is a private business. Yet core banking functions, including access to credit, smooth functioning of the payments system and access to deposits/checking accounts, have a public interest dimension since externalities are involved. In order to align private costs with social costs, banking must be regulated. In the aftermath of the crisis, it is clear that banks had too little capital, that is too thin a buffer to absorb losses and that those capital requirements were inadequate. Basel III is an attempt to respond to the limitations of its predecessors. Basel III is the name given to the new capital and liquidity standards adopted by the Basel Committee on Banking Supervision in December 2010.[2] As

[2] The Basel Committee on Banking Supervision, 'Basel III: A global regulatory framework for more resilient banks and banking systems', December 2010, http://www.bis.org/publ/bcbs189_dec2010.pdf (last accessed 17 September 2012). The Basel Committee on Banking Supervision, 'Basel III: International framework for liquidity risk measurement, standards and monitoring', December 2010, http://www.bis.org/publ/bcbs188.pdf (last accessed 17 September 2012). The Basel Committee subsequently conducted a review resulting in a small modification of

an international standard it should contribute towards establishing a level playing field. However, some 'fault lines' are already apparent, since some countries will actually prescribe more onerous capital rules. Furthermore, capital regulation is no panacea. Good banking and finance also rest upon asset quality, management (including compensation and other incentives), earnings and risks. Some rules might prove counterproductive, while others – notably in the area of resolution and insolvency of cross-border institutions – fall short of what is needed.

There is a perception that banks have already influenced the Basel III rules ('hijacked' the process?), given the long implementation period for the new capital regime. One could be forgiven for thinking that we might find ourselves enmeshed in Basel IV before Basel III is in place, thus repeating the history of Basel II, an agreement that was never fully implemented.

A more relevant question is why should strict capital requirements be limited to commercial banks (credit or depositary institutions) when the 'shadow banking system' – a rather imprecise term encompassing a variety of non-bank financial intermediaries – is engaged in similar types of risky activities? Moreover, emphasis on capital, important as it is as an indicator of soundness, should not be the sole regulatory focus. As Robert Litan, insightfully stated in the 1980s, regulators focus so much upon capital requirements because it is difficult to assess and control the quality of the asset portfolio and, of course, potential mismatches between the duration of liabilities. As well, assets provide a cause for concern about liquidity management and controls.

Whether more stringent capital requirements, by themselves, will be sufficient to prevent financial crises is not clear. Regulation is most needed in good times, when rapid credit expansion and exuberant optimism cloud the exercise of sound judgement in risk management, yet regulation is typically designed in bad times, in response to a crisis. We need appropriate counter-cyclical regulation, bearing in mind the biblical stories of

---

the credit valuation adjustment; the revised Basel III capital rules were published in June 2011. The Basel Committee on Banking Supervision, 'Basel III: A global regulatory framework for more resilient banks and banking systems', June 2011, http://www.bis.org/publ/bcbs189.pdf (last accessed 17 September 2012). The core aspects of Basel III are scheduled to be adopted into national laws by 1 January 2013; certain aspects of the new standards are slated to become effective upon adoption, while others will be phased in over several years during 2013–2019. In terms of liquidity standards, after an observation period beginning in 2011, the Liquidity Coverage Ratio (LCR) will be introduced on 1 January 2015 and the Net Stable Funding Ratio (NSFR) will move to a minimum standard by 1 January 2018.

Joseph in which provisions were gathered in good times to be used in bad times. Regulation and supervision should aim at protecting the interests of society (by identifying, preventing and containing systemic risk, as well as by guaranteeing the continuing operation of and access to critical banking and financial functions), rather than the interests of individuals or institutions.[3]

With regard to the range of institutions that should be regulated, Andrew Crocket[4] advocated the need to 'widen the net' beyond the three pillars upon which financial regulation has traditionally rested (that is, banking, securities and insurance) to a broader range of institutions that are now critical to financial stability, such as those involved in the originate-to-distribute model of credit intermediation, service providers such as clearing and settlement systems, credit rating agencies and auditing firms, and private pools of capital such as hedge funds and private equity funds. Perhaps the answer in some cases – for example, with regard to derivatives markets – is not more regulation, but more transparency and accountability, a well-functioning clearing and settlements system, and on balance sheet accounting. In other cases, the answer might be found through litigation.[5]

Both the Basel Committee and the Financial Stability Board have been busy issuing new 'soft-law' rules. For example, a new 'Core Principles for Effective Banking Supervision' consultation paper was issued in December 2011;[6] it addresses issues not covered in the original 1997 document, such

---

[3] See Charles Goodhart and Rosa Lastra, 'Border Problems', (2010) 13(3) Journal of International Economic Law 705–18.

[4] See Andrew Crocket, 'Rebuilding the Financial Architecture', (2009) 46(3) Finance & Development 18.

[5] Goodhart and Lastra, n.3 above.

[6] The Basel Committee on Banking Supervision, 'Core Principles for Effective Banking Supervision: Consultative Document', December 2011, http://www.bis.org/publ/bcbs213.pdf (last accessed 17 September 2012). This document updates the Core Principles and the associated Core Principles Methodology and merges the two documents into a single comprehensive one. The Consultative document has increased the number of Core Principles from 25 to 29, introduced 36 new assessment criteria comprising 31 new essential criteria and 5 new additional criteria, and upgraded 33 additional criteria from the existing assessment methodology to essential criteria that represent minimum baseline requirements for all countries. Moreover, it has reorganized the revised set of 29 Core Principles to foster their implementation through a more logical structure commencing with supervisory powers, responsibilities and functions, focusing on effective risk-based supervision, the need for early intervention and timely supervisory actions and followed by supervisory expectations of banks, emphasising the importance of good corporate governance and risk management, as well as compliance with supervisory

as: corporate governance, the treatment of systemically important banks, and recovery and resolution plans. The Financial Stability Board has recently published a number of documents containing regulatory and supervisory principles, the most relevant being the 'Key Attributes of Effective Resolution Regimes for Financial Institutions' published on 4 November 2011.[7] Those key attributes – which are the result of work undertaken by the FSB jointly with its members including the IMF, World Bank and the standard-setting bodies – are new internationally agreed standards that lay out the responsibilities, instruments and powers that national resolution regimes should have to deal with a failing systemically important financial institution (SIFI). They also establish the requirements for resolvability assessments and recovery and resolution planning for global SIFIs, as well as for the development of institution-specific cooperation agreements between home and host authorities. In addition, they are aimed at addressing the TBTF problem by making it possible to resolve any financial institution in an orderly manner, without exposing taxpayers to the risk of loss, and protecting essential economic functions through mechanisms for losses to be allocated between shareholders and unsecured and uninsured creditors.

II. WHO REGULATES AND HOW TO REGULATE – THE INTENSITY OF SUPERVISION

All national 'architectures', whether one authority, twin-peak, or many regulators, failed to prevent the crisis.[8] Inadequate systemic risk control

standards. The revision aims to address many of the significant risk management weaknesses and other vulnerabilities highlighted in the last crisis. It also responds to several key trends and developments that emerged during the last few years of market turmoil: the need for greater powers and resources to deal effectively with systemically important banks; the importance of applying a system-wide, macro perspective to the micro-prudential supervision of banks to assist in identifying, analysing and taking pre-emptive action to address systemic risks; and the increasing focus on effective crisis management, recovery and resolution measures in reducing both the probability and impact of a bank failure.

[7] See Eva Hüpkes 'Resolving systemically important financial institutions: – The Financial Stability Board key attributes of effective resolution regimes', Chapter 4 in this volume. Also see http://www.financialstabilityboard.org/publications/r_111104cc.pdf (last accessed 17 September 2012).

[8] Luis Garicano and Rosa Lastra, 'Towards a new Architecture for Financial Stability: Seven Principles', (2010) 13(3) Journal of International Economic Law 597–621.

is a feature of the 2008 financial crisis. In recognition of this, the concept of macro-prudential supervision is now embraced by financial authorities in the EU, UK, US and other jurisdictions. Macro-prudential supervision is analogous to the oversight of the forest, while micro-prudential supervision is analogous to the oversight of individual trees.

A quick overview of some recent developments in the UK casts some light on the relative weight given to reforms of the institutional structure, even though the safety net architecture, *per se*, was not a cause of the crisis. From 1997 to 2010, the UK presented a unified picture in terms of supervision, following the transfer of supervision from the Bank of England and the establishment of a single supervisory agency, the Financial Services Authority (FSA), governed by the Financial Services and Markets Act 2000. The tripartite model of dividing responsibilities between the Bank of England, the FSA and HM Treasury with regard to crisis management was in principle a suitable structure to respond to the problems of transferring supervision from the central bank to a new agency, while keeping the Treasury involved. However, this structure was heavily criticised at the time of the problems surrounding Northern Rock and thereafter for its lack of effective and timely communications and coordination among the authorities and because of an apparent absence of a clear leadership structure – shared power had led to muddled decision making. In response to the financial crisis, following its electoral victory in May 2010, the UK government decided to change the supervisory structure.

In July 2010, HM Treasury released a consultation document which argued that the tripartite system had failed to ensure financial stability due to inherent weaknesses and contradictions. In reaction to the failings of the tripartite model, the Treasury suggested the establishment of a new supervisory architecture with the following components: (1) a Financial Policy Committee (FPC) housed within the Bank of England, with primary statutory responsibility for maintaining financial stability across the financial system using macro-prudential tools to ensure that systemic risks to financial stability are dealt with; (2) a Prudential Regulation Authority (PRA), a subsidiary of the Bank of England, responsible for prudential regulation of all deposit-taking institutions, insurers and investment banks; and (3) a Consumer Protection and Markets Authority, later renamed the Financial Conduct Authority (FCA), with a primary statutory responsibility to promote confidence in financial services and markets.[9]

The details of the new system were fleshed out during the first six months

[9] HM Treasury, 'A New Approach to Financial Regulation: Judgment, Focus and Stability' (July 2010).

of 2011. In February 2011, HM Treasury issued a second consultation document.[10] With respect to the PRA, the Bank of England and the FSA jointly published 'The Bank of England, Prudential Regulation Authority: Our approach to banking supervision' in May 2011, which describes how the PRA will approach the delivery of its statutory objectives.[11] Finally, HM Treasury issued a White Paper in June 2011, which includes a draft bill regarding the proposed reforms.[12] The Financial Services Bill was published in January 2012.[13]

While the repatriation of a financial stability mandate to the Bank of England, to be pursued in tandem with its price stability mandate, is a welcome development, I am much less persuaded of the wisdom of the

---

10 HM Treasury, 'A New Approach to Financial Regulation: Building a Stronger System' (February 2011).

11 The Bank of England and the FSA, 'The Bank of England, Prudential Regulation Authority: Our Approach to Banking Supervision' (May 2011), http://www.bankofengland.co.uk/publications/other/financialstability/uk_reg_framework/pra_approach.pdf (last accessed 17 September 2012).

12 HM Treasury, 'A New Approach to Financial Regulation: the Blueprint for Reform' (June 2011), http://www.hm-treasury.gov.uk/d/consult_finreg__new_approach_blueprint.pdf (last accessed 17 September 2012).

13 The Government published the Financial Services Bill on 27 January 2012, See http://www.hm-treasury.gov.uk/press_08_12.htm (last accessed 17 September 2012).

The Bill:

- gives the Bank of England responsibility for protecting and enhancing financial stability, bringing together macro and micro prudential regulation;
- abolishes the Financial Services Authority (FSA) and creates a strengthened regulatory architecture consisting of the Financial Policy Committee, the Prudential Regulation Authority and the Financial Conduct Authority, also providing them each with clarity of responsibility and the necessary powers to ensure the stability of the financial sector and the protection of consumers; and
- empowers authorities to look beyond 'tick-box' compliance and fosters a regulatory culture of judgement, expertise and proactive supervision.
- The Bill has been shaped by extensive consultation with both stakeholders and Parliament and, while the fundamental elements of the new framework are in line with the model put forward by the Chancellor in 2010, contains a number of refined policy proposals, including measures to:
  - legislate for a new crisis management regime, providing greater clarity and accountability to protect the taxpayer during times of crisis by providing the Chancellor with new powers over the Bank of England where public money is at risk; and
  - enable the transfer of responsibility for regulating consumer credit to the Financial Conduct Authority to better protect consumers.

proposed structural changes. Since all supervisory structures failed during the crisis (whether a single authority, twin-peak or multiple authorities), changes in structure, *per se*, are unlikely to lead to a better system of supervision. The failure was not in the 'who' to supervise, but in the 'how', and in the priority given to the objective of financial stability. What is needed is better supervision and regulation, an efficient and credible resolution process and a better ranking of objectives.

There is also a concern about the issues of coordination – which, if anything, have become more relevant and problematic given the multiplicity of authorities – and about accountability. The Bank of England has a clear mandate with regard to monetary policy, and since the Banking Act of 2009, it has also had a mandate for financial stability, as well as crisis management responsibilities (the Special Resolution Regime) for troubled banks.

With the new changes, the supervisory powers of the Bank of England will be substantially expanded, both with regard to macro-prudential supervision through its new Financial Policy Committee and to micro-prudential supervision through the Prudential Regulation Authority. As the Treasury Select Committee concluded in its inquiry in July 2011, there are serious concerns about the accountability of the revamped Bank of England.[14] With power comes responsibility and accountability, an issue which was covered in my contribution to a Parliamentary Brief in July 2011. (Lord Acton's dictum, 'Power tends to corrupt, and absolute power corrupts absolutely'[15] – resonates in the background of the corridors of power, as a key reminder of the importance of accountability.)

When it comes to objectives, it is widely accepted that the neglect of financial stability prior to the crisis was an important enabling factor. Financial stability should be the ultimate goal of supervision, regulation and crisis management. It is a national, a European and an international goal, but a commonly accepted definition is still lacking, complicating its pursuit.

International comparisons can provide a useful perspective on proposals in this area. For example, while the FSA is going to be dismantled in the UK, in the US there have been calls 'to end the Fed', which is the title of a book by Republican candidate Ron Paul.[16] The US has redesigned

---

[14] Twenty-first Report of Session 2010–12, Accountability of the Bank of England (HC 874).

[15] Lord Acton in a letter to Mandell Creighton dated 5 April 1887, published in *Historical Essays and Studies*, (Macmillan, London 1907).

[16] Ron Paul, *To End the Fed*, (1st edn, Grand Central Publishing, New York 2009).

its financial regulatory system through the enactment of the Dodd-Frank Wall Street Reform and Consumer Protection Act (Dodd-Frank Act 2010), though in the end the structural changes were relatively minor.[17] The Act creates the Bureau of Consumer Financial Protection and abolishes the Office of Thrift Supervision, distributing its powers among the Federal Reserve System, the Office of the Comptroller of the Currency and the Federal Deposit Insurance Corporation (FDIC). Even after the Dodd-Frank Act, the US financial safety net architecture remains fragmented and 'multi-peaked'. The US's complex regulatory system is still based upon a combination of federal law (financial laws enacted by Congress), state law, regulation by agencies (the Fed and the Securities and Exchange Commission have rule-making powers), and self-regulation (in the field of securities, the rules of the self -regulatory organizations). One significant change, contained in the Dodd-Frank Act, is the establishment of a Financial Stability Oversight Council (chaired by the Secretary of the Treasury and with representation from all the regulatory agencies) tasked with identifying risks to financial stability that could arise from the activities of both firms and markets and determining how best to respond to emerging threats. The Fed has also expanded its remit, since its supervisory power can be extended to systemically significant non-bank financial institutions. Under the orderly liquidation authority regime, the FDIC can be appointed as a receiver for SIFIs.

In response to the crisis, two trends can be identified internationally: first, a reinforcement of the role of the central bank and second, because of the fiscal costs of the bailout or rescue packages, there is greater political interference and reduced independence for central banks and supervisory agencies. This latter trend is in stark contrast with the movement towards independence that characterized the framework of central banks prior to the crisis.

What is still rather puzzling is the inadequate response in the UK and elsewhere to a key challenge: the dichotomy between national law and global markets. The reshuffling of supervisory responsibilities, *per se*, does not address the fundamental problem, which is the 'illusion' of relying upon national regulation and supervision to confront the challenges of international markets and globalization. There are two possible solutions at the extreme: de-globalization, with reduced international financial inter-connectivity; and a retrenchment to national law and structures or the internationalization of rules and structures.

---

[17] Dodd-Frank Wall Street Reform and Consumer Protection Act, Pub. L. 111-203 (2010) (the Dodd-Frank Act).

The need for an 'international financial architecture' has been addressed elsewhere.[18] Given the rise in systemic risks, noted by all the reports on the current global financial system and its interconnectedness, the way forward must involve the substitution of this loose network by a hierarchical structure more akin to that of the WTO. That is, in the same way as the governance of trade has required a new multilateral organization with a clear hierarchical structure that superseded the previous morass of bilateral relationships, the evolution of financial system oversight requires the creation of a new multilateral financial body with authority to settle disputes and to impose its decisions.

The challenge posed by the dichotomy between global financial institutions and markets and the constraints of national law is best exemplified by the problems posed by the resolution of cross-border systemically important financial institutions, for which living wills may provide at least a partial answer.[19]

III. BANKERS' BEHAVIOUR

A third group of proposals[20] concern the behaviour of the banking industry and bank management, whether through better risk management, enhanced corporate governance, or simply through the responsibility that comes with the job of banking and the need to internalize the costs associated with providing financial stability protection.

IV. FISCAL AND COMPENSATION CONSIDERATIONS

There have been a number of proposals on the fiscal side;[21] the issue of rents, rather than normal profit making, is controversial for banking and financial markets which have been largely subsidized by government

---

18 Luis Garicano and Rosa M. Lastra, 'Towards a New Architecture for Financial Stability: Seven Principles' (2010) 13(3) Journal of International Economic Law 599–600.

19 See Thomas F. Huertas and Rosa M. Lastra, 'Living Wills' No: 21 Estabilidad Financiera (November 2011).

20 See Rosa Lastra and Geoffrey Wood, 'The Crisis of 2007–2009: Nature, Causes and Reactions', (2010) 13(3) Journal of International Economic Law 531–50.

21 Ibid.

rescue packages and through monetary and fiscal policies. Acute moral hazard problems persist. Governments have targeted compensation (for example, the 50 per cent one-off bonus tax on bonus compensation pools of a number of financial institutions in the UK) and the proposals adopted have varied among countries. Some economists and politicians have advocated the imposition of a global tax on financial transactions, akin to the Tobin tax, and one which is similar to the proposed EU financial transaction tax.

V. STRUCTURAL REFORMS

The aim of these reforms is to change the structure of the banking industry and the balance sheets of commercial banks and other financial institutions. This is a key thrust of the so-called 'Vickers Report' and its ring-fencing proposals. The Independent Commission on Banking was established by the UK Government in June 2010 to consider structural and related non-structural reforms to the banking sector intended to promote financial stability as well as competition. The Commission was asked to report to the Cabinet Committee on Banking Reform by the end of September 2011. Its members, Sir John Vickers (Chair), Clare Spottiswoode, Martin Taylor, Bill Winters and Martin Wolf, published an interim report in April 2011 and their final report in September 2011 (hereinafter, referred to as 'the report'). The report recommends that UK retail deposit takers (Barclays, HSBC, Lloyds, RBS and Santander UK) and the largest building society (Nationwide) keep equity capital at a minimum of 10 per cent of risk adjusted assets (Basel III called for 7 per cent). It also recommends that large banking groups should have a loss absorbing capacity of 17–20 per cent. It suggests that the UK introduce depositor preference, thus giving depositors higher priority status. It also tackles a range of 'competition issues', bearing in mind – as a September 2011 briefing entitled 'Resolving the Dilemma of British Banking' by the law firm Slaughter and May LLP clarified – competition in the context of the report refers to two different concepts: first, competition within the UK amongst its retail banks (taking into consideration consumer protection) and second, competition between the UK (London in particular) and other global centres, since the relative competitiveness of doing banking and finance in the UK is affected by legislative changes at home and elsewhere.

The most controversial part of the report is the proposed structural separation between domestic retail services and global wholesale and investment banking operations. According to the Vickers Report, the best

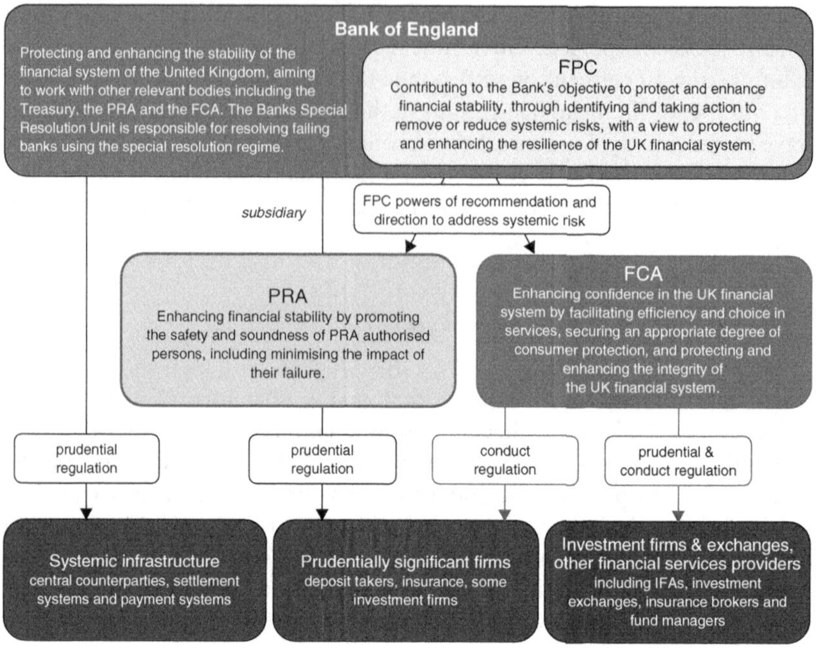

Note: See http://www.hm-treasury.gov.uk/

Figure 6.1 New supervisory structure in the UK

policy approach is to require ring-fencing of UK domestic retail banks. The report argues that a structural separation should make it easier and less costly to resolve banks that get into trouble and should help insulate retail banking from external financial shocks, thus diminishing problems arising from global interconnectedness and increasing the resilience of the UK retail banking system.

Though the rationale for many of the reforms is sound, a number of legal and policy issues need to be worked out (the devil is usually in the details). First, whenever a fence or boundary is established, the challenge arises: what should be inside the fence or boundary, and what should be outside? Boundaries and fences provide various incentives for institutions to place themselves on one side or the other, depending on what appears to be more beneficial to them. The Commission's view is that domestic retail banking services should be inside the ring-fence, global wholesale/investment banking should be outside, and the provision of straightforward banking services to large domestic non-financial companies can be in or out. Second, would these structural reforms place UK institutions at a competitive disadvantage? Given the limitations of regulation to promote good conduct, is perhaps too much being asked of it and not enough of improved governance? Finally, the focus of the report is on the UK, independent of European and international efforts that are taking place in tandem.[22]

The Commission did a commendable job in putting together an outline of the main problems and challenges for the UK banking system and tried to come up with pertinent recommendations. As in the case of the De Larosière report[23] – which set out the blueprint for the new supervisory structure in the EU – the members of the Committee had a mandate that focused on economic issues. It will be up to the legislators to consider the important legal issues that arise from this blueprint. After all, the law provides the framework for the licensing, expansion, regulation, supervision and resolution of banks and other financial institutions and the key attributes of a clear legal framework are certainty and predictability. It is these last attributes, and the cross-border dimension, that must be considered in depth in the structural reforms proposed in the UK.

The narrow banking proposals were endorsed by John Kay in, 'Narrow Banking. The Reform of Banking Regulation',[24] while Lawrence J. Kotlikoff made a case for the mutualization of the financial industry in his book, *Jimmy Stewart is Dead: Ending the World's Ongoing Financial Plague with Limited Purpose Banking*.[25] The so-called 'Volcker rule' (section 619 of the Dodd-Frank Act 2010) is also a structural reform. As acknowledged, the Volcker rule prohibits federally insured 'banking entities' from engaging in proprietary trading (subject to certain exceptions) and restricts their relationships with hedge funds and private equity funds.

Plans to establish a high-level expert group on structural aspects of the European banking sector were announced in the European Parliament in

---

[22] For example, how realistic is the possibility that existing UK banking groups could relocate elsewhere in the European Union (or European Economic Area) and use the single banking passport to establish branches in the UK (which would not be affected by the ring-fence)? The same considerations apply to non EU banks seeking to do business in the UK. Will they have an incentive to establish a subsidiary in another EU jurisdiction and choose to operate in the UK through branches? These are points made in the note written by Slaughter & May.

[23] See http://ec.europa.eu/internal_market/finances/docs/de_larosiere_report_en.pdf (last accessed 17 September 2012).

[24] http://www.johnkay.com/2009/09/15/narrow-banking (last accessed 17 September 2012).

[25] John Wiley & Sons, Chichester 2010.

November 2011 and shortly thereafter Commissioner Barnier appointed Erkki Liikanen, Governor of the Bank of Finland, as the Chair of the group. The 'Liikanen Group' is scheduled to start working in February 2012.[26]

The aim of these structural proposals is to circumscribe the scope of institutions that receive governmental protection, that is to separate 'utility banking' from 'casino banking'.

VI. A NOTE ON SIFIS[27]

Until the financial crisis of 2007–2009 the term TBTF was mostly associated with size and with banks. However, in 2008 Bear Stearns brought a new dimension to this notion: some institutions were too interconnected to fail, as confirmed by AIG. Bear Stearns and Lehman Brothers were investment banks, while AIG was an insurance company. The TBTF concept had moved from commercial banks to securities firms and insurance companies. Systemic risk is as likely to arise from activities in securities and derivatives markets as it is in banking. This makes systemic risk prevention a fundamental goal of securities regulation and of financial regulation more broadly, and not 'simply' of banking regulation.

Today's SIFI is an extension of the TBTF idea. Some institutions are considered to be too important to fail and/or too complex to manage, and if they are too complex to manage, they are obviously too complex to control/supervise. Supervision should never be a substitute for good management.

The problems in Iceland in 2008 showed that some institutions were 'too big to save'. Systemically important financial institutions or SIFIs are institutions that are so important for the functioning of the financial system that their problems (in particular, their failure) can trigger systemic risk. SIFIs – according to the FSB Recommendations of October 2010 – are financial institutions 'whose disorderly failure, because of their size, complexity and systemic interconnectedness, would cause significant disruption to the wider financial system and to overall economic activity'.[28] Though as individual institutions SIFIs may be subject to micro super-

[26] http://ec.europa.eu/commission_2010–2014/barnier/headlines/news/2012/01/20120116_en.htm (last accessed 17 September 2012).

[27] See Rosa Lastra, 'Systemic Risk, SIFIs and Financial Stability', (2011) 6(2) Capital Markets Law Journal 197–213.

[28] See http://www.financialstabilityboard.org/publications/r_101111a.pdf (last accessed 17 September 2012).

vision (though some SIFIs can be part of the shadow banking system and thus subject to lesser regulation or no regulation), their systemic significance implies that they should also be subject to macro-prudential supervision.

The size or importance of SIFIs is a source of concern not only nationally, but globally. SIFIs raise numerous concerns and issues, including: problems of definition, problems of effective regulation and supervision and problems of resolution and crisis management. SIFIs enjoy an implicit government guarantee, which generates pernicious moral hazard incentives. That implicit protection should be priced according to market mechanisms (perhaps best referred to as 'market discipline in protection'). Adequate resolution mechanisms for SIFIs are fundamental to limiting SIFI moral hazard and reducing systemic risk.

A major challenge lying ahead in the treatment of SIFIs is the boundary problem or perimeter issue. Once a definition of SIFI or global SIFI is established, a clear boundary is drawn and with it an incentive for financial institutions to position themselves on one side or another of the boundary, whichever seems most advantageous to them. The definition of a SIFI is also dynamic: what is systemic today is not necessarily what will be systemic in future and vice versa. The fact that most systemically significant financial institutions have a cross-border dimension, calls for a cross-border solution, supra-nationally and/or internationally.

CONCLUSION

Though financial markets and institutions have grown more integrated internationally in recent years, regulation remains constrained by the domain of domestic jurisdictions.[29] How best to deal with this is the ultimate challenge for financial regulation, supervision and resolution. It will require the application of coherent and consistent international rules, as well as improved cooperation amongst national authorities.

---

[29] See Rosa Lastra (ed.), *Cross Border Bank Insolvency* (Oxford University Press, Oxford 2011).

7. The Federal Agency for Financial Market Stabilisation: From rescuing to restructuring

Christopher Pleister

I. INTRODUCTION

The financial market crisis worsened steadily after summer 2007. Distressed banks, rattled investors, the real economy's need for fresh capital and central banks' attempts to address the most severe liquidity needs led to a bundle of problems which seemed to be spiralling out of control. All developed economies were affected, albeit to varying degrees. The effects of the fall of the US investment bank Lehman Brothers were particularly dramatic for Germany. The order of the day was to act as fast as possible because survival of the German banking sector was at stake.

A key element of the response to the crisis in Germany was to establish a new institution, in order to supplement the range of tasks already performed by the Deutsche Bundesbank and the *Bundesanstalt für Finanzdienstleistungsaufsicht* (Germany's Federal Financial Supervisory Authority, hereinafter BaFin). Neither prudential instruments nor German insolvency laws were adequate for rescuing German banks that had got into difficulty. The government needed to take action: it set up the *Bundesanstalt für Finanzmarktstabilisierung* (Financial Market Stabilisation Agency, hereinafter FMSA), originally to function as a temporary institution.

II. RESCUE PHASE: POST-LEHMAN BROTHERS TO THE END OF 2010

There were several options for reacting to such a crisis. Paying due consideration to the principles of a free-market economy, one option would have been to let individual banks exit the market through an orderly procedure provided by the state. Insolvency proceedings could have been launched for stressed banks. Contrary to common assumptions, German insolvency proceedings don't necessarily lead to liquidation. There can indeed be a restructuring on the basis of an insolvency plan with the participation of creditors and shareholders. But, this is a long drawn-out process and whether it will succeed or not is difficult if not impossible to forecast. During the crisis, decisions need to address two things: quickness and sustainability. Hence, aspects of timing and confidence played an overriding role in overcoming the financial crisis. However, the legal framework existing in Germany at that time was inadequate. The German banks that had got into difficulty were themselves not in a position to raise the necessary funds.

A. The Creation of the FMSA

In the third quarter of 2008 the financial crisis peaked with the failure of Lehman Brothers. The ensuing loss of confidence in the interbank market and the subsequent liquidity and capital problems for banks led to the creation of the FMSA on 17 October 2008. Within a week the German lower house of parliament, the Bundestag, passed the Act on the *Establishment of a Financial Market Stabilisation Fund* (*Gesetz zur Errichtung eines Finanzmarktstabilisierungsfonds*), which was subsequently ratified by the upper house, the Bundesrat. The purpose of the FMSA was to stabilise German financial markets. Banks that had got into difficulty due to the crisis were to be rescued quickly and banks in an apparently hopeless situation provided with the necessary 'help to help themselves', that is, banks taken out of the market by the crisis were to be reintegrated into the German banking scene. The aim was to avoid incalculable consequences for the German banking system and to quickly regain market confidence. The FMSA and the Financial Market Stabilisation Fund (*Sonderfonds für Finanzmarktstabilisierung*, hereinafter SoFFin) were set up temporarily with that aim in mind.

Under the Act on the *Establishment of a Financial Market Stabilisation Fund*, SoFFin could grant measures only upon application from the recipient of those measures. Hence, as regards the applicant, the recourse to SoFFin measures was on a voluntary basis.

B. SoFFin Instruments

The Act provided for the granting of three support measures for banks:

1. Guarantees: the fund was able to guarantee up to EUR400 billion to secure bank refinancing and hence overcome short-term liquidity bottlenecks.

2. Recapitalisation: measures to strengthen the capital base in the form of shares or silent participations, for which EUR80 billion was available.
3. Assumption of risk positions: in principle, the fund was able to take on or otherwise hedge limited quantities of risk positions (claims and securities) of banks.[1]

A further part of the German rescue package was the Supplementary Act to Stabilise the Financial Market (*Gesetz zur weiteren Stabilisierung des Finanzmarktes*) of 7 April 2009. It enabled the FMSA in particular to take over banks more easily, that is expropriation for compensation. That Act originated in the context of the particularly dire straits of Hypo Real Estate Holding AG.

In the course of the financial crisis the Financial Market Stability Fund Act was supplemented with 'bad bank legislation'. The resolution agency model allowed the applicants to move risk positions and non-core business lines to an agency set up by SoFFin in order to free up capital to promote lending to the real economy. At the same time, by using the resolution agency the bank was supposed to be able to 'reinvent itself' through a promising business model.

The FMSA set up two resolution agencies, over both of which it has supervisory responsibilities. The conditions under which the loss settlement obligations function are governed by the statutes of each respective agency. In principle, the obligation to settle losses and to provide fresh liquidity rests with the 'former owners' with a stake in the transferring bank at the time of transfer. The resolution agencies are dissolved after all transferred risk positions and business lines have been wound up.

SoFFin was also able to grant guarantees to special purpose vehicles to which a recipient of SoFFin measures could have transferred structured securities in advance. However, in practice, that instrument was not used.

The maximum guarantees of up to EUR400 billion were drawn down in peak periods with amounts up to EUR168 billion (42 per cent) and are currently still at EUR28 billion (7 per cent), which will be terminated by the start of 2015. Therefore, much of the assistance made available has never been called on or is no longer at risk. Generally speaking, the taxpayer incurs no payments when granting guarantees but only if the issue suffers a default. In the case of such a default, the SoFFin would have recourse to the bank's assets. To date no guarantee has defaulted and the

[1] Only one recipient drew on this instrument in 2009 for some months until their positions were transferred to a resolution agency.

FMSA is currently assuming that none of the outstanding guarantees are going to default.

Of the capital assistance of a maximum of EUR80 billion, an amount not exceeding EUR30 billion was drawn, of which approximately EUR20 billion is currently still outstanding. The capital provided, at a maximum of 8 per cent of German banks' tier 1 capital (about EUR380 billion as at December 2008), has saved the German banking system from a Lehman Brothers-like event.

The fees and interest SoFFin had received as of the end of 2010 for the guarantees granted exceeded expenses. Although, for its capital measures, SoFFin received interest on its hidden deposits, as well as special payments, it also had to write down some of these measures. The FMSA had to make value adjustments to the participations in 2009 and 2010, leading to loss carry forwards currently amounting to approximately EUR8 billion, or about 2 per cent of the capital of the German banking system as at the end of 2008. Given the current situation on the financial markets, the losses carried forward will likely be higher. The provisions for impending losses result from lower receipts expected in the future and do not constitute realised losses to the taxpayer. The exact result and the timing of SoFFin's closing statement after repayment of all instruments are still open and will depend greatly on the trend in the capital markets and among banks.

By law, SoFFin has not granted any new stabilisation benefits to credit institutions since 1 January 2011. However, it continues to discharge responsibilities based on the existing stabilisation measures, for example, the controlling of the conditionality of the measures and the legal supervision of the resolution agencies. In addition, SoFFin may, beyond 2010, augment its previously acquired capital participations in order to prevent dilution. SoFFin may also inject new capital into the existing resolution agencies and provide them with guarantees.

C. FMSA's Successes

Retrospectively, it could be said that German banks were rescued successfully. The lines of credit provided by the Federal Government did not have to be drawn in full, and the banks have already successfully repaid a large portion of the assistance received. In comparison to other international initiatives, the costs of the stabilisation measures have remained fairly moderate.

A run on deposits by small investors typical of a banking crisis has been avoided and the provision of funding to the economy has been assured. The Deutsche Bundesbank and the European Central Bank have confirmed that there has been no credit crunch in Germany and hence no restrictions on the availability of financing. Insurance corporations and the fund industry have been benefiting indirectly from the FMSA and its work. The various policy actions taken prevented the financial crisis from spilling over to the real economy. Indeed the problems of the banking sector have not prevented the German economy from recovering.

However, the successful short-term stabilisation of markets has not contributed to the necessary adjustment process in the German banking sector. Individual rescue measures stabilised a given bank but they have weakened the system over the longer term. The crisis has not led to a healthy restructuring because the policy measures have taken a lot of pressure off the banks. In addition, the stabilisation measures were based on the naïve assumption that all the banks that encountered distress did so because of the crisis and as a result of their own wrongdoings. But there has been, and doubtless still is, a long-term need to restructure German banks, irrespective of the financial crisis, as German banks have always suffered from extremely weak capitalisation and low profitability.

III. RESTRUCTURING PHASE: ROLLOUT OF THE *RESTRUCTURING ACT* IN JANUARY 2011

When the Restructuring Act was passed at the beginning of 2011 it marked a turning point in the inception of the FMSA. From that time on, its focus broadened to be not only on the short-term rescue and stabilisation of banks but also to provide a proper framework for the restructuring of the banking industry. The idea of helping to recover from the crisis lost momentum. Instead, the aim has become to create the necessary balance between short-term restructuring and the overdue restructuring of the German banking sector by providing an institutionalised legal framework for resolving systemically important banks. The purpose of the framework is to prevent a systemically important bank from pushing the German banking market into a downward spiral, making a financial crisis even worse. In the event that support measures are necessary, the required funds ought to be provided by the banks themselves and not by taxpayers.

The passage of the Restructuring Act turned the FMSA into a fixed addition to the architecture of the German financial system.

A. Instruments of the Restructuring Act

The German Banking Act (*Kreditwesengesetz* (KWG)) has been amended as a result of the Restructuring Act. The Banking Act now authorises

BaFin to order the transfer of systemically relevant assets to a new legal entity if a distressed bank endangers the stability of the system as a whole. Those assets which remain with the transferring bank and are not classified as systemically important are normally to be dealt with in an orderly resolution procedure.

The *Restructuring Act's* toolbox contains the following measures:

1. Restructuring and reorganisation procedures for banks which are based on an insolvency plan procedure and initiated by the banks. They involve a two-stage procedure to support banks' independent and voluntary efforts to restructure ahead of any insolvency.
2. Extended competencies for supervisors and regulators: the right to appoint a special commissioner, the obligation to submit restructuring plans and the option of issuing a transfer order.
3. Introduction of a bank levy to finance the measures.

When a bank applies for a restructuring procedure this does not mean a legal intervention in the rights of shareholders and creditors. The restructuring plan, its implementation and the appointment of a restructuring consultant, are aimed at helping to restructure the bank. The shareholders and creditors can decide on a reorganisation plan if the reorganisation process would involve more far-reaching interventions. These procedures involve BaFin, but in either case it is necessary for a bank to apply for them.

BaFin can however implement a far-reaching intervention, a transfer order. A transfer order can be decreed against the will of shareholders and creditors. The prerequisite for this measure is that the bank's continued existence be threatened, which would in turn endanger the stability of the financial system. Under a transfer order, BaFin is entitled to transfer a bank's systemically important assets to a private buyer or to a bridge bank established by the Restructuring Fund. Insolvency proceedings are commenced for the remaining parts of the distressed bank that are not systemically relevant. At the end of those proceedings, the distressed bank is either restructured or liquidated. The creditors of the distressed bank are paid on a *pro rata* basis. The law states that the financial status of creditors, after the transfer order and the resolution of the distressed bank, should not be worse than absent a transfer order.

Figure 7.1 shows the effects of a transfer order on the balance sheets of the remaining rump and the bridge bank, when systemically relevant assets and liabilities are separated from those which are not.

To strengthen market discipline, BaFin may decide only at the time

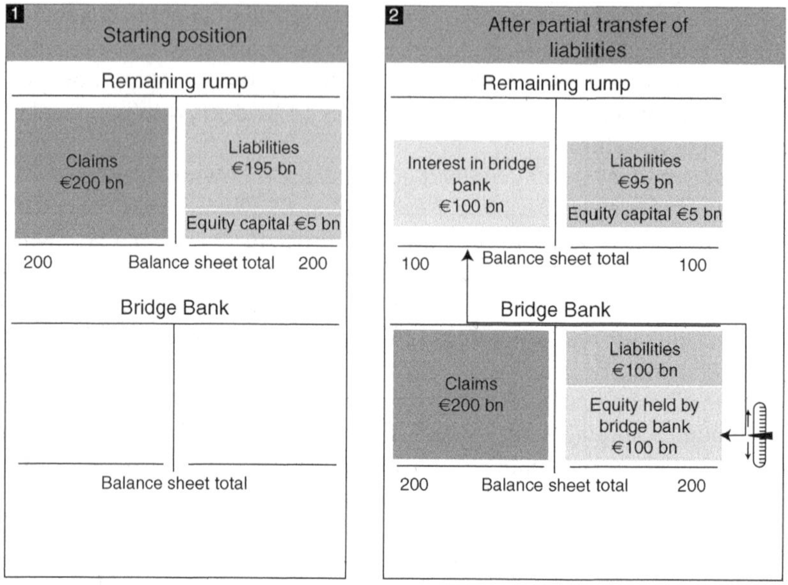

Figure 7.1 Creating a safe heaven

of the transfer order which assets are to be transferred to a bridge bank. Hence, there is no certainty *a priori* about which assets or liabilities will remain with the distressed bank or be transferred to the bridge bank. This new set of instruments has not been used so far. As a purely precautionary measure the Restructuring Fund has set up three bridge banks without a specific purpose. This measure is precautionary; it allows for being prepared for worst-case scenarios, in which a transfer order would have to be issued under extreme time constraints.

The Restructuring Fund is aimed at creating a solid financial foundation for the orderly resolution of banks, as well as at protecting systemically important assets by taking measures vis-à-vis the legal entity accepting those assets. The financial resources from this fund are available for payments under a transfer order and especially for granting guarantees and recapitalisation in the case of a bridge bank. But, unlike under the Financial Market Stabilisation Fund Act, it is no longer possible to provide support for any applicant bank.

In principle, the idea is to exempt the public sector from paying for bank rescues. This aim is to be achieved with an annual bank levy. The levy is raised, collected and managed by the Restructuring Fund, and all banks licensed to operate under the German Banking Act are required to pay the levy, except for so-called promotional banks (German public banks set up to promote investment activity by granting loans at preferential rates). The bank levy is geared to the size of the bank and its interconnectedness with the financial system, using a proper weight between the assessment base and levy rates in order to take appropriate account of the risk involved: banks with lower systemic risk carry lower charges than systemically important banks. In any case, the banks will bear the cost of restructuring measures themselves in the future, thus relieving taxpayers of that burden.

The target funding to be accrued over time through the annual levy for the Restructuring Fund is EUR70 billion. If the funds required during a crisis exceed the financial resources accrued under the banking levy the Federal Republic of Germany will provide any additional financial assistance required.[2] The additional financing gap will be recovered from the Restructuring Fund over time through the annual levy and a separate exceptional contribution rate to recover the amount in excess. This structure ensures that the Fund is ready to act at any time and that it does not depend on accrued financial means.

Under the Restructuring Act, the FMSA is no longer the saviour of failed banks but the fiduciary of healthy ones. This situation enhances market discipline and increases the pressure on German banks to restructure.

IV. EUROPEAN COMMISSION CONDITIONALITY

The granting of assistance by SoFFin was predicated on meeting various conditions laid down in laws and regulations, such as a sustainable business model for the core bank or adherence to remuneration standards. EU state aid legislation is just one of many reasons why banks have to obtain this assistance at market rates and repay them. Furthermore, owing to commitments by the Federal Government to the European Commission in order to avoid competitive distortion, recipients of assistance who drew on recapitalisation measures or resolution agencies were required to make adjustments and changes to their business models which, in some cases, were massive.

At the same time, the European Commission has emphasised the role of involving owners and creditors in the costs of the restructuring measures and is seeking to secure this participation by means of a directive.

---

[2] If needed, the fund can draw on a guarantee authorisation amounting to EUR100 billion and a recapitalisation authorisation of EUR20 billion.

A. Digression

Crises are inherent in market economies as a necessary corrective to unsustainable developments. Corrective measures should be implemented not only by regulators but also by those bearing responsibility in the finance industry. What this means is that, although regulatory measures can contribute to stabilising financial markets, they can never replace confidence created by market participants 'walking the walk'. Achieving that confidence requires a change in the attitude of decision makers in banking and the set of values underlying observed practices. When all is said and done, laws and regulations cannot replace a proper code of professional ethics. The banking sector must recognise that the freedom accorded by free markets comes with responsibilities as well. Only when market participants have fully understood this relationship can the current crisis serve as a genuine turning point for the better.

SUMMARY AND OUTLOOK

Prior to the Lehman event there had not been any concerted state assistance in Germany but only one-off bank rescues. When Lehman Brothers became insolvent in 2008, the FMSA was established temporarily as a government lifeline to help banks that had become distressed due to the crisis. Thanks to its cooperation with the Bundesbank, BaFin, the Federal Ministry of Finance and the European Commission, the FMSA succeeded in rescuing German banks. No German bank had to be wound up and a second Lehman-type situation was avoided. This has buttressed systemic stability in the short run. A one-off rescue of a distressed bank may strengthen that individual institution, yet at the cost of weakening the overall banking system in the long run, because government measures have taken considerable pressure from the banks. In addition, it is a naïve assumption to say that all the banks encountered distress through no fault of their own, just because of the crisis.

Since the end of 2010, SoFFin has no longer been permitted to grant new stabilisation measures. Since that time, Germany has had a Restructuring Act and hence an institutionalised legal framework for resolving systemically important banks. This means that the task of the FMSA is no longer a temporary one. It is a new addition to the German banking system and is under instructions to rescue only the systemically important parts of a bank, the failure of which would endanger financial system stability. The other parts are to be resolved. In the future, banks will bear the costs of restructuring themselves, by paying a bank levy into the Restructuring

Fund. This fund will relieve a burden on taxpayers. Uncompromising restructuring will sacrifice an individual bank in order to save the banking system in the long run. There is no justification for keeping unsustainable business models on life support. The Restructuring Act thus ensures an appropriate balance between rescue on the one hand and overdue restructuring on the other.

When a shock occurs, the preferable approach would be to provide individual banks with crisis assistance, as it achieves short-term bank stabilisation and quickly restores confidence in the entire system. Otherwise, the afflicted banks are to be restructured. Owing to the current state of financial markets, politicians have already indicated that, if need be, they are prepared to take the requisite measures.

8. Extraordinary measures for extraordinary times and the need for effective bank resolution laws in Europe

Gillian G. Garcia and Maria J. Nieto[1]

INTRODUCTION

In the fall of 2011, when this chapter was being prepared, a number of EU member states were struggling to overcome problems with their sovereign debt. Many of those problems were attributed to measures that they felt compelled to take during the financial crisis that began in 2007. During the two years beginning in October 2008, member states committed 39 per cent and expended 9.3 per cent of 2009 GDP levels in rescuing their banking systems. At the same time the crisis revealed an inadequacy of financial system safety nets, notably legal frameworks for resolving failed banks along with arrangements for funding bank resolutions.

In Section I we analyse bank support operations by member states whose final cost to taxpayers is still to be determined. Section II summarizes the legal reforms that were undertaken in two EU countries that were seriously harmed by the financial crisis – Germany and the UK. The measures enacted were designed to better protect the public interest when banks fail in the future. Those countries led reform efforts whose spirit was eventually enshrined in the European Commission's (EC) proposal for an EU framework for bank recovery and resolution laws, which explicitly sets out the following objectives: maintenance of financial stability and public confidence and a reduction or elimination of costs to taxpayers.[2] The chapter concludes by emphasizing the need for adequate tools and powers to enable regulators to effectively resolve failed banks in the future.

---

1 The views expressed in this chapter are the responsibility of the authors.

2 See http://ec.europa.eu/internal_market/bank/crisis_management/index_en.htm#consultation2011 (last accessed 25 September 2012).

I. BACKGROUND: PUBLIC INTERVENTIONS IN THE EU BANKING SECTORS

The focus of this section is on the extraordinary tools being used to deal with the most important financial crisis since the Second World War. First, central banks felt compelled to respond to the challenge of restoring normal money market functionality. To that end, they provided ample liquidity by extending the maturity of refinancing operations, provided foreign currency liquidity through local operational frameworks at harmonized market prices and they accepted less liquid collateral in their operations (that is, Asset-Backed Securities). As well, central banks made outright asset purchases of targeted specific securities and in addition to their support to the money markets, they also lent to individual credit institutions in their traditional role of lenders of last resort (emergency liquidity assistance in the context of the Eurosystem).

Second, deposit protection, the other element of the safety net aimed at alleviating financial distress, proved to be insufficient as has been well documented elsewhere.[3] The turn taken by the crisis in late 2008 triggered an abrupt increase in the harmonized minimum coverage levels of insured deposits from EUR20 000 to EUR100 000 by the end of 2010, an end to co-insurance, and an increase in the speed of repayment to insured depositors resulting from a bank failure.

In light of the inability of the safety net players' actions to stem the financial crisis, national governments scrambled to guarantee financial institutions' debts, acquire good assets and also, in some cases, poorer quality assets. Moreover, government support often led to recapitalizations of financial institutions. All such support was initially granted in an uncoordinated manner within the EU. Coordination of subsequent actions was led by the EC in the context of its state aid policy, which was aimed at preserving an integrated EU financial market.

It is noteworthy that in the early stages of the crisis, national governments' support was initially directed to individual institutions. As the crisis intensified, in late 2008 assistance was extended to a larger number of banks and even to the financial system as a whole. Accordingly, more comprehensive schemes were adopted in a number of countries – the Irish and Danish blanket-guarantee schemes that covered virtually all bank

3 Gillian G. Garcia, Rosa Lastra and María J. Nieto, 'Bankruptcy and reorganization procedures for cross-border banks in the EU: Towards an integrated approach to the reform of the EU safety net', (2009) 17(3) Journal of Financial Regulation and Compliance 240-27.

liabilities (including retail, corporate and interbank deposits) are two such examples.

The advantage of the explicit schemes as compared to *ad hoc* measures, resides in the transparency surrounding the institutions eligible, the volume of support available, the pricing and the duration. However, the existing rescue and restructuring guidelines of the EU State aid policy were not adequate to address promptly the level playing field issues raised by countries' immediate responses to the banking crisis. In this context, the EC's coordinating role materialized in guidance covering government guarantees on bank debt issuance; recapitalization of financial institutions; treatment of banks' impaired assets; and the assessment of the restructuring measures by drawing up recommendations on the appropriate framework for pricing government support measures for the euro area countries.

The EC-approved schemes and the *ad hoc* interventions from October 2008 to October 2010 give a good insight into the dimension of government support to the EU banking system stemming from the financial crisis. The maximum volume of EC-approved measures amounted to EUR4 588.90 billion or 39 per cent of EU-27 GDP for 2009,[4] although the nominal amount of financial support actually used and reported to the EC was EUR1 106.54 billion or 9.3 per cent of EU-27 GDP. However, the percentages do not reflect the wide differences among countries within the EU that range from almost 3 per cent Portuguese GDP to almost 141 per cent of Irish GDP. Government support was highly concentrated – between 37 and 63 per cent of the support extended under capital, guarantee and asset protection schemes – and was absorbed by the largest three recipient institutions.

A. Specific Characteristics of Bank Debt Guaranteed by Governments

Since October 2008, government guarantees of new issuance of bank senior debt have been aimed at easing solvent banks' liquidity problems. Other measures included government guarantees higher temporary coverage limits for retail deposits (and debt held by retail clients), certain types of wholesale deposits (excluding interbank deposits) and short- and

---

[4] Only Bulgaria, the Czech Republic, Estonia, Malta and Romania did not grant any State support to their financial systems. Close to 70 per cent of the maximum volume (both schemes and *ad hoc* interventions) relates to the UK, Ireland, Denmark, Germany and France (see http://ec.europa.eu/competition/state_aid/studies_reports/studies_reports.html#scoreboard (last accessed 25 September 2012)).

medium-term debt instruments, to the extent that such liabilities were not already adequately protected by existing arrangements. In order to avoid protecting shareholders and other risk capital investors, coverage excludes subordinated debt (Tier 2 capital) and blanket guarantees (which would indiscriminately cover all liabilities).

In the euro area, pricing of government guarantees discriminates by the maturity of the guaranteed debt and it is based on banks' five year CDS spreads plus add-on fees. Historically high levels of the CDS spreads and the stigma associated with accepting government guarantees partly explain banks' reluctance to use government support. Furthermore, spreads on government debt rose to mirror spreads on government-guaranteed bank bonds and so the advantage of the guarantee was less obvious.

B. Specific Characteristics of Government Bank Recapitalizations

As acknowledged by the EC, government capital injections were aimed to 'respond to the widespread perception that higher capital ratios are necessary in view of the past underestimation of risk and the increased cost of funding'.[5] Although initially capital support came in the form of Tier 2 capital and non-core Tier 1 (for example, preferred shares) in order to avoid acquiring minority voting rights, ultimately government financial support shifted to acquiring banks' ordinary shares and some even led to full nationalization (for example, Hypo Real Estate and Anglo Irish). In some instances, the capital injections went to the banks' holding company structures, which provided significant evidence that governments intended to provide support to the entire legal entity. In other cases, recapitalizations involved support by several governments simultaneously (that is, Dexia and Fortis).

Both the EC and the ECB provided guidance on remunerating governments for their capital assistance by setting out a methodology based on market prices, specific bank risk, the level of subordination and the corresponding risk of the specific instrument (via CDS spreads and equity risk premiums), and the country risk (via government bond yields). Most important, pricing was set to incentivize the temporary nature of the government's involvement by using add-on fees, call options, and/or conditional payment for dividends.

Government-induced bank recapitalization has (or should have) been taking place without prejudice to supervisors' ability to decide whether

[5] Please see 'State Aid Scoreboard Report on State aid granted by the EU Member States', Report from the EU Commission COM, 701 Autumn 2010.

banks should be restructured or wound up. Furthermore, distressed banks that received state aid in the form of recapitalization and/or impaired asset support that together exceeds 2 per cent of the bank's total risk-weighted assets are obliged to present a restructuring plan to their supervisor.

C. Specific Characteristics of Asset Support by Governments

The acquisition of impaired assets was also part of the governments' strategy to clean up banks' balance sheets in a context of high refinancing costs due to uncertainty, particularly in the interbank market. Government asset support had two forms: asset insurance schemes that maintained the assets on the banks' balance sheet and asset removal schemes, which transferred the assets to a separate institution (bad bank) as in Germany and Ireland. In either case, asset support faces the challenge of pricing the impaired assets.[6] If the guaranteed asset remains on the bank's balance sheet, the bank usually assumes a first loss (plus an additional buffer) to cover losses, for example, a 16 per cent share of the portfolio in the case of Royal Bank of Scotland and 20 per cent in the case of ING. The government assumes the subsequent (and larger share) of the potential losses related to the insured portfolio of assets. Although assets continue to be shown on the banks' balance sheet, some or all of the associated 'tail risk' is removed. This improves, *prima facie*, banks' solvency ratios to the extent that asset purchase prices are above their book values. In return, the bank pays a fee or insurance premium based on the riskiness of the insured portfolio by taking into consideration the difference between the asset's book value and some measure of its 'fundamental value'. Moral hazard is thus at least partly limited by conditioning government capitalization to the banks that have minimum core capital and whose shareholders pay insurance premiums from distributable profits.

Most relevant is the relationship between the different types of government intervention. First, as Panetta et al. show, almost all banks that received capital injections also participated in impaired asset support schemes (for example, Hypo Real Estate, Commerzbank, ING and Royal Bank of Scotland).[7] Moreover, purchases of impaired assets often occurred

---

6 In most case, the assets were impaired. Only in Spain did good quality assets receive government support.

7 See Fabio Panetta, Thomas Faeh, Giuseppe Grande, Corrinne Ho, Michael King, Aviram Levy, Federico M. Signoretti, Marco Taboga and Andrea Zaghini, 'An assessment of financial sector rescue programmes', BIS Working Papers, No 48, July 2009. Those authors focus on the experience of Australia, Canada, France, Germany, Italy, Japan, the Netherlands, Spain, Switzerland, the UK and the US.

after earlier government capital injections. Second, in the case of bank debt guarantees, approximately one-half of those that received capital injections also received government guarantees for their bank debts (for example, Commerzbank, Bayern LB, ING and Erste).[8] Third, banks that received bigger capital injections also tended to be the ones that had borrowed more under government debt guarantees, confirming the substitutability between capital and liquidity in the short term. Liquidity provides a buffer from adverse shocks, but it comes in the form of time rather than loss absorption. Empirical evidence seems to support the argument that governments used liquidity support measures to deal with banks' solvency problems because their national legal frameworks for failed bank resolution were inadequate. Government support programmes thus created *ex ante* moral hazard, undermined market discipline, and subsidized bank creditors at the taxpayer's expense.

II. NEW BANK RESOLUTION LAWS FOR GERMANY AND THE UK

Taxpayers in Germany and the UK supported their banking systems throughout the crisis. For example, the UK government nationalized Northern Rock and Bradford and Bingley, and gave substantial aid to the Royal Bank of Scotland and Lloyds Banking Group.[9] The German government rescued IKB, Hypo Real Estate, Commerzbank and several Landesbanks. In doing so, both countries acknowledged deficiencies in their abilities to resolve failing banks that relied heavily on ordinary insolvency laws and subsequently revised their laws.

A. Germany's Bank Restructuring Act[10]

In the past German law on bank resolution relied on ordinary insolvency procedures with the exception that the supervisor, BaFin, could file to close a bank on insolvency grounds and the proceedings were normally started by a BaFin-imposed moratorium on the bank. These rules remain

---

8 The Irish and Greek banks that received capital injections also received debt guarantees.

9 Thomas F. Huertas, *Crisis: Cause, Containment and Cure* (2nd edn, Palgrave Macmillan, Basingstoke 2011).

10 This section draws heavily on Deutsche Bundesbank, German *Bank Restructuring Act, Monthly Report,* June, 2011, pp. 62–75 and Germany, *Draft Law of the Federal Government,* SEC/GovC/X/10/414b, 2010.

in place and may well be used to resolve small banks with a large retail customer base.[11]

Germany's Bank Restructuring Act came into effect at the beginning of 2011 to provide three additional restructuring procedures. Two are voluntary under civil law – a stabilization proceeding and a reorganization proceeding that may both be initiated and managed by the troubled bank's managers with the consent of the different constituencies that are affected. The Act's third procedure that falls under public law allows BaFin to transfer viable assets and liabilities to a sound bank and might become the relevant procedure for systemically important German banks.[12]

1. Stabilization Proceeding (Article 1: Credit Institution Reorganization Act (CIRA)

In the CIRA's early restructuring phase, once it appears likely that a bank will breach its capital and liquidity requirements and not be able to meet them on a sustainable basis, the bank can offer a restructuring plan to BaFin that does not affect the rights of third parties without their prior consent. If BaFin approves the plan, the bank can apply to the Higher Regional Court to approve the plan and appoint a Recovery Advisor with extensive powers to control the plan's implementation by monitoring bank actions and developments and reporting to the Court. Under the plan existing unsecured creditors may be asked (possibly required) to provide a restructuring loan (limited to 10 per cent of the bank's own funds) that is granted super priority over other unsecured credits should the bank file for bankruptcy within the next three years. BaFin can then take strong supervisory actions against a restructuring bank. On advice from BaFin and the advisor and after hearing the credit institutions' views, the courts may order changes in management to prevent owners and managers from taking certain actions or distributing profits, require changes in remuneration, and ultimately end the recovery procedure. Otherwise the bank would retain its managers, directors and owners and its identity.

2. The Reorganization Proceeding (Article 1: CIRA)

A second phase of recovery action can occur *ab initio* or after a restructuring plan has failed. Bingham considers it to essentially be an acceleration

---

11 Bingham, *German Bank Restructuring Act*, 9 February 2011, available at www.bingham.com/Media.aspx?mediaID=11986 (last accessed 25 September 2012).

12 Ibid.

of existing insolvency proceedings in which either the credit institution or BaFin (if the bank has or threatens to have, capital and/or liquidity below 90 per cent of the required thresholds or if its collapse would endanger financial stability) can ask a court to approve a Reorganization Plan.[13] After consulting with BaFin, the Bundesbank and the credit institution, a court can approve or reject the plan and appoint a Recovery Advisor to oversee the plan's execution.

The plan is comparable to an insolvency plan in that it may impair the rights of third parties by ordering a debt-for-equity swap, increasing or decreasing capital, transferring assets and liabilities, or cancelling contracts. A court can override shareholder disapproval of the Reorganization Plan and must confirm it within three months of its approval by creditors and owners – then its provisions become effective. Consequently, it may involve a slow process.

3. Transfer Order (Article 2: Amendments to the Banking Act)

The Act gives BaFin broad powers to intervene at an early stage to prevent a bank's financial distress once capital or liquidity requirements are breached. It can, for example, appoint a special representative who can assume the powers of the bank's governing board. BaFin may also issue a transfer order if (i) the going concern value of the bank is jeopardized, (ii) its collapse would endanger financial stability, and (iii) no easier alternative is available. In an attempt to balance the rights of those affected by the transfer order with the need to maintain systemic stability, BaFin may allow the bank to present a recovery plan in which it would acquire adequate capital and liquidity within six weeks. There is no need to obtain shareholder approval.

BaFin can transfer overnight the viable assets and secured liabilities of a systemically important troubled bank, for example to a good existing bank or a new private bank (NewCo) while leaving excess unsecured liabilities and toxic assets in a bad bank from which creditors would have to seek recovery. If the value of assets transferred (as assessed by a court-appointed expert appraiser) exceeds that of transferred liabilities the distressed bank may be compensated by receiving shares in the recipient bank or cash. The distressed bank will owe a cash contribution where the value of liabilities transferred exceeds that of assets transferred. The transferee bank's ability to pay dividends and interest will be impaired until any financial aid it has received from the state has been repaid.

---

13 Ibid.

4. The Restructuring Fund Act (Article 3 of the Bank Restructuring Act)
The Act allows for the creation of a temporary bridge bank that would be assisted and held by the Restructuring Fund (BRRF), which is managed by the Authority for Stabilization of Financial Markets (FMSA) and is mainly funded by German banks. Some or all of the assets and liabilities of the troubled bank that threatens financial stability could be moved to the bridge bank under a BaFin/FMSA transfer order.

B. Bank Resolution in the UK: The Banking Act 2009[14]

Until 2008, the UK relied on the Insolvency Act 1986, under which the bank's supervisor or its creditors could petition the court to declare bankruptcy when the bank failed (or threatened to fail) to meet its financial obligations.[15] The government noted that these arrangements made no provision to protect financial stability or the public interest, but were more concerned with achieving an orderly resolution, maximizing returns to creditors, channelling resources to more productive uses, and achieving a fair outcome. Moreover, the government considered that the existing laws were more likely to lead to the disposal of the assets of the failed bank than to its revival.[16]

Following the collapse of Northern Rock, Parliament enacted the Banking (Special Provisions) Act in February 2008 to give the authorities a temporary third option that would sunset in 12 months – to take over a problem bank, to facilitate its orderly resolution and to maintain financial stability. The share capital, business, assets, and liabilities of banks could be transferred in whole or in part to the Bank of England, the Treasury, or a commercial entity. This provision was applied to Bradford and Bingley, Northern Rock and two UK subsidiaries of Icelandic banks.[17] The Banking Act 2009 was enacted speedily to come into force just before

---

[14] This section draws on HM Treasury (2009) and the UK Statute Data Base. Banking Act 2009 available at at http://www.legislation.gov.uk/ukpga/2009/1/contents (last accessed 25 September 2012). The authors wish to thank Dalvinder Singh for his comments on an earlier draft of this section.

[15] Andrew Campbell and Peter Cartwright, *Banks in Crisis: The Legal Response* (Ashgate Publishing Limited, Aldershot 2002).

[16] Roman Tomasic, 'Creating a template for Banking Insolvency Law Reform after the Collapse of Northern Rock', available at http://ssrn.com/abstract=1416823 (last accessed 25 September 2012).

[17] Maximilian J.B. Hall, 'The Sub-Prime Crisis, the Credit Crunch and Bank Failure: an Assessment of the UK Authorities' Response' (2009) 17(4) Journal of Banking Regulation and Compliance 427–52 and Andrew McKnight, 'The *Banking Act* of 2009', June 2009, available at http://www.salans.com/en-GB/

the temporary Act expired. The first three of the Act's seven parts that relate to bank resolution are relevant to this chapter and they are discussed below. To remedy the former neglect of financial stability, it became one of the Act's objectives and the Act also establishes the Financial Stability Committee in the Bank of England.[18]

1. Stabilization Options (Part 1 of the Act, ss. 1–89)

Part 1 of the Banking Act 2009 establishes a special resolution regime (SRR) to enable the authorities to deal quickly and decisively with banks facing insolvency. The government wanted to retain as much as possible of the existing insolvency laws that cover winding up by the courts under the insolvency provisions and resuscitation under court administration. Consequently, Parts 2 and 3 of the Act retain these two options, but enact special provisions to apply only to banks (incorporated and authorized to take deposits in the UK).[19]

The bank's supervisor, in consultation with the Bank of England and the Treasury, can trigger the SRR by determining that the bank (regardless of its size or complexity) is failing, or is likely to fail, to meet the 'Threshold Conditions' that are necessary for it to conduct regulated activities and that the bank is not likely to meet these conditions quickly without action under the SRR. Section 7(3) of the Act has been criticized for setting a low standard for the supervisor to trigger the SRR: 'having regard to timing and other relevant circumstances it is not reasonably likely that . . . action will be taken by or in respect of the bank that will enable the bank to satisfy the threshold conditions'. Requiring the supervisor to meet a higher standard – such as being beyond a reasonable doubt, for example, would have been likely to delay the proceedings that needed to be taken in a timely manner in order to avoid a disorderly and costly outcome.

Several authorities have parts to play in the SRR. While the supervisor takes responsibility for deciding when a bank has failed (or is likely to fail) and initiates an SRR action, the Bank of England and HM Treasury are responsible to execute the SRR action. The two agencies can transfer a troubled bank's shares, other securities, property, rights, and liabilities.

Locations/~/media/Assets/Salans/Publications/2009/20090604-The-Banking-Act-2009.ashx (last accessed 1 October 2012).

[18] Peter Bierley, 'The UK Special Resolution Regime for Failing Banks in an International Context', Bank of England Financial Stability Paper, no 5, July, 2009 and Dalvinder Singh, 'The UK *Banking Act* 2009, Pre-Insolvency and Early Intervention: Policy and Practice,' (2011) 1 Journal of Business Law 20–42.

[19] The SRR, as well as the insolvency and administration procedures can also be extended to cover building societies and credit unions.

This is done after first determining that such action is in the public interest and, after consulting with the supervisor and the Treasury, the Bank of England can sell all or part of the bank to (i) a private purchaser or (ii) transfer it to a bridge bank whose board it will appoint and whose strategic direction it will oversee (although it requires HM Treasury consent where public funds or international obligations are involved). After consulting with the supervisor and the Bank and determining that such action is necessary to protect against a serious threat to UK financial stability or to protect the public interest, the Treasury may nationalize the bank.

These actions are effected by transfer instruments, issued by the Bank of England, that convey shares (and other securities) and property (assets and liabilities) to a private purchaser or bridge bank or by transfer orders, issued by HM Treasury that transform the bank into public ownership. Compensation orders (approved by Parliament) may compensate the transferors or third parties for the losses they suffer. The extent of such losses is to be determined by an independent assessor, appointed by HM Treasury, who must consider the principles that are laid out in the Act. A 'Banking Liaison Panel' is to advise HM Treasury on the SRR's likely effects on banks, their customers and financial markets. After consultations, the Treasury laid before Parliament a 'Revised Code of Practice' to govern the conduct of the SRR on 22 November 2010. The Act also gives HM Treasury extraordinary powers to amend existing statutory or common law even retrospectively (subject to subsequent approval by Parliament) in order to better achieve its objectives.[20]

2. A New Bank Insolvency Procedure (Part 2 of the Act, sections 90–135)
The new procedure applies specifically to banks and 'reflects the Authorities' intention to adhere, where possible, to existing insolvency laws and practices, so that the formal insolvency of a bank will be dealt with along similar lines to an ordinary liquidation' (para. 4.5, Bank, HM Treasury and FSA, 2008).[21] The Act adjusts, however, the existing

---

[20] Chuck Grieve, 'The *Banking Act* 2009: Implications for the Financial Markets', Clifford Chance Banking Note, May, accessed July 10 2009 at http://www.cliffordchance.com/publicationviews/publications/2009/06/clifford_chance_commentthebankingact20091.html (last accessed 1 October 2012) and Andrew McKnight, '*The Banking Act of 2009*', June 2009, available at http://www.salans.com/en-GB/Locations/~/media/Assets/Salans/Publications/2009/20090604-The-Banking-Act-2009.ashx (last accessed 1 October 2012).

[21] Bank of England, HM Treasury and FSA, *Financial Stability and Depositor Protection: Special Resolution Regime,* Cm 7459, July 2008, see especially para. 4.5.

insolvency procedures to enable insured depositors to receive priority and to be compensated rapidly.

The Bank of England, the FSA, or the Secretary of State can apply to a court for a bank insolvency order. The Act extends the grounds for seeking an insolvency order to refer not only to (i) the bank's inability, or likely inability, to repay its debts, but also to (ii) its winding up being in the public interest and (iii) whether it is fair.[22] The court can grant the application, dismiss it or adjourn it.[23] The Act also limits the rights of the bank, its shareholders, creditors, and others from applying to the court for insolvency or administration. When the bank enters insolvency via a court order, it is to be wound up under a court-appointed liquidator, who operates under the supervision of a liquidation committee but has broad powers to achieve two objectives. The primary objective is to ensure that each eligible depositor is paid promptly. In the insolvent bank's subsequent winding up, the liquidator will pursue the secondary goal – 'to achieve the best result for the bank's creditors as a whole' (s. 99).

3. A New Bank Administration Procedure (Part 3 of the Act, sections 136–168)

Part 3 of the Act creates a new form of administration that will keep in operation those parts of the bank that were not transferred by the Bank of England under the SRR to a private purchaser or a bridge bank but are judged to be still necessary to enable the acquirer to operate effectively. In this respect, creditors must be protected from losses that would be caused by delaying the normal insolvency processes. The Bank of England can apply to a court for a bank administration order after it has decided to make a transfer to a private purchaser or bridge bank and that the residual bank will be unable, or is likely to become unable, to pay its debts as a result of the transfer. The court will then appoint an administrator that the Bank nominates. The administrator has broad powers (including new powers to disclaim onerous property and bring proceedings for wrongful or fraudulent trading) to achieve two objectives. The primary objective is to provide support to the private purchaser or the bridge bank. The secondary objective is the traditional one – to rescue the bank as a going concern or achieve a better result for the (residual) bank's creditors than would be attained under an immediate winding up.

---

22 The Banking Act Explanatory Notes states that 'fair' means 'just and equitable'. For more detail please see HM Treasury, *Explanatory Notes to the Banking Act of 2009*, 12 February 2009, available at http://www.legislation.gov.uk/ukpga/2009/1/notes/contents (last accessed 25 September 2012).

23 Tomasic, above, n.16.

The new processes are largely administrative – that is, the courts are not involved. By late 2011, the SRR had already been used twice – to resolve Dunfermline Building Society in 2009 (by transfer of part to a TSP and part to a bridge bank) and South Sea Mortgage and Investment Company in 2011, which being a very small institution was placed into a bank insolvency procedure to be liquidated.

CONCLUSIONS

The systemic character of the recent international financial crisis has tested not only the perimeter of the safety net policy action but also the traditional safety net mechanisms themselves. Government financial support to banks in this context has highlighted the importance of developing effective procedures for bank resolutions, that is, procedures that will make it possible to deal with a bank in difficulty without violating the principles of private responsibility and liability and without putting at risk financial stability and the overall economy.

It is widely recognized that laws and procedures for bank resolution importantly influence the safety net's ability to succeed and might even be construed as a fourth arm of the safety net. In light of their experience in the present financial crisis, Germany and the UK have made changes in the measure for bank resolution that are aimed at limiting the taxpayers' exposures involved in dealing with a banking crisis. This chapter briefly analyses both laws.

The new laws formally express similar objectives in explicitly emphasizing the maintenance of financial stability and public confidence, the reduction or elimination of costs to taxpayers and protection for depositors. On the one hand, the German Bank Restructuring Act 2010 seems to provide a less clear and less workable set of procedures for dealing with failing banks than the UK banking law. On the other hand, Germany has an *ex ante* bank industry funding mechanism for bank resolutions (BRRF) that is not envisaged in the UK law. The BRRF allows for a more balanced share of tail-risk costs involved in bank resolution between private investors and taxpayers.

PART III

Using government guarantees

9. The fault lines in cross-border banking: Lessons from the Icelandic case

Már Guðmundsson[1]

INTRODUCTION

In the panic that gripped global financial markets after the collapse of Lehman Brothers, Icelandic banks – like so many internationally active banks around the world – were faced with a wholesale run on their foreign currency liabilities, and were therefore heading towards a default on them in the absence of a lender of last resort assistance in foreign currency. However, given the size of the balance sheets involved (10 times GDP overall, with over two-thirds in foreign currency), it was impossible for the Icelandic authorities to provide such assistance on their own. It would indeed have been catastrophic if they had made a full-scale attempt to do so.

The background to these events was that the Icelandic banking system expanded very rapidly in just less than five years. Their balance sheets grew from under twice GDP at the end of 2003 to almost 10 times GDP by mid-2008. At the same time, it extended across national borders. Just before its collapse, the three major cross-border banks that constituted the bulk of the banking system had over 40 per cent of their total assets in foreign subsidiaries, 60 per cent of total lending was to non-residents, 60 per cent of income was from foreign sources, and over two-thirds of total lending and deposits were denominated in foreign currencies.

1 Some of the topics discussed in this chapter are dealt with at greater length in the following two sources: Már Guðmundsson, and Thorsteinn Thorgeirsson 'The fault lines in cross-border banking: lessons from the Icelandic case' in SUERF Studies – 2010/5, *Contagion and Spillovers: New Insights from the Crisis* (2010), available at http://suerf.org/index.php?option=com_k2&view=item&id=177&Itemid=133 (last accessed 25 September 2012) and Már Guðmundsson, 'The fault lines in cross-border banking', speech at the FIBE meeting in Bergen on 7 January 2010 available at http://www.bis.org/review/r100129a.pdf (last accessed 25 September 2012).

I. THE EU FRAMEWORK AND THE ICELANDIC BANKS

How did this happen, and why was it allowed? I do not think we yet have the research and the consensus to provide a reasonably undisputed list of the main causal factors in this process; however, I think four factors will rank highly on that list. These are Iceland's membership in the European Economic Area (EEA) in 1994, privatisation of the Icelandic banking system in the early 2000s in a manner that placed the major banks in the hands of risk-loving investment bankers, the global conditions of ample and cheap credit that prevailed in the years prior to the international financial crisis, and the tendency in Iceland both to adopt international and EU regulations without critical analysis of Iceland-specific risks and to base supervision to a significant degree on mechanical checks of adherence to those regulations.

Let me expand a bit on the EEA part, as it is highly relevant to my topic. The EEA Agreement provides a legal and regulatory framework based on European Union Directives, including a framework for free movement of capital and provision of financial services. The underlying principles are those of home licensing for operation anywhere in the area and of a level playing field for competition where size and location are not supposed to matter. This European 'Passport' enabled the Icelandic banks to operate throughout the EEA, including through branches in other EEA countries.

I will discuss the flaws in this set-up in regards to banking later in this chapter, but in order to provide a proper perspective of the story, I must make two points. First, it goes against the grain of the underlying principles of the European Passport to consider the size of banks relative to GDP as a metric for concern, as is now rightly in fashion. Second, we should see this more in the nature of a necessary rather than a sufficient condition, and it does not exonerate Icelandic banks and authorities of blame for their part in the story.

The financial crisis revealed major fault lines in cross-border banking, the most important being large foreign currency balance sheets with significant maturity mismatches but with limited lender of last resort facilities in foreign currency. The nature and magnitude of this phenomenon were not well understood before the crisis.[2]

---

[2] My former colleagues at the Bank for International Settlements have been doing important research in this area, please see, for example, Patrick McGuire and Goetz von Peter, 'The US dollar shortage in global banking and the international policy response', BIS Working Papers, No. 291 (2009), Naohiki Baba and Frank Packer, 'Interpreting deviations from covered interest parity during the

Maturity mismatches are, of course, the bread and butter of modern banking, although they make banks vulnerable to runs. In the case of solvent institutions, we have known theoretically since Thornton in 1802 – and probably over a century, as a practical policy – how to deal with that vulnerability in a domestic setting: with central bank lender of last resort (LOLR) operations, later complemented by deposit insurance.

In the current setting, it is far from guaranteed that this process can be replicated at the international level. Of course, in normal times and with developed capital markets, banks can use foreign exchange swap markets to convert domestic liquidity into foreign exchange liquidity swiftly and relatively cheaply. However, this process broke down almost completely during the global run on cross-border non-US bank liabilities in the immediate aftermath of the Lehman collapse.

In a situation like this, the home central bank's ability to assist banks in acquiring the foreign liquidity denied them on the market and thus avoid a failure to deliver on their foreign currency payments is limited by the size of its reserves or the willingness of the central bank issuing the international currency in question to help. Although the provision of foreign currency liquidity through reserves was clearly important during the crisis, most studies seem to support the conclusion that dollar swap lines made the pivotal difference, especially when they were uncapped vis-à-vis some key central banks. To a significant degree, this was the domestic LOLR process replicated at the international level.

Does this mean that we have the solution? At the conceptual level, yes, but at the practical level, maybe not. At present, such swap lines are not a permanent and reliable feature of the international monetary system, and there are important unresolved governance issues, such as who should decide which countries get a swap line and which ones do not.

Let us now move back to the EU/EEA level, where we have the contradiction between the European Passport, on the one hand, and national supervision, a national safety net of deposit insurance and LOLR, and national crisis management and resolution regimes, on the other. The crisis revealed that this framework is deeply flawed. First, it ignores the foreign exchange liquidity risk that I discussed earlier. Banks from small countries with independent currencies are more exposed to this risk than, for instance, banks within the euro area. Second, country size and bank

financial market turmoil of 2007–08', BIS Working Papers, No. 267 (2008) and Naohiki Baba, Frank Packer and Teppei Nagano, 'The spillover of money market turbulence to foreign exchange swap and cross-currency swap markets' (2008) BIS Quarterly Review, March, 73–86.

size relative to countries are important factors in the viability of bailout options. The Icelandic banks are a good example of this.

Keeping in mind what I have said about the fault lines in cross-border banking, let us go back to the collapse of the Icelandic banks. What were the options facing the authorities? At that time, the official view was that the banks were solvent but faced a foreign currency liquidity problem. Their published CAD ratios were well above the 8 per cent limit, and as late as August 2008, the Icelandic Financial Supervisory Authority had deemed them able to withstand severe capital shocks. Now, however, we know that this was probably not truly the case. Even if they had been solvent in the sense that equity was positive, in the aggregate they were below the 8 per cent threshold when corrected for 'weak' capital in the form of equity financed by lending to each other. Furthermore, we know that, over time, an unchecked liquidity problem will turn into a solvency problem.

Be that as it may, with the solvency assumption in mind, the authorities had tried to build defences against potential foreign currency liquidity problems at the banks by negotiating swap lines and by tapping foreign capital markets, in both cases with limited success. The problem was surely exacerbated by the handling of an LOLR request from one of the banks in late September 2008. The announced solution was to nationalise the bank. This would have been a disaster if it had been carried out because it would have made the Government responsible for refinancing a bleeding foreign currency balance sheet, which it did not have the resources to do. Foreign exchange reserves and swap lines amounted to only 35 per cent of GDP, and at that point the Government itself was shut out of international capital markets. Nationalising the bank would have turned a bank foreign currency financing problem into a sovereign problem with the serious risk that the sovereign might have defaulted on such foreign currency payments. The decision was, however, never implemented because of the ensuing full-scale run on the foreign liabilities of the banks and the domino effects inside the Icelandic economy. But the time to consider the options was rapidly running out.

II. THE EMERGENCY ACT

Given the lack of international cooperation, the Icelandic authorities were forced to consider some radical solutions. Although they were not necessarily articulated fully at the time, the solutions had several goals: to preserve a functioning domestic payments system, to ring-fence the state in the case of bank failures, to limit the socialisation of private sector losses, and to create the conditions for rebuilding a domestic banking system.

The adopted solution incorporated several elements. The Government declared that all deposits in Iceland were safe. Second, on 6 October 2008, the so-called Emergency Act (see Box 9.1) was rushed through Parliament, giving the Financial Supervisory Authority broad-based powers to intervene in failing institutions, granting all deposits seniority over other unsecured claims in case of bank failures, and giving permission for Government capital injections into new domestic banks.

The Emergency Act allowed new domestic banks to be created when the old cross-border banks failed and were placed in special resolution regimes followed by winding-up proceedings. In essence, the old banks became the property of the creditors, which were mostly foreign. The new banks were created by carving the domestic assets and liabilities out of the old banks, so it was not a good bank/bad bank split. The idea, then, was that the Government would recapitalise the banks and place compensation bonds in the estates of the failed banks. However, valuing the assets and liabilities proved a complicated process in the middle of an economic and financial crisis, and a solution emerged where the creditors of the failed banks became majority owners of two of the banks and kept a small equity stake in the third. This saved the Government significant expense in recapitalising the banks. The new banking system amounted to 1.7 times GDP.

As a result, the domestic payments system functioned more or less seamlessly throughout, and customers had continuous access to their deposits. The run on the domestic banks stopped, but at its peak, demand for cash tripled and the Central Bank almost ran out of banknotes. Nonetheless, international payment flows were seriously affected by the freezing order imposed by the UK, and the British authorities' suspicion that Iceland would not honour deposit insurance in UK branches of the failed Landsbanki and by general distrust among foreign counterparties. With heavy Central Bank involvement, international payment flows were gradually restored in the months that followed.

I have expanded at some length on the measures taken when the banks failed, as there are still a number of misconceptions about the process. Some have claimed that the banks were nationalised. They were not. The old banks are private companies. They are in winding-up proceedings governed by law; they are not under the control of the Government. The Government has a majority stake in only one of the new banks. Others have claimed that Iceland defaulted and got away with it. The opposite is true. The credit of the sovereign was preserved, and all debt obligations have been paid on time. This is why the sovereign was able to tap

BOX 9.1 THE EMERGENCY ACT OF 6 OCTOBER 2008

The aim of the Act was to ensure a functioning payments system and create the conditions for continued domestic banking operations in the event of failure of major banks.

Measures:

- to permit the Minister of Finance, on behalf of the Treasury, to provide financing to establish new financial firms and acquire existing such firms, wholly or in part. Financing to savings banks was limited to 20 per cent of net worth;
- to grant the Financial Supervisory Authority (FME) broad-based powers to intervene in the operation of distressed financial firms by:
  - convening shareholders' meetings;
  - appropriating the power of shareholders in order to make what may be necessary decisions to limit the power of the Board or remove it, wholly or in part; to take over the assets, rights and responsibilities of the financial firm, wholly or in part; and to dispose of the firm, including merging it with another such firm;
  - appointing a Resolution Committee;
  - limiting or prohibiting the disposal of funds and assets by the financial firm, safeguarding assets earmarked to meet liabilities, having asset values assessed for payment of claims;
  - requiring financial firms to apply for a moratorium on payments, request composition of creditors, or file for bankruptcy;
- to improve the financial safety net by making the following amendments to legislation on deposit guarantee schemes:
  - identifying deposits as priority claims in case of receivership;
  - redeeming deposits in the Icelandic króna;
  - providing for repayment of term deposits in harmony with the accounts' existing requirements, so as to avoid the development of liability for the Depositors' and Investors' Guarantee Fund until withdrawal is permitted;

  - setting rules on netting out deposits and debts within the same financial firm;
- to protect homeowners, the Government-owned Housing Financing Fund was given permission to take over the mortgages of the banks.

Implementation:

In October 2008, in accordance with the Act, the FME placed Landsbanki, Glitnir and Kaupthing banks into receivership managed by separate resolution committees under its auspices. The domestic assets and liabilities of the old banks were transferred to new banks, and the assumptions behind the division of accounts were explained. In November and December 2008, the old banks entered formal winding-up proceedings, first with a moratorium on payments and then with a resolution.

international capital markets last summer, and why its CDS spread is currently around 300 points.

III. DEPOSIT GUARANTEES

Before leaving the topic of crisis management and resolution in the case of the Icelandic banks, I would like to say a few words about deposit guarantees. Why did the Government give a verbal blanket guarantee only for domestic deposits and not the deposits in the banks' foreign branches? After all, this distinction probably added fuel to the fire of the so-called Icesave dispute about the settlement of deposit guarantees in Landsbanki's Dutch and British branches. The short answer is that such a guarantee would never have been credible. As a result, it would not have stopped the run on these deposits and, if attempted, might have bankrupted the Government. At the time, the Central Bank of Iceland's foreign exchange reserves amounted to EUR2.5 billion, while the foreign currency deposits in Landsbanki's Dutch and British branches totalled EUR11.5 billion and payment of the EU minimum deposit insurance would have required EUR4.5 billion.

In economic terms, given that these deposits were used to a significant degree to finance illiquid assets in these same countries, such a payment would have amounted to a net transfer of resources from Iceland to these countries at a time when Iceland was going through its deepest financial and economic crisis in the post-war period. That made no sense, and the only solution was for the governments concerned to pay out the insurance in their own currency with the aim of settling later with Iceland. There are legal arguments about the merit of such claims that I will not comment on here. The fact of the matter is, however, that the Icelandic Government made three good-faith attempts to close the issue through negotiated settlements but got caught up in political dynamics and the case might be on its way to the EFTA Court. But the financial risks for the parties involved are dwindling, as it now appears that the estimated recovery from the estate of Landsbanki will cover almost 100 per cent of all deposits in the foreign branches. And, of course, the priority given to deposits in the Emergency Act is of vital importance to that result.

IV. LESSONS LEARNT

Let us now turn to some of the lessons learnt from the crisis.

First, as regards the EU/EEA framework, the bottom line is that we cannot have a level playing field in banking, except perhaps in risk-adjusted terms, as long as the EU passport is not matched by EU supervision and an EU-wide safety net, which is the logical solution. Furthermore, EU-active banks from small countries with their own currencies should have reduced passport rights and/or face higher capital charges, as they have a less credible LOLR and are therefore more risky, other things being equal. Subjecting all banks in the EU to supervision by an EU supervisor is probably too much, and in practical terms, it might make sense to have two types of bank licences. In such a case, national authorities would licence and supervise domestic banks, which would face significant restrictions on the type and scope of their cross-border activities. Their deposits would be insured by the domestic deposit insurance system, and the national central bank would be their LOLR. Banks wanting a European passport would be licensed and supervised by an EU authority; they would be part of an EU-wide deposit insurance system, and in most cases, their LOLR would be the ECB.

Second, at the national level the key issue is that, as long as global risks and EU flaws are not dealt with, individual countries are forced to take action to protect themselves: actions that might contribute to a further retreat of cross-border banking. Such action might take the form of restricting international activities of home banks and placing much stricter prudential limits on foreign currency maturity mismatches. For example, when Iceland lifts its current capital controls on outflows, it will probably impose restrictions on the size and composition of the foreign currency balance sheets of home-headquartered banks. Some might see such restrictions as capital controls in another form, but I see them as prudential rules.

Finally, deposit insurance and the LOLR are logically related and should be in the same currency. Part of the rationale behind them is to prevent and stop runs. In the final analysis, it only works if the bank liabilities are flowing into a central bank that has the duty, willingness and capacity to recycle them against collateral and expand its balance sheet as needed. The question therefore arises whether national deposit insurance systems should cover domestic deposits only and the payout should likewise be in domestic currency only, even for foreign-denominated deposits.

In closing, let me note that the saga of the financial crisis in Iceland and its interaction with the European and global financial system is a complex one. The analysis in this chapter has only given you glimpses here and there. But as with other sagas, Icelanders will be writing about this for decades, if not centuries, and I think we can be confident that they will be better at writing about it than at running and supervising cross-border banks.

10. Government guarantees and contingent capital: Choosing good shock absorbers

David G. Mayes

INTRODUCTION

This chapter considers government guarantees in the context of recent experience and proposals for enabling shocks to the banking system to be absorbed without the need for taxpayer-funded bailouts. The chapter argues that guarantees have an important but limited role to play in the financial safety net, when the operation of financial markets is impaired. It argues further that where possible such guarantees should be priced and reflect the costs that financial institutions would have incurred had markets been functioning normally. With interconnected international markets, guarantees offered by one country can have implications for others. For example, when Australia offered guarantees in the spring of 2008, both for wholesale funding and for deposits, New Zealand had little choice but to follow within a day or two. Similarly, when Sweden introduced guarantees for its banks around the same time, after the collapse of Lehman Brothers, this had unintended adverse consequences for the domestic banking system in Latvia, where the authorities could not afford a matching offer.

We explore the range of guarantees employed in a broad sample of countries during the global financial crisis (GFC) and other recent crises, particularly the Nordic crises, and contrast them with alternative means of achieving the same objective. Norway for example did not resort to blanket guarantees, while Sweden and Finland did. Guarantees are particularly important when it comes to deposit insurance. For example, to be credible, deposit insurers, with limited funds contributed by the industry, have to be backed up by guarantees of public support until they can be recapitalized after the crisis.

I. BACKGROUND

Guarantees form part of the normal financial system safety net in dealing with banking problems and are particularly helpful in restoring and maintaining confidence in the event of large shocks when there is a fear of contagion. Up until the GFC, guarantees were well thought of, particularly since they formed an important feature of the quick recovery in the 1990s' Nordic crises. However, the experience of Ireland in the GFC has revealed a significant downside in that they can impose major burdens on taxpayers, particularly when an important proportion of those being compensated are actually outside the country. Guarantees may take many forms and in the GFC were used successfully in protecting and assuring lenders against further loss. In the cases of Australia and New Zealand, wholesale funding guarantees permitted a rapid return of the banks to international markets. In the main, guarantees are designed not to be drawn down, but simply to underwrite tail risks. In many cases the alternative to an explicit guarantee is the absorption of losses by the private sector, while in others it is investment by the government in the troubled institution, whereby the public sector takes a stake in any upside gains, not just residual losses.

There is an important distinction to be made between guarantees against losses that have already been made, but are yet to be revealed fully, and guarantees against further losses. The inherent problem of underestimating existing losses has been vividly illustrated by Ireland, where a sweeping guarantee, entered into on the expectation that the losses would be limited, proved capable of threatening the solvency of the country as a whole. The contrast between Iceland and Ireland is striking. In the former case no attempt to guarantee the creditors of the main banks against loss would have been credible, even if limited to depositors, as the country's resources were completely inadequate. Here a successful solution has been achieved by requiring creditors to bear much of the loss and to protect foreign depositors simply by giving them priority in the insolvencies. Guarantees have been issued against further losses by depositors in the case of the new successor domestic banks. The key ingredient in guaranteeing against further loss being that the authorities are in a position to monitor and manage the actions of the new banks closely and are therefore not subject to the normal risks from arm's length supervision and regulation.

Temporary guarantees against further losses make sense where there has been a government-initiated or backed reorganization of a financial institution and where the government has a close say in its future risk-taking activities. It can therefore limit its exposure. Where the purpose of guarantees is to enable financial institutions to regain access to markets, which have become severely affected by the fear of losses in a crisis, it should normally be possible to price such guarantees in a way to avoid providing an unintended subsidy.

During the GFC government guarantees in many cases were adopted because the appropriate tools for resolving severe problems were not in place. In the main this has now been addressed in most countries through the introduction of a *lex specialis* for handling troubled banks that enables early intervention and rapid restructuring without the need for government funding, except perhaps temporarily, say, through a bridge bank. There are thus routes available for avoiding unacceptable costs arising from insolvency and also other means of restoring confidence to the rest of the financial system, particularly ill-informed depositors with small balances that there will not be contagion to otherwise healthy institutions and that deposit insurance will prevent any credit or significant liquidity losses.

Guarantees have been needed in the case of organizations that are 'too-big-to-fail' (TBTF), as in the UK. It has been possible not only to price such guarantees, but also make them convertible into equity in a way which ensures that the government does not simply participate in downside risk without any potential benefit from a recovery. Furthermore, the concept of TBTF is itself being weakened with the development of living wills, funeral plans and contingent capital. Together these measures should limit the role of government guarantees in the future.

One problem in the GFC has been that the widespread use of guarantees may have led to the expectation that come any future crisis, similar methods would be used again, with the attendant moral hazard. Making the alternative routes to resolving such a crisis explicit and credible will go a long way towards restricting guarantees to market failures where potential losses to the taxpayer can be manageable and the costs normally recouped.

An area which remains difficult is policy spillovers from one jurisdiction to another. No doubt guidelines are possible through the Basel Committee on Banking Supervision and the Financial Stability Board, *inter alia*, but unless the financial system is to become less interconnected such spillovers are inevitable. This means that countries have to structure their own systems in the expectation that other countries might introduce sweeping guarantees that they do not wish to emulate. To maintain financial stability they will need to have worked out in advance how they would counter the difficulty. One of the problems in the GFC was that authorities had to react rapidly without a worked-out plan and have exposed the taxpayer to major potential and actual losses as a result.

II. LESSONS FROM THE NORDIC CRISIS

In many respects the Nordic crises at the beginning of the 1990s set the standards for the use of emergency guarantees. Finland, Norway and Sweden all found that the losses incurred by the banks in the crisis exceeded the resources of funds set up in more normal times to handle banking problems and as a result they had to issue government guarantees. The nature of the guarantees differed considerably, with Norway providing specific guarantees and the others more general or 'blanket' guarantees. The Finnish guarantee took the form of a declaration by Parliament that all claims on banks would be honoured on time[1] and the Swedish arrangement was similar.

The use of guarantees to quite some extent reflected the resolution methods available. In the case of Finland, initially the central bank stepped in and bought control of Skopbank, the first bank to get into difficulty. This holding was then sold to the Government Guarantee Fund after its formation in 1992. Sweden also assumed control of its most troubled banks by share purchase, although in the case of Nordbanken it was already the majority shareholder. Loans and options to buy stock were used for those whose problems were more limited. Having gained control both Finland and Sweden used asset management companies to buy the impaired loans so that the banks could recover swiftly, in some cases assisted by mergers. In the Norwegian case the authorities were able to write down the existing shareholders to zero in failing banks and hence were able to reduce the cost of acquiring the banks. By taking over banks in difficulty and guaranteeing their future, it was able to give general confidence and also avoid using asset management companies.

The Finnish guarantees were quite expensive, amounting to 7 per cent of GDP in fiscal terms by the end of the crisis,[2] although the exact amount after recoveries is rather soft. The higher cost reflected the more severe economic and banking problems in Finland. Finland was, for example, much more exposed to the collapse of the former Soviet Union. The Norwegian and Swedish guarantees proved to be relatively costless,[3] however, and this suggested that guarantees, if well handled, need not result in any great loss to the government. The principal ingredient in such

---

1 K. Sandal, 'The Nordic banking crises in the early 1990s: Resolution methods and fiscal costs' in T.G. Moe, J.A. Solheim and B. Vale, *The Norwegian Banking Crisis*, (Norges Bank, Oslo 2004) pp. 77–116.

2 B. Drees and C. Pazarbasioglu, 'The Nordic Banking Crisis: Pitfalls in Financial Liberalisation', IMF Occasional Paper 161, 1998.

3 Moe et al., above, n. 1.

successful guarantees is either that the banking system should recover sufficiently so that any contributions that have to be made can be repaid or that the form of the guarantee should allow the government to participate in the upside of the recovery through holding equity in the surviving institutions, such that it outweighs the losses from those that fail. Where fees are charged for the guarantees this can also help in contributing to a positive financial return to the government or at least offset the cost by the end of the process.

The opportunities for such favourable outcomes are by no means a foregone conclusion and depend crucially on the extent of the problem, which is not normally revealed until well after the guarantees have been issued. In all three cases the eventual extent of the crisis was heavily underestimated in the first phase.

III. LESSONS FROM THE NEW ZEALAND EXPERIENCE

Unlike most OECD countries, before the GFC New Zealand had very little by way of a conventional safety net for banks: no deposit insurance and light-handed supervision, with very limited rules for non-bank deposit takers. Its main recourse was to statutory management in the event of failure so that the Reserve Bank, as the supervisor, had wide powers in administering a resolution, subject to agreement by the courts. Beginning in 2006, large banks were compelled to operate as properly capitalized subsidiaries, operating independently of their parents (all Australian) within the value day.[4] Thus, in theory it would have been possible to limit losses by performing a rapid resolution. Work is still in progress to make this process, labelled Bank Creditor Recapitalisation, operational. Depositors, as junior unsecured creditors, would be written down in this process.

The position in Australia was and remains rather different, with conventional close supervision of all deposit-taking institutions, domestic deposit preference and implicit support for the four major banks. Plans were in place to introduce retail deposit insurance at the time of the onset of the GFC. All the main New Zealand banks are Australian owned and Closer Economic Relations between the two countries mean that they

---

[4] Governed by BS11 'Outsourcing Policy", RBNZ (2006) available at: http://www.rbnz.govt.nz/finstab/banking/regulation/bs11.pdf (last accessed 25 September 2012).

have many of the characteristics of a single financial market. Hence if Australia makes major changes to its system, in practice New Zealand has to follow suit. This is precisely what happened during the GFC.

Following the collapse of Lehman Brothers, when wholesale financial markets froze, the Australian banks were substantially affected as a major proportion of their financing came from overseas and some of this needed to be rolled over. Thus, while the banks themselves had little exposure to derivative or sub-prime related losses in the US, they did face a funding problem.[5] The Australian authorities responded on 12 October 2008 by issuing two guarantees: a temporary wholesale funding guarantee, from AUD1 million upwards, for which issuers had to pay and a deposit guarantee for which they did not.[6] The wholesale guarantee made sense for a country which believed it had strong banks. There was a clear short-term market failure, where the creditworthy could not borrow, whose existence would have threatened the financial stability of the system unnecessarily. The chances of serious exposure were small. The deposit guarantee is more difficult to understand. The programme called for a ceiling of AUD20 000 per depositor per bank. There was no sign of any depositor uncertainty or fear of a run on the banks. It might have reflected an extension of the concern over 'wholesale' deposits, which are more mobile.

New Zealand implemented a very similar arrangement, also on 12 October 2008, with the same $1 million limit, but this time in New Zealand dollars. The NZD was worth about 20 per cent less than the AUD, although this also reflects a difference in measured income per head. The New Zealand deposit guarantee was also slightly different in character. It was for two years and eligible institutions could opt in. Furthermore, the four largest institutions had to pay for the guarantee, while it was free for the others, given the threshold of NZD5 billion in assets. After the initial launch a number of changes were introduced, including a ceiling to the guarantee, only institutions with investment grade ratings were eligible

---

[5] Christine Brown, Kevin Davis, Mervyn Lewis and David Mayes, 'The Global Financial Crisis and Financial Regulation in the Antipodes', in Robert Litan (ed.) *The World in Crisis: Insights from Six Shadow Financial Regulatory Committees From Around the World* (Wharton Financial Center 2011), available at http://finance.wharton.upenn.edu/FIC/FICPress/crisis.pdf (last accessed 1 October 2012).

[6] The deposit guarantee was rapidly amended on 28 October, both to include deposits in branches of foreign banks and to cap the non-contributory scheme at AUD1 million. Above that banks could apply for coverage at a risk-weighted fee. While the initial terms of the retail guarantee were temporary it was clear that a permanent scheme would be established at the end of the crisis period in 2011.

without a fee.[7] (New Zealand did not introduce a wholesale guarantee scheme until 1 November 2008. This was also an opt-in, ratings-based fee system.) It is immediately apparent, from all the various adjustments that were made, that the New Zealand authorities were not prepared for the introduction of such crisis tools and put them together hurriedly.[8]

The differences between the two countries' responses, while small, were significant. Australia's wholesale guarantee scheme was among the least costly of the OECD countries[9] and its deposit guarantee was free.[10] New Zealand's wholesale guarantee was towards the upper end of the charges,[11] while the deposit guarantee scheme had a reverse risk weighting, making the highly rated banks (and the taxpayer) bear the risks (the scheme was changed and risk-weighted premia introduced in two stages on 15 and 22 October 2008).

The guarantees achieved their immediate aim. Deposits increased rapidly in both countries[12] and longer term wholesale funding was resumed as soon as the guarantee came into effect; as a result short-term wholesale funding declined as a share of the total. The deposit guarantees in New Zealand, however, had rather adverse results and provide an example of moral hazard at work. Because it was only accompanied by an increase in supervision after the event, those institutions most at risk took the opportunity to increase deposits and in some cases to increase risky lending, thus increasing the exposure of the taxpayer to risk and allowing some private sector lenders to exit.

In both countries it was not banks that were really at risk, it was non-bank deposit takers. In New Zealand the majority of these deposits were

---

7 On 15 October it was announced that unrated institutions and those with a rating below BB had to pay a premium on any increase in deposits. Australia also introduced a premium if deposits grew by more than 10 per cent. This was also introduced in New Zealand, with a ratings-based tariff.

8 This is clear, not merely from the flurry of changes, but from the Reserve Bank Governor's autobiographical account of the period. See A. Bollard (with S. Gaitanos), *Crisis: One Central Bank Governor and the Global Financial Collapse* (Auckland University Press, Auckland 2010), pp. 60–66.

9 C. Schwartz, 'The Australian Government Guarantee Scheme', March 2010, *Reserve Bank of Australia Bulletin*, pp. 19–26.

10 The Australian scheme was changed on 24 October, capping the free deposit guarantee at AUD1mn and providing guarantees for larger deposits according risk-weighted fees. These changes came into force on 28 November.

11 Op. cit.

12 *Banking Facts and Figures*, Australian Bankers Association, available at http://www.bankers.asn.au/Banks-in-Australia/Facts-and-Figures (last accessed 1 October 2012).

with finance companies, which were very lightly regulated.[13] They merely needed to have a trust deed to regulate their activities and the trustee would be responsible for ensuring that they complied with it, the main requirements being under the Companies Act 1983. If they issued securities, these were covered by the Securities Act 1978 and the Securities Regulations 1983. The Securities Commission was responsible for compliance. There was no prudential supervision or responsibility by the Reserve Bank. Although legislation had been introduced in 2007, after reviews of the position amendments to the Reserve Bank giving it limited prudential responsibility for the sector, it was not passed until 3 September 2008 and would only come into force progressively from September 2009.[14]

By the time the Act came into force most of the sector had disappeared with the firms being closed, in liquidation, receivership or at least moratorium (see Table 10.1). The principal concern of the guarantee scheme was therefore with the few remaining companies. The companies were all vetted against a set of criteria for eligibility set out on 22 October 2008 comprising:

- size of the entity and the number of depositors;
- creditworthiness;
- related party exposure;
- quality of the information provided by the entity and whether its financial statements are audited;
- character, business experience, and acumen of controlling individuals;
- business practices and track record of the entity (that is, meets reasonable standards, bank-like in nature, length of time in business, meeting payments, and maintaining solvency);
- importance to the financial system; and
- any other factors relevant to the maintenance of public and depositor confidence.

---

13 What principally determined whether a financial institution was a bank regulated by the RBNZ was whether it wanted to call itself a bank. Otherwise building, societies, credit unions and finance companies could operate outside the net if they wished. Just one, the Southland Building Society, the largest in the country at the time, had decided to apply to become a bank before the guarantee was issued, succeeding on 7 October 2008.

14 While there is still considerable responsibility on the trustee rather than the Reserve Bank for supervision, the overall responsibility for conduct of business has now been taken over by the Financial Markets Authority, which came into being on 1 May 2011. Thus between them the sector is now covered in a much more straightforward manner even though the framework is still 'light-handed' by international standards.

Table 10.1 Summary of troubled NZ financial institutions

Institution		Date failed	Status at October 2008	Deposits at risk (NZDmn)
1	National Finance 2000 Limited	May 2006	receivership	25.5
2	Provincial Finance Limited	Jun 2006	receivership	296.0
3	Western Bay Finance Limited	Jul 2006	receivership	48.0
4	First Step Trusts	Nov 2006	closed	457.0
5	Bridgecorp Limited	Jul 2007	receivership	458.7
6	Bridgecorp Investments Limited	Jul 2007	liquidation	29.0
7	Nathans Finance NZ Limited	Aug 2007	receivership	174.0
8	Chancery Finance Limited	Aug 2007	liquidation	17.5
9	Property Finance Securities	Aug 2007	moratorium	80.0
10	Five Star Consumer Finance Limited	Aug 2007	receivership	54.0
11	Antares Finance Holdings Limited	Aug 2007	liquidation	3.2
12	Five Star Finance Limited	Jun 2008	liquidation	43.0
13	LDC Finance Limited	Sep 2007	receivership	22.0
14	Finance & Investments	Sep 2007	receivership	16.0
15	Clegg & Co	Oct 2007	receivership	15.1
16	Beneficial Finance Limited	Oct 2007	moratorium	12.7
17	Geneva Finance NZ Limited	Oct 2007	moratorium	51.0
18	Capital + Merchant Finance Limited	Nov 2007	liquidation	167.0
19	C&M Investments Limited	Nov 2007	receivership	1.5
20	Numeria Finance Limited	Dec 2007	receivership	6.7
21	OPI Pacific Finance Limited	Mar 2008	liquidation	335.0
22	Boston Finance Limited	Mar 2008	receivership	24.0
23	ING funds x2	Mar 2008	suspended	520.0
24	QED Limited	Mar 2008	liquidation	4.5
25	Lombard Finance & Investments Limited	Apr 2008	receivership	111.0
26	Kiwi Finance Limited	Apr 2008	receivership	1.7
27	Tower Mtg + Fund	Apr 2008	closed	242.0
28	Cymbis / Fairview	May 2008	receivership	6.9
29	Belgrave Finance	May 2008	receivership	20.5
30	IMP Diversified	Jun 2008	moratorium	15.8
31	Dominion Finance	Jun 2008	liquidation	232.0
32	North South Finance	Jun 2008	receivership	100.0
33	St Laurence	Jun 2008	receivership	253.0
34	Dorchester	Jun 2008	moratorium	176.0
35	Canterbury Mtg Trust	Jul 2008	closed	250.0
36	Hanover Finance	Jul 2008	moratorium	465.0
37	Hanover Capital	Jul 2008	moratorium	24.0

Table 10.1 (continued)

Institution	Date failed	Status at October 2008	Deposits at risk (NZDmn)
38 United Finance	Jul 2008	moratorium	65.0
39 Guardian Mtg Fund	Jul 2008	closed	249.0
40 Totara Mtg Fund	Jul 2008	closed	60.0
41 AMP NZ Property Fund	Aug 2008	suspended	419.0
42 AXA Mtg bonds	Aug 2008	closed	117.0
43 Strategic Finance	Aug 2008	liquidation	391.0
44 St Kilda	Aug 2008	receivership	6.9
45 Compass Capital	Aug 2008	receivership	15.0
46 Waipawa Fin	Aug 2008	liquidation	20.0
		Total	6102.2

Under the circumstances a depositor could not be sure whether the more marginal institutions would be covered. Since there was no prior prudential supervision, it took some time to decide which firms would be admitted and the first company (Mascot Finance) failed on 2 March 2009, before the process was completed. Mascot, however, had passed the eligibility test and was covered as from 12 January 2009.[15] Eventually, 73 institutions were covered by the scheme, 12 of them banks – not surprisingly no information was revealed on who had applied.

There proved to be more problems with the scheme when it came to paying out, not least because interest still had to be paid to depositors after default until the principal was repaid. The scheme was therefore revised as from 1 January 2010.

The main problem for the scheme was the failure of South Canterbury Finance (SCF) in August 2010 (Table 10.2). On failure SCF had approximately NZD1.6 billion in assets and later estimates of the loss suggested it might be as high as NZD1.2 billion. On entry into the scheme SCF was rated BBB – and was generally thought sound. It appears that on entry the company was able to raise considerable new finance from depositors and was able to increase its loan portfolio by a third, at a time when the economy was in trouble. Thus, far from using the guarantee to reduce its risks and improve the solidity of its position, SCF expanded its risk base,

[15] Having an institution fail so soon after admission not surprisingly resulted in an outcry and was a major reason for the Auditor General being required to conduct a review of the deposit guarantee scheme; see n. 9.

Table 10.2 Finance company failures in New Zealand following the deposit guarantee

Company	Date of failure	Payout $mn	Depositors
Mascot Finance Limited	2 March 2009	70.0	2494
Strata Finance Limited**	23 April 2009	0.5	17
Vision Securities Limited	1 April 2010	30.0	967
Rockforte Finance Limited	10 May 2010	4.0	66
Viaduct Capital Limited	14 May 2010	7.6	88
Mutual Finance Limited	14 July 2010	9.2	329
Allied Nationwide Finance Limited	20 August 2010	131.0	4094
South Canterbury Finance Limited	31 August 2010	1580.3	30404
Equitable Mortgages Limited	26 November 2010	140.2	3852
TOTAL		1972.8	42311

by booking loans outside its main geographical coverage, for example. In the early stages of the guarantee there was no supervision of the guaranteed entities and no detailed assessment of where the risks might lie. These deficiencies were corrected eventually, but by then moral hazard had taken its toll and the damage was irreparable.

SCF also presented an additional problem. The guarantee scheme was under an obligation to pay interest on outstanding deposits after failure. If payouts to depositors were to be made rapidly, the authorities, after putting in a statutory manager, would need to treat creditors according to their priority. Paying out depositors would therefore be likely to be drawn out, as more senior and other junior creditors would have to be dealt with as well. The government therefore decided to take on SCF as a whole and pay out all creditors in full, so it could then manage the remaining assets in a manner that would maximise their value, without having to pay anything more than a few days interest to depositors. It is not clear whether this minimised the loss to taxpayers, but it did enable a swift payout. Clearly, as a result of this one failure alone, without adding in the other eight, one of which, Mascot, was mentioned above, taxpayers are going to incur a net loss. Without the guarantee, no doubt these finance companies would have failed earlier and some that survived might also have failed in the end. In retrospect it is not clear whether the guarantee increased or diminished the loss. None of those thought likely to fail by the authorities were either singly or jointly of systemic importance.

The scheme also faced the usual exit problem. Any institution that is in trouble and actually needs the guarantees will fail just before the scheme ends, as those depositors who can withdraw their funds will do so. Hence, exit requires that some credible scheme be put in place for the longer term survival of the remaining institutions or alternatively they should be closed. The scheme was duly extended from 12 October 2010, when the original two years were complete, until the end of 2011. By the end of 2011 only three institutions were left: Fisher & Paykel Finance, Wairarapa Building Society and Heartland Building Society, the last of which is an amalgamation that hopes to become a bank and hence regain credibility with depositors and potential bondholders.

In the extended scheme most of the awkward features of the initial one were removed, coverage limits were reduced to NZD250000 for non-banks, a rating of BB or above was required for acceptance and interest was not payable after failure. Most importantly controls are now placed on the activities that the subject institutions could perform so that they do not use the guarantee to advantage related parties and thereby shift the risk onto taxpayers. However, it did not include an overall objective for the management of the system, such as loss minimisation.

Clearly the taxpayer was exposed to loss from the failure to have prudential supervision of the whole deposit-taking sector. Introducing guarantees without clear prior knowledge of the possible exposures is a risky choice.

The wholesale guarantee scheme turned out well. The New Zealand scheme, which was closed to new issues on 30 April 2010, not only enabled new issues, but earned substantial fee income for the government as no payouts were needed.

IV. LESSONS FROM ICELAND

While of course it was those running the banks who were primarily responsible for their failure, as the reports on the Icelandic debacle make clear,[16] much of the blame for the over-expansion of the three main Icelandic banks and their failure in October 2008 can be laid on poor supervision and the unwillingness by the authorities to take prompt corrective action. However, equally blame can be placed on the shareholders and bondholders who were willing to permit the obvious excessive risk-taking and to continue to lend increasing amounts to the banks. However, once the crisis

16 K. Jannari, 'Report on Banking Regulation and Supervision in Iceland: past, present and future', available at www.island.is/media/frettir/KaarloJannari%20_2009_%20Final.pdf (last accessed 25 September 2012); only some chapters of the report of the Special Investigation Commission into the financial crisis set up by the Icelandic Parliament, Althingi, are available in English at http://sic.althingi.is/ (last accessed 25 September 2012).

struck, the Icelandic authorities managed to resolve banks, which at their height had assets more than 10 times as large as GDP, without bankrupting the country, although it was a close call.[17]

The key element in the Icelandic response was not to offer implausible guarantees with an impossible burden for the state, but rather to leave the losses mainly with private sector risk-takers. Iceland was also poorly prepared for the crisis and had to introduce emergency legislation on 7 October 2008 so that it could handle the bank failures the following day. The legislation had two key elements. First, it gave the authorities powers to undertake a resolution rather than simply place the banks in insolvency and second, it conferred depositor priority in the resolution. The resolution itself involved the authorities transferring the domestic deposit balances and sound domestic assets to new banks, with adequate capitalization from the state, while leaving foreign depositors and the remaining creditors and the foreign assets in the insolvency. It appears likely that there will be sufficient funds in two of the banks to reimburse the foreign depositors in full and very close to sufficient in the third case (Landsbanki). The remaining creditors are likely to receive little or nothing.

The Icelandic authorities faced a considerable dilemma because of the nature of the deposits, particularly in Landsbanki and their consequent deposit insurance liability. In the European Economic Area (EEA), of which Iceland is a member, as in the EU, the home country is responsible for insuring deposits not just in the home country, but also in branches of the bank in other countries in the area. Because interest rates were very high in Iceland, the Icelandic banks could get cheaper and secure funding by raising deposits elsewhere. This they did, particularly in the UK and the Netherlands, where they could offer higher rates of interest than domestic banks, while still having high margins for lending. In many instances there was not a currency mismatch because the Icelandic borrowers wished to finance operations in the UK and the Euro area.

The potential exposure to the deposit insurance fund, however, was

---

17 According to A. Sighvatsson and G. Gunnarsson, 'Iceland's Financial Disaster and its Fiscal Impact', in J.R. LaBrosse, R. Olivares-Caminal and D. Singh, *Managing Risk in the Financial System* (Edward Elgar, Cheltenham, UK and Northampton, MA, USA 2011), the gross direct fiscal cost of the financial crisis was 57 per cent of GDP, 30.5 per cent net, which is at the upper end of what can be withstood without a default (G. Hoggart, R. Reis and V. Sapporta, 'Costs of Banking System Instability: Some Empirical Evidence', Bank of England Working Paper no.144, 2001).

clearly beyond its ability to pay out. As with so many other deposit insurance funds it was predicated on not having to contemplate the failure of the major institutions. By splitting the banks in the resolution the Icelandic authorities found a way of overcoming the difficulties, in that the deposit insurer did not have to pay out all depositors immediately; some could be reimbursed, eventually, from the insolvency. Clearly, this would have disadvantaged foreign depositors, particularly as under EU law depositors were supposed to be paid out within 90 days, although this could be renewed twice in the event of difficulty. Nevertheless a complex insolvency is going to take more like nine years than nine months to work through. The Icelandic authorities were therefore assisted by the Financial Services Compensation Scheme in the UK and the Dutch Central Bank, who covered depositors in their respective countries, with the prospect of being compensated later from Iceland.

Despite the fact that it will take a very long period for Iceland to repay its creditors and get back on a more normal footing, it has been possible for the economy to continue despite a sharp downturn and devaluation and for the debt position to be stabilized with the help of an IMF loan and support from other Nordic countries.

V. LESSONS FROM IRELAND

Ireland reacted rapidly to the deteriorating situation, after the demise of Lehman Brothers, by introducing a blanket guarantee on 29 September 2008. Initially foreign-controlled banks were not eligible; however, it was extended to them on 9 October. The guarantee was to last for two years. Virtually all uncollateralized liabilities were included, not just retail deposits. The immediate spur to action was that wholesale funding for the Anglo-Irish Bank was eroding rapidly. However, the speed of the introduction of the guarantee meant that the magnitude of the likely obligations was not known with any certainty and turned out to have been grossly underestimated. Not only were the problems with the Anglo-Irish Bank much larger than initially thought, but a second institution, the Irish Nationwide Building Society, also failed and the Bank of Ireland had such major losses that it had to be recapitalized.

The key determinant in the issuing of the guarantee was that the Anglo-Irish Bank was judged to be too-big-to-fail and had to be kept open by one means or another. It is not clear that the guarantee *per se* was necessarily a very poor choice in the circumstances. Using outright nationalization instead would probably not have had much impact on the losses incurred by the taxpayer according to the Honohan Report on the whole episode.[18] What made the action so expensive – the Irish deficit was 14.5 per cent of GDP in 2009 and 32 per cent in 2010 – was that only taxpayers and shareholders bore the losses. Bondholders, even those who were subordinated, did not suffer losses under the initial guarantee.

Since then Ireland has introduced a new special resolution regime so that it can handle problem banks and organize an orderly resolution, where at least some of the cost would be borne by junior debtholders and not entirely by taxpayers.[19] The proposed legislation has a lot in common with the Banking Act 2009, implemented in the UK after it too found that it could not handle the failure of Northern Rock in 2007 adequately. Since the guarantee expired in September 2010, it has proved possible to impose some losses on subordinated debtholders.

The Irish action also had some unexpected spillover effects in that other EU countries felt obliged to follow the Irish lead in extending substantial guarantees, although in these cases the losses incurred were small. It is not at all clear that this experience was the result of good judgement rather than good luck in the way the crisis evolved in these countries.

VI. A BETTER WAY FORWARD

In the light of these experiences, it is clear that the role of emergency guarantees to restore confidence in crises needs to be limited. In particular they should not stand instead of a comprehensive Special Resolution Regime that enables the authorities to handle the failure of any financial institution in an orderly manner. Large institutions in particular have to be resolved in a manner that keeps their functions vital to the maintenance of systemic financial stability in being. Such continuity in operation requires that neither shareholders be bailed out nor should other junior creditors not suffer losses. The Bank Creditor Recapitalisation arrangements in New Zealand provide an example of how far such an arrangement might go, with the possibility of no losses to taxpayers, except in respect to guarantees that are implemented in the resolution of a bank to limit further

---

[18] According to the Honohan Report, *The Irish Banking Crisis Regulatory and Financial Stability Policy 2003–2008, A report to the Minister of Finance by the Governor of the Central Bank*, May 2010, p. 136, available at http://www.bankinginquiry.gov.ie/The%20Irish%20Banking%20Crisis%20Regulatory%20and%20Financial%20Stability%20Policy%202003-2008.pdf (last accessed 25 September 2012).

[19] The Central Bank and Credit Institutions (Resolution) Bill received its second reading in July 2011.

losses.[20] All other OECD countries have deposit insurance, so depositors would be protected in part in these cases, either through contributions from the banking industry or through the taxpayer, depending on the design of the scheme. However, it is common in crises for such compensation to be extended as has been demonstrated in the GFC.

The main problem with such guarantees is that they can work well under some circumstances and be disastrous under others. They can make a lot of sense when the authorities have good reason to believe that the institutions that they propose to cover are solvent and that the problems being encountered in funding in the market represent a market failure or panic in response to rumour. The potential exposure is then relatively small. The New Zealand and Australian wholesale funding guarantees fit into this pattern and have actually resulted in a small return to the taxpayer as premiums were charged and no institution raising these funds failed. However, there is a serious risk that guarantees will be offered before the solvency status of the eligible institutions has been determined, with the risk that considerable losses could be unnecessarily imposed on taxpayers rather than existing lenders. Wholesale funding guarantees can be limited to new finance although depositor protection, by necessity, applies to existing funds as they can be withdrawn on demand. Deposit guarantees, on the other hand, only carry a reasonable risk if the institutions they cover are already being carefully supervised by the authorities and if there are clear rules in place to avoid such guarantees being used to shift the risks from other sources of funding onto the taxpayer, as appears to have been the case in New Zealand.

Advances in the structuring of bond contracts with contingency clauses that would enable them to be swapped into equity in the event of a decline in capital below a trigger point, as with the bonds that have already been issued by the Lloyds Banking Group, offer a further way or resolution without the need to call on the taxpayer. This, in conjunction with an improved special resolution regime and careful restructuring or organization of large institutions through living wills so that they can be handled, could largely obviate the need for the risky guarantees that have been used in the GFC, particularly by Ireland. In this way the major potential for moral hazard that has been caused by the stepping in of the authorities to backstop or impose the losses on taxpayers in the GFC may be avoided.

---

[20] Since relabelled Open Bank Resolution, see 'Pre-positioning for Open Bank Resolution' Reserve Bank of New Zealand Consultation Paper, March 2011, available at http://rbnz.govt.nz/finstab/banking/4335146.pdf (last accessed 25 September 2012).

11. Public guarantees on bank bonds: Effectiveness and distortions

Giusèppe Grande, Aviram Levy, Fabio Panetta and Andrea Zaghini[1]

I. GUARANTEED BANK BONDS IN THE CONTEXT OF THE RESCUE MEASURES ADOPTED IN 2008

The exacerbation of the financial crisis which followed the collapse of Lehman Brothers in October 2008 led the governments of several advanced economies to use unprecedented amounts of state aid to support the financial sector. The immediate aim of this massive intervention was to avoid widespread failures and to restore normal financial intermediation.

The financial sector support measures can be divided into three main groups: (i) guarantees on new debt securities; (ii) capital injections; and, (iii) asset purchases and asset guarantees.[2] In most countries guarantees on bank debt turned out to be one of the favourite tools, largely because guarantees do not have an immediate impact on budget deficits since they represent a contingent liability. As can be seen in Figure 11.1, in several countries the volume of 'indirect support' through guaranteed issuance (in terms of GDP) was larger than or equal to the amount of 'direct support' via capital injections and asset purchases. Explicit government guarantees against default on bank fixed income debt and other non-deposit liabili-

---

1 The authors wish to thank the participants of the Symposium 'Financial crisis management and the use of government guarantees', held in Paris on October 2011, and Sebastian Schich for helpful comments on an earlier draft. The views expressed in the article are those of the authors and do not involve the responsibility of the Bank of Italy.

2 See F. Panetta, T. Faeh, G. Grande, C. Ho, M. King, A. Levy, F.M. Signoretti, M. Taboga, and A. Zaghini (2009), 'An assessment of financial sector rescue programmes', BIS Papers, No.48, and S. Schich, 'Expanded Guarantees for Banks: Benefits, Costs and Exit Issues' (2009) 2 OECD Journal: Financial Market Trends, (available at http://www.oecd.org/dataoecd/53/48/44260489.pdf (last accessed 25 September 2012)).

(percentage of GDP)

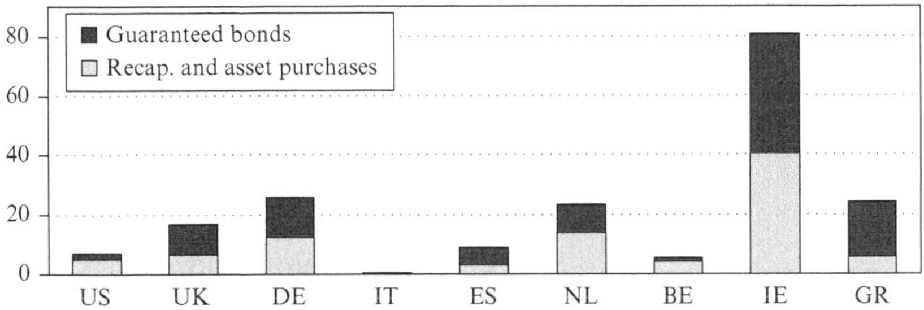

Source: Authors' estimates based on IMF Fiscal Monitor 2011; Bloomberg

Figure 11.1 Government support to banking systems as a ratio to GDP

ties proved effective in restoring bank funding, offsetting the drying-up of alternative sources (such as securitization) and the widening of spreads.[3]

In most countries, issuance of guaranteed bonds by banks was sizeable right from the very beginning of the guarantee programmes in October 2008. Figure 11.2 shows the monthly profile of guaranteed and non-guaranteed gross issuance for the combined banking systems of the euro area, the US and the UK. Bank bond issuance, which had sharply declined during the summer months of 2008, was revived by the adoption of the guarantee schemes; issuance picked up in October and November and in the following two months reached the highest levels in many years. During late 2008 and early 2009 the bulk of issuance was represented by guaranteed bonds, but a considerable volume of non-guaranteed bonds was also issued, suggesting that guarantees were successful in reducing the funding liquidity risk of banks and encouraged investors to buy also non-guaranteed bonds.

In the second half of 2009 tensions on bank funding markets declined significantly and an increase in investors' appetite for risk supported the demand for non-guaranteed bank bonds. In the first half of 2010 the actual usage of guarantees continued to decline, despite the fact that

---

[3] See A. Levy and S. Schich, 'The design of government guarantees for bank bonds: lessons from the recent financial crisis', (2010) 1 OECD Journal: Financial Market Trends (available at http://www.oecd.org/dataoecd/46/47/45636972.pdf (last accessed 25 September 2012)) and G. Grande, A. Levy, F. Panetta, and A. Zaghini, 'Public Guarantees on Bank Bonds: Effectiveness and distortions' (2011) OECD Journal: Financial Market Trends, October (available at www.oecd.org/daf/fin (last accessed 25 September 2012)).

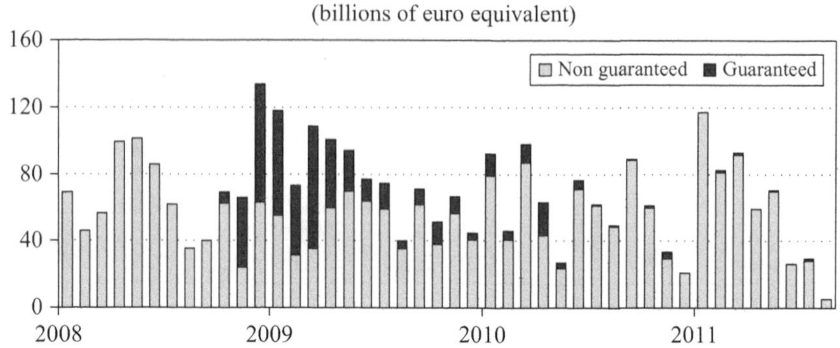

Source: Authors' estimates based on Bloomberg and Datastream

Figure 11.2 Gross issuance of bank bonds in the Euro area, the UK and the US

the first wave of sovereign debt tensions started to affect banks' funding conditions. In that period, the decline of guaranteed issuance also reflected the discontinuation of guarantee schemes in several countries, among them the US, UK and France.

In the rest of the chapter we review the experience of the guarantee schemes adopted in the autumn of 2008, assessing with hindsight their effectiveness and their costs (including those represented by distortions and moral hazard). The assessment is carried out not only in order to provide a stocktaking exercise, three years after their adoption and with most schemes having been discontinued, but also with a view to judging whether those schemes may be resumed in the current juncture (late 2011), taking into account the changed financial landscape.

II. GOVERNMENT GUARANTEES ON BANK BONDS: WERE THEY EFFECTIVE?

A. Impact on Banks' Access to Medium-Term Wholesale Funding

The main short-term goal of the schemes providing explicit government guarantees on bank bonds was to help banks maintain access to medium-term funding at a reasonable cost, ensuring solvency and offsetting the drying-up of alternative sources of funding as well as the increase in credit spreads.

The available evidence reviewed in Section I suggests that debt guarantees did help banks to resume medium-term funding. The overall gross issuance of bank bonds on the international market, which had declined markedly with the onset of the global financial crisis in the summer of 2007, picked up significantly after the launch of the guarantee programmes in the last quarter of 2008. While some degree of substitution between government-guaranteed and non-guaranteed bonds cannot be ruled out, banks' reliance on government-guaranteed bonds declined markedly since the second quarter of 2009, as the strains in funding markets started to ease. Evidence of a contribution of debt guarantees to the recovery of banks' medium-term funding also has been found in other studies.[4]

B. Impact on the Perceived Riskiness of Bank Bonds

The effect of debt guarantees on the likelihood of banks' insolvency can be gauged by looking at credit risk premiums on bank bonds, which are proportional to banks' creditworthiness as it is perceived by financial market investors. In what follows, we focus on two types of indicators: the yield spreads on bank bonds and the premiums on the credit default swap (CDS) contracts written on banks. We will also have a look at an *ex post* measure of banks' riskiness, namely the number of defaults on guaranteed bank bonds.

Figure 11.3 shows the yield spreads of non-guaranteed bonds issued by banks of selected countries. In the months that followed the announcement of a public backstop (and other rescue measures), the spreads of unsecured bonds stabilized and then started to decline, indicating that bank bonds had become less risky.[5]

A second way of measuring the impact of bond guarantees on banks' riskiness is to look at the reaction of financial market variables to the announcement of the guarantees programmes. If the guarantees succeeded in reducing banks' riskiness, their introduction should have led to a decline in the credit risk premiums required by investors on banks' securities. Some econometric studies have attempted to make such an

---

[4] See International Monetary Fund, *Global Financial Stability Report* (IMF, Washington DC 2009); European Central Bank, 'Measures taken by euro area governments in support of the financial sector' (2010) Monthly Bulletin April 75–90; and C. Schwartz, 'The Australian government guarantee scheme' (2010) *Reserve Bank of Australia Bulletin*, March Quarter.

[5] See Panetta et al. above, n. 2; and CGFS (Committee on the Global Financial System), 'The impact of sovereign credit risk on bank funding conditions' (2011) CGFS Papers 43.

(option-adjusted spreads over comparable Treasury bonds; daily data, in basis points) (1)

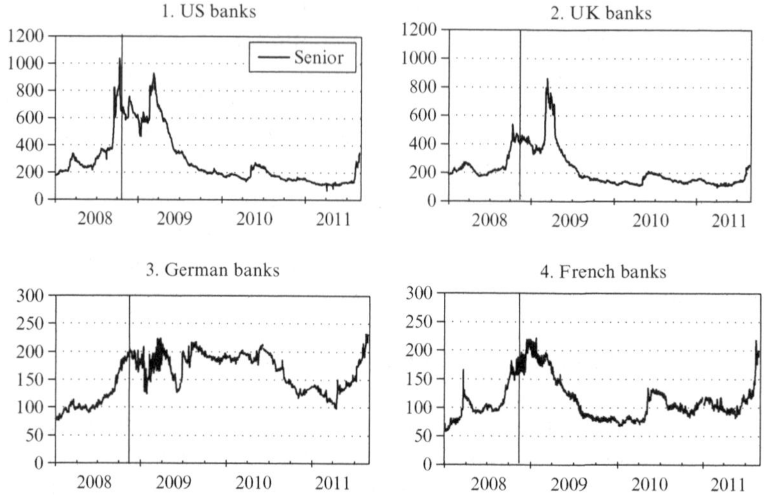

Source: Committee on the Global Financial System, 'The impact of sovereign credit risk on bank funding conditions', (2011) CGFS Papers 43

Figure 11.3 Yield spreads on banks' unsecured bonds

assessment by resorting to event study analysis.[6] An appropriate proxy for the credit risk premiums on banks is represented by the premiums on the CDS contracts written on banks. Other things being equal, the introduction of a credible bond guarantee should lower CDS premiums. By means of event study analysis, Panetta et al.[7] study the impact of the announcement of bond guarantees programmes and the other two types of rescue packages (capital injections and asset purchases/guarantees) on indexes of the bank CDS premiums for the countries where the schemes were adopted.

According to this study, debt guarantees turned out to be quite effective: (1) they lowered bank CDS premia; (2) they had a sizeable impact (about 25 basis points); (3) their effect was quite persistent. Note that the support

6 See Panetta et al. above, n. 2; M. King, 'Time to buy or just buying time? The market reaction to bank rescue packages' (2009) BIS Working Paper 288; Y. Aït-Sahalia, J. Andritzky, A. Jobst and N. Tamirisa, 'How to Stop a Herd of Running Bears? Market Response to Policy Initiatives during the Global Financial Crisis' (2009) IMF Working Paper 204; and IMF above (n. 4) and references therein.

7 Panetta et al. above, n. 2.

measures were to some extent anticipated by market participants, as bank CDS premia started to decline before the announcement. With regard to the other rescue measures, capital injections also had quite a sizeable negative impact, while the announcement of asset purchases/guarantees apparently led on average to an increase in bank CDS premia. These results are consistent with those found by the IMF[8] on the basis of a comparable, though somewhat different methodology. When considering the post-Lehman phase of the global financial crisis (from 15 September 2008 to 30 June 2009), the IMF finds that for euro area countries the introduction of liability guarantees led to a statistically significant decline in bank CDS premiums in the three days after the announcement.

While the prices of debt securities and credit derivatives provide some clues on how bond guarantees are viewed by financial market investors, additional evidence on their effectiveness in preventing banks' insolvency is provided by the actual incidence of defaults on guaranteed bonds. Despite the widespread use of government guarantees on bank bonds and the high vulnerability of banks in many of the countries that introduced this policy tool, guarantee calls on bank bonds have been rare so far. There is evidence of one case in Portugal, where the liquidation of one troubled bank in April 2010 resulted in the activation of the state guarantee, and one case in Denmark in early 2011. This confirms that bond guarantees programmes may have a very limited impact on budget deficits, because the actual liabilities generated by them may be much lower than the contingent liabilities.

C. Impact on the Supply of Credit to the Private Sector

The ultimate goal of public intervention was to resume and support financial intermediation. It is thus important to know whether public guarantees on newly issued bank bonds contributed to the recovery in bank lending. The size and timing of the impact on credit supply may have varied depending on whether financial institutions decided to use public funds to strengthen their balance sheets or to support lending.[9]

---

8 IMF above, n. 4.

9 Brei, Gambacorta and von Peter provide an econometric analysis of the impact of equity injections on loan growth for a sample of 108 large international banks headquartered in 14 major advanced economies for the period 1995–2010. They find significant non-linearities: recapitalisations may not translate into greater credit supply until bank balance sheets are sufficiently strengthened to boost risk-weighted capital ratios. See M. Brei, L. Gambacorta and G. von Peter, 'Rescue Packages and Bank Lending' (2011) BIS Papers 357.

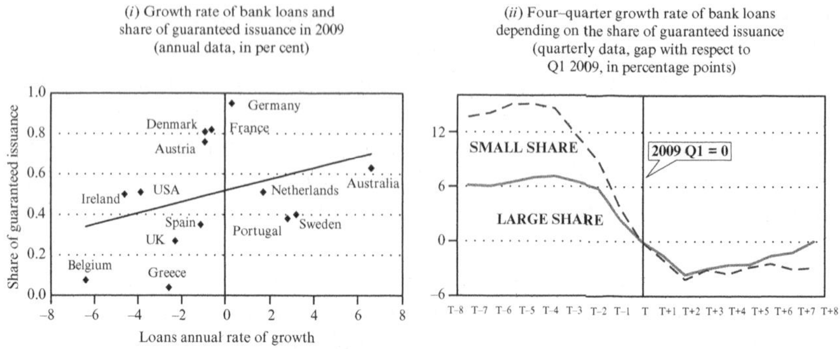

Source: Authors' estimates based on national data

Figure 11.4 Public guarantees on bank bonds and trends in bank lending

It goes without saying that such an assessment is fraught with plenty of challenges. Besides the fact that rescue measures included several tools, the definition of the counterfactual is particularly difficult, because banks' lending behaviour has been affected by many macroeconomic factors, such as the strongly expansionary monetary policies and the general economic conditions. Moreover, credit supply factors are very difficult to identify in their own right, as the lending standards applied by banks typically reflect a range of different characteristics, some of which are hard to measure or may take time to fully emerge after a major financial crisis (for example, losses).

That said, a bird's eye view on aggregate trends in bank lending may provide some hints about a possible contribution of bond guarantees to the resumption of the supply of credit to the real economy. For the countries that have adopted public guarantees on bank bonds, the left-hand panel of Figure 11.4 plots the growth rate of bank lending in 2009 against the portion of total issuance that is accounted for by guaranteed bonds. The graph suggests a broadly positive relationship between the intensity of the recourse to guaranteed bonds and lending growth in 2009.

For the same set of countries, the right-hand panel of Figure 11.4 looks at the evolution of lending growth since 2007. Countries are divided in two groups: the red (blue) line is a weighted average of countries with a share of guaranteed bonds at issuance in 2009 above (below) the median value of 51 per cent. For each group of countries, the graph plots the gap (in percentage points) between the four quarter growth rate in a given quarter and the same growth rate in Q1 2009, the latter being the first quarter in which issuance of guaranteed bonds was significant. The graph suggests that the countries in which banks had a higher recourse to bond guarantees tended on the whole to have a stronger rebound of bank lending.

It is worth emphasizing that inferences from simple bivariate and aggregate analyses such as the ones shown in Figure 11.4 can only be very tentative. In order to get deeper insights, one should be able to assess the contribution of bond guarantees against those of other determinants of bank lending.

III. WHAT ARE THE DRAWBACKS OF A RESUMPTION OF 2008's GUARANTEE SCHEMES? DISTORTIONS AND INEFFICIENCIES

The evidence presented in the previous sections seems to suggest that government guarantees and, more generally, financial support measures to the banking system have contributed to prevent severe disruptions in financial markets after Lehman's default. This evidence raises a more general question on whether and how those support schemes may be resumed and made available again in the current juncture (late 2011), characterised by severe strains in bank funding markets (as in 2008) and by a fully fledged sovereign debt crisis in the euro area (unlike 2008). In order to answer this question, it is worth examining, first, whether guarantees are 'desirable' (this will be done in the present section), when considering the significant distortions to the banking sector implied by the 2008 schemes and, secondly, whether guarantees are 'feasible' in view of the sharp worsening of sovereign risk observed since 2010 (see Section IV).

An important aspect of guarantee schemes of 2008 is how they affected the cost of new debt issuance (guaranteed or not) by banks. As reported by Levy and Zaghini,[10] a striking feature of the guaranteed bond market in 2009 was the significant 'tiering' of spreads by country. In particular, the spreads at launch were not monotonically related to bank ratings: better-rated banks in some countries paid larger spreads than weaker banks in other countries. In other words the spread seemed to reflect the nationality of banks rather than their soundness.

[10] A. Levy and A. Zaghini, 'The pricing of government-guaranteed bank bonds' (2011) 6 Banks and Bank Systems 16–24.

A. The Estimation Approach

In principle, the dispersion of the spreads paid on guaranteed bonds could reflect several factors: the characteristics of the issuer, the characteristics of the bond, the characteristics of the guarantor (and of the guarantees' scheme) and, finally, market conditions. In order to disentangle the contribution of each factor, the following cross-country regression framework is adopted:

$$Spread_{jk} = a_0 + \sum_j a_j D_j^{BANK} + \sum_k a_k D_k^{BOND} + \sum_i a_i D_i^{GOV} + \sum_z a_z D_z^{MKT\_COND} + \varepsilon \qquad (11.1)$$

where $Spread_{jk}$ is the spread at launch between the yield of the bond k of bank j and the swap rate on the contract of corresponding maturity, D^{BANK} are binary dummies for each of the characteristics of the issuer (rating, CDS spread, size), D^{BOND} are dummies for bond characteristics (issue size, maturity, currency, rating), D^{GOV} are dummies for the sovereign (rating, CDS spread, characteristics of the guarantees scheme) and D^{MKT_COND} are dummies for market conditions (quarter of issue).

In the following Sections III.B to III.D this equation will be estimated over three sample periods (2009, the banking crisis; 2006, a pre-crisis, tranquil period; 2010, the sovereign debt crisis) in order to address the following questions: During the banking crisis of 2009, did the cost of issuing government-guaranteed bank debt reflect mainly the characteristics of the bank or those of the sovereign guarantor? What is the relative role of bank vs. sovereign characteristics in determining the issuing cost in tranquil times, such as 2006? Does the result change when we consider non-guaranteed bank debt issued during the sovereign debt crisis of 2010?

B. Cost of Issuance in 2009 (Initial Peak of Banking Crisis)

The first regression analyses 414 guaranteed bonds issued in 2009. The first column of Table 11.1 shows the estimation results when only significant coefficients are taken into account. A general property of the regressions shown in Table 11.1 is that the exogenous variables are constrained so as to have only negative coefficients. In this way, thanks to the fact that we use only dummy variables, each coefficient can be seen as the estimated saving an issuer would achieve if one of the 'worst case' characteristics foreseen by the intercept were removed. In fact, on the one hand, each coefficient shows the (negative) contribution in basis points to the spread at launch, on the other hand the intercept, by construction,

Table 11.1 OLS regression results

Dependent Variable: SPREAD AT LAUNCH				
Variable	2009 G	2006 NG	2010 NG	2009 NG
Constant	116.1***	67.3***	346.4***	332.5***
Rating Gov AAA	−36.4***		−61.5***	
Low Sovereign CDS	−25.1***	−18.0*	−59.0***	−34.6**
Maturity low	−9.1*	−9.1*	−94.2***	−62.7***
Volume high	−9.7*			
Issue rating high		−19.0**	−44.6***	−106.1***
Euro denomination	−7.9*	−48.8***	−68.7***	−47.7***
Fav. Market condition	−30.6***	−28.8***	−13.6*	−44.2***
Bank CDS low	−8.7*	−14.4**	−21.0**	−27.5*
Bank rating high		−10.3*	−31.7*	−64.2**

Notes: One, two and three asterisks denote statistical significance at 90%, 95% and 99%, respectively. 'G' and "NG' denote guaranteed and non-guaranteed issuance respectively.

can be interpreted as the estimated spread of the weakest issuer, namely the spread that a hypothetical bank would pay at launch in the worst case scenario, that is, if the state were rated below AAA, premia on sovereign CDS were high, the maturity of the bond were long, the issuance volume were low, the issue had a low rating, the issuer had high premia on CDS, the issuer had a low rating and issuance occurred under adverse market conditions.

Independently of the negative sign that was imposed, each variable has the expected influence on the cost of bond issuance. For instance, it is not surprising that a favourable bank outlook (that is, a low CDS) would reduce the cost of issuing a bond or that a small volume or a long maturity would negatively affect the cost for the issuer.

The most relevant result is that sovereign characteristics (AAA rating and low CDS) account for almost 50 per cent of the whole spread at launch, suggesting that the guarantee from a strong guarantor can almost halve the cost of the issuance for a troubled bank.[11] At the same time the characteristics of the issue account for only 21 per cent of the total spread, whereas only 7 per cent of the spread could be deducted from the cost if a bank had a good market assessment (that is, a low CDS).

[11] Moreover, if we introduce additional dummy variables for the characteristics of the guarantees' scheme the overall weight of the government reaches 2/3 of the total cost. This result is in line with Levy and Zaghini above, n. 10.

C. Cost of Issuance in 2006 (Pre-crisis Period)

Is the role of government always so important in determining the cost of issuance of a bank bond? In order to answer the question we apply the same methodology to 287 bonds issued by 79 banks of 13 countries between January and December 2006, a year in which market conditions and investor sentiment can be described as very stable and favourable.

Based on the estimates of the coefficients presented in the second column of Table 11.1, we analyse the contribution of each variable to the overall cost at launch in 2006. Even though statistically significant, it is immediately clear that the role of the government is a minor one (12 per cent). As expected, what matters most for the pricing of an individual bond are the characteristic of the issuance (71 per cent) together with the bank's soundness (17 per cent).[12]

D. Cost of Issuance in 2010 (Sovereign Debt Crisis)

As a third sample period, the cross-sectional regression (1) was run also for 534 bank bonds issued in 2010, a year characterized by severe tensions in sovereign debt markets which had a strong negative effect on bank funding.[13] Predictably, the weight of sovereign variables in the estimated cost at issuance of non-guaranteed bank bonds is significantly higher in 2010 than in previous tranquil periods (2006). The role played by government's creditworthiness rises to 30 per cent of the total cost while the characteristics of the issuance and issuer decline to 56 and 13 per cent, respectively (column 3 of Table 11.1). One possible interpretation of this pattern is that although in 2010 explicit public guarantees were not actively used (and our sample includes only non-guaranteed bonds), the reliability of the sovereign helped banks from solid countries to reduce by around 30 per cent the cost of bond issuance, suggesting that these banks enjoyed an implicit guarantee.

E. Interpretation of Results: Distortions and Inefficiencies

The bottom-line of the statistical evidence provided in this section is that the guarantees that were granted in 2008–09 to distressed banks created

---

[12] Rather interestingly, analysing non-guaranteed issuance in 2009 (fourth column of Table 11.1) leads to a result which is very similar to the one derived for 2006, namely that the sovereign's characteristics played a negligible role in determining banks' cost of issuance.

[13] See CGFS above, n. 5.

severe distortions: the fact that the cost of issuing guaranteed bonds reflected by more than 50 per cent the guarantor's creditworthiness (rather than the issuer's) implies that banks with lower profitability and weaker balance-sheet positions – but enjoying guarantees from highly rated sovereigns – were able to raise funds at a much lower cost than sounder and better-rated banks.

This distortion in the pricing of bank bonds has two main negative effects. First, the absence of a 'level playing field' is detrimental to competition and leads to a misallocation of resources that lowers the banking system's productivity. Second, the measures could create expectations of further intervention, thus influencing and distorting banks' business strategies and encouraging excessive risk-taking (that is, moral hazard).[14] One way in which the authorities might have mitigated these distortionary effects is the adoption of an appropriate mechanism for pricing the guarantees,[15] such as a fee that is inversely related to sovereign risk, so as to broadly align across countries the 'fee-adjusted' subsidy (in terms of lower interest payments) benefiting the issuing banks.[16]

---

[14] Gropp et al show that public guarantees on saving banks in Germany – which ended in 2001 – were indeed associated with substantial moral hazard. See R. Gropp, C. Gruendl and A. Guettler, 'The impact of public guarantees on bank risk taking: evidence from a natural experiment' (2010) ECB Working Papers 1272.

[15] See Panetta et al. above, n.2.

[16] For a more expanded discussion of the costs of the bond guarantees see S. Schich, 'Financial Crisis: Deposit Insurance and Related Financial Safety Net Aspects' (2008) 2 OECD Journal: Financial Market Trends (available at http://www.oecd.org/dataoecd/36/48/41894959.pdf (last accessed 25 September 2012)); Schich, above, n. 2; S. Schich, 'Challenges Associated with the Expansion of Deposit Insurance Coverage during Fall 2008' (2009) 16 Economics: The Open-Access, Open-Assessment E-Journal; Organization for Economic Co-Operation and Development, 'The Financial Crisis – Reform and Exit Strategies' (OECD, Paris 2009) (available at http://www.oecd.org (last accessed 25 September 2012)); and Levy and Schich, above, n. 3. Economic distortions are a common drawback of public guarantee schemes that provide insurance against financial risks generated in the private market. A good deal of the literature has focused on deposit insurance. In a general equilibrium analysis of a multi-region economy with banks, Bruche and Suarez find that deposit insurance causes a misallocation of credit and argue that one possible solution to the distortions would be to introduce fair risk-based premia. M. Bruche and J. Suarez, 'Deposit Insurance and Money Market Freezes' (2010) 57 Journal of Monetary Economics 45–61. See also V. Acharya, 'Comment on "The Macroeconomics of Money Market Freezes" by Max Bruche and Javier Suarez', (2010) 57 Journal of Monetary Economics 62–3; V. Acharya, J.A.C. Santos and T. Yorulmazer, 'Systemic Risk and Deposit Insurance Premiums' (2010) FRBNY Economic Policy Review 89–99; and G.G. Pennacchi,

(in percent of total issuance)

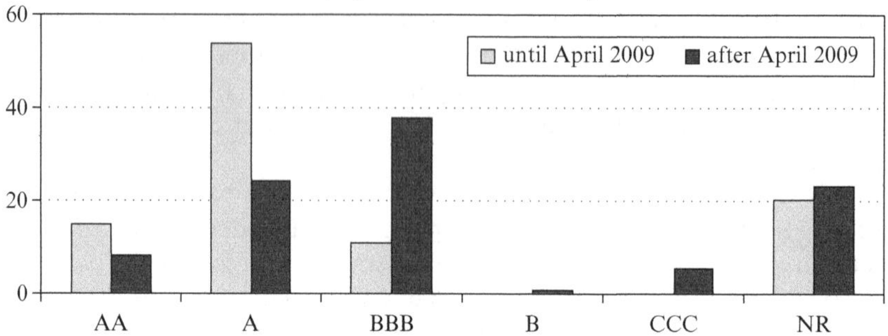

Source: Authors' estimates based on Bloomberg and Datastream

Figure 11.5 Issuance of guaranteed bank bonds by rating of issuing banks

Indirect evidence of these inefficiencies is provided by the fact that the credit quality of banks that issued guaranteed bonds declined over time: Figure 11.5 shows that the average credit rating of banks that made use of guarantees in the period October 2008-April 2009, at the peak of market tensions, was much higher than the rating of those banks that issued between May 2009 and June 2010.

IV. IS A RESUMPTION OF BOND GUARANTEES FEASIBLE? THE DECLINE IN THE VALUE OF SOVEREIGN GUARANTEES

The financial crisis that began in 2008 after Lehman's default has undergone two major stages. The first phase lasted until the end of 2009 and can be characterised as a bank crisis. By the end of 2009 investors realised that the fiscal landscape was changing and during 2010 the repricing of risk reflected the emergence of a fully fledged sovereign debt crisis.[17]

Severe funding pressures were experienced by banks in both stages of the crisis, especially in non-triple-A sovereigns, but there is a major difference between the two episodes; while in 2008 the increase of banks'

'Deposit Insurance Reform', in J.R. Brown (ed.), *Public Insurance and Private Markets* (The AEI Press, Washington, DC 2010).

[17] See Grande et al. above, n. 3.

credit risk reflected concerns about banks' exposure to private sector toxic assets, in 2011 the concern was about exposure to sovereign debt.[18]

Reflecting the severe strains on bank funding conditions since July 2011, in October the EU Heads of State or Government acknowledged 'the need to ensure the medium-term funding of banks, in order to avoid a credit crunch and to safeguard the flow of credit to the real economy, and to coordinate measures to achieve this.' At the same time the EU leaders were aware that: 'A simple repetition of the 2008 experience with full national discretion in the setting-up of liquidity schemes may not provide a satisfactory solution under current market conditions. Therefore a truly coordinated approach at EU-level is needed regarding entry criteria, pricing and conditions.'[19]

Following the request of the EU summit, European authorities have been devising a new guarantee scheme for bank bonds that avoids the distortions induced by the 2008 programme and that can be effective despite the sharp deterioration of the fiscal landscape. The main purpose of the new guarantee scheme is to resuscitate the market for wholesale funding for banks.

In achieving this goal it is important to make sure that the scheme does not introduce distortions to competition; for this purpose it is crucial to take into account that differences exist across countries in the value of the sovereign guarantee as well as in the riskiness of banks.

For some countries the value of sovereign guarantees was indeed already low in the first stage of the crisis in 2008–09. For instance, in the context of the guarantee scheme adopted in the EU in 2008, for banks located in fiscally weak countries such as Italy it was not worth buying insurance from the Treasury because the cost for the bank (the insurance fee) was roughly of the same order of the yield reduction (that is, the interest saving) made possible by the guarantee. Mainly for this reason no Italian bank relied on the guarantee scheme.[20] In 2010–11 things got worse and in several euro area countries sovereign credit risk rose above banks credit risk, implying that the value that banks may extract from a public guarantee is close to nil. As a consequence, in the case of Italy and many other euro area countries a government guarantee on bank bonds would not be able to improve funding conditions of banks to a significant extent, while it would likely

---

[18] See CGFS, above, n. 5; and M. Davies and F. Panetta, 'How does sovereign risk affect bank funding conditions? What can policymakers do?', VoxEU.org, 26 July 2011 (available at http://www.voxeu.org (last accessed 25 September 2012)).

[19] European Union, 'Statement of EU Heads of State or Government', 26 October 2011.

[20] See Levy and Zaghini, above, n. 10.

worsen the country's fiscal position, as a consequence of the increase of contingent liabilities.

A non-distortionary pricing mechanism should make sure that the 'insurance premium' is adjusted in order to reflect both the value of the sovereign guarantee (banks enjoying a less valuable guarantee should pay a lower fee) and the 'standalone' riskiness of the insured bank (riskier banks should pay a higher fee than 'safer' banks). As for the latter adjustment, in analogy with the programmes adopted in 2008, authorities may rely on a bank's CDS premium as recorded over an appropriate time period. One caveat when using a bank's CDS premium as a measure of a bank's riskiness is that the CDS does not reflect only the bank's 'standalone' riskiness but it also incorporates the benefit coming from any kind of sovereign guarantee.[21]

Concerning the adjustment related to the value of the sovereign guarantee, two cases can be considered depending on whether a national or a 'mutualistic' guarantee scheme is adopted. In case a national approach is adopted, the premium could be a function of the gap between the credit standing of the bank's sovereign and the average credit standing of advanced economies, so that the insurance fee decreases for those banks that obtain a less valuable guarantee.[22]

An alternative solution would be a 'mutualistic' approach, in which the guarantee is not provided at the national level but rather by a supranational institution (such as the European Financial Stability Fund) or by a pool of countries that provide a 'several' and, possibly, 'joint' guarantee. In this case the value of the sovereign guarantee would be equal across countries and there would be no need to adjust the price of the guarantee for this factor.

The 'mutualistic' approach is more attractive in terms of relief for bank funding costs but it may raise a number of objections. First, it may be

---

[21] In principle, the very announcement of a guarantee scheme should lead the difference across banks' CDS to reflect only the difference in standalone risks and possible differences across countries in the value of the guarantees. In practice, it may take some time until the guarantee is priced in and therefore the authorities would need to take this into account when choosing the pricing formula.

[22] See Panetta et al., above, n. 2; Levy and Panetta, 'Government guarantees on bank funding: should we extend them into 2010 despite the improved bank profitability and the schemes' distortionary effects?', VoxEU.org, 3 November 2009 (available at http://www.voxeu.org (last accessed 25 September 2012)); A. Estrella and S. Schich, 'Sovereign and banking sector debt: interconnections through guarantees', OECD Journal: Financial Market Trends October 2011 (available at http://www.oecd.org/dataoecd/38/7/48963986.pdf (last accessed 25 September 2012)).

argued that a mutualistic approach implies fiscal subsidies and transfers across countries and thus violates the Treaty provisions. Second, it may be objected on economic grounds that the contingent liabilities taken up by the European supranational institution or, equivalently, by the 'joint guarantors' might negatively affect the latter's rating. These drawbacks make the adoption of mutualistic guarantee schemes highly unlikely.

12. The impact of sovereign guarantees on the quality of bank debt: Theory and evidence from Europe

Arturo Estrella and Sebastian Schich[1]

I. MOTIVATION

The financial crisis has put a sharp spotlight on the use of government-supported guarantees as a policy tool to support financial stability. Together with the provision by some public authorities of additional capital and by central banks of additional liquidity for banks, these measures meant that the sovereign effectively provided the function of the 'guarantor of last resort'[2] in response to the banking crisis of 2008–09. The immediate concern was financial stability and these policies were helpful in stabilizing markets and institutions. That said, guarantees – even if not triggered – are not costless. For the guarantor, they create contingent liabilities and underpriced guarantees can create fiscal challenges further down the road and lead to distortions to competition and incentives and produce moral hazard.

While many of the explicit emergency guarantees have been withdrawn already, recent tensions in funding markets have led to renewed calls for the creation of explicit government-supported arrangements for guaranteeing debt. Some proposals foresee that the debt guarantees will be provided jointly by several sovereigns or specific international institutions

---

1 The authors are grateful to Joseph Saia for his excellent research assistance, for comments and suggestions by Blaise Ganguin, Stephen Lumpkin and Hans Wright, and comments from participants at the Symposium 'Financial crisis management and the use of government guarantees', held at the OECD in Paris on 3 and 4 October 2011. This chapter draws in parts on A. Estrella, and S. Schich, 'Sovereign and Banking Sector Debt: Interconnections Through Guarantees' (2011) 2 OECD Financial Market Trends.

2 Schich, S. (2009), 'Expanded Guarantees for Banks: Benefits, Costs and Exit Issues' (2009) 2 OECD Financial Market Trends, November, available at: http://www.oecd.org/dataoecd/53/48/44260489.pdf (last accessed 25 September 2012).

or facilities, noting that the value of the guarantees that currently could be provided by some weak sovereigns alone would be insufficient to reassure investors of the quality of their domestic banks' debt.

This chapter develops a framework for valuing (and pricing) sovereign debt guarantees based on concepts of contingent claims analysis (Section II). In particular, it investigates the value of insurance of risky bank debt when the sovereign providing a guarantee can itself be risky. The conceptual approach developed here applies in principle to both explicit and implicit guarantees, and the chapter reports the results of an empirical application of the framework to data on external (mostly government) support for the debt of a cross-section of large European banks (Section III). Section IV discusses selected policy implications and is followed by conclusions.

II. THE CONCEPTUAL FRAMEWORK

A. Motivation for the Model

All debt is risky. This principle is generally acknowledged in the modelling of the debt of private entities, including banks, and of debt issued by sovereigns in emerging economies, but is more likely to be downplayed or even overlooked in the case of sovereign debt or debt guarantees in more advanced economies. However, as Gray, Merton, and Bodie contend,[3] the ability of the sovereign to pay off its debt or to make good on guarantees on private sector debt can play a major role in the valuation and risk assessment of private sector debt instruments.

Merton[4] developed a framework for the valuation of risky debt of a single issuer, which has been applied and extended in various ways in the finance literature. The Merton approach, for instance, forms the theoretical basis for the well-known KMV ratings, as indicated in Crosbie and Bohn.[5] The framework is particularly helpful in the case of banks, which tend to have thin capital margins (high leverage) and thus a propensity for large proportional equity losses in response to changes in asset value.[6]

---

3 D.F. Gray, R.C. Merton and Z. Bodie (2007) 'Contingent Claims Approach to Measuring and Managing Sovereign Credit Risk' 5(4) Journal of Investment Management 1–24.

4 R.C. Merton, 'On the Pricing of Corporate Debt: The Risk Structure of Interest Rates', (1974) 29 Journal of Finance 449–70.

5 P. Crosbie and J. Bohn *Modeling Default Risk*, (Moody's KMV Company, San Francisico: 2003).

6 See, for instance, Kealhofer for an application of KMV methods to banks.

This chapter considers the valuation and risk assessment of bank debt guaranteed by a sovereign. Thus, our model is designed to include two sources of risk, as well as the correlation between them. In that sense we follow the theoretical lead of Gray, Merton and Bodie, though in that paper they only model explicitly one source of risk. Other earlier work has extended Merton's approach to two sources of risk. For example, Johnson and Stulz[7] calculate the value of a debt guarantee provided by a risky guarantor under the assumption that the latter has no debt outstanding. Lai[8] proposes an approximate closed-form expression for the value of such a guarantee, also under the assumption that the guarantor has no debt, and provides numerical results in the case in which the guarantor has non-zero debt.

Our approach is a general extension of the Merton model to two sources of risk, possibly correlated, using a bivariate counterpart to Merton's univariate stochastic assumptions. The resulting form of the model does not lend itself to closed-form expressions for the value of guaranteed debt, so we generate numerical values from a calibrated version of the model. Since the empirical distributions of financial asset returns have been shown to be prone to leptokurtosis or 'fat tails', we also consider the effects of such stochastic properties on the robustness of our results.

Section II.B, which follows, presents technical details of the model and Section II.C provides numerical valuation results and sensitivity analysis.

B. Model

Our model includes two agents operating in a single-country setting, a bank and the sovereign, and both issue risky debt. For valuation purposes, we consider the debt of each agent on a standalone basis, but our main focus is on the debt of the bank under the assumption that the sovereign provides a financial guarantee. We look at the bank's debt from the perspective of an investor in the bank, with or without a guarantee. As to the guarantor, our assumption here is that the sovereign's own liabilities are senior to its guarantee of bank debt. Thus, the guarantee does not directly affect the value of the sovereign's direct debt issuance. Other assumptions are possible and could induce changes in the valuation of sovereign debt, but we leave those alternatives for future research.

Stephen Kealhofer, *The Economics of the Bank and of the Loan Book* (Moody's KMV Company, San Francisco 2002).

[7] H. Johnson and R. Stulz, 'The Pricing of Options with Default Risk' (1987) 42(2) Journal of Finance 267–80.

[8] V.S. Lai, (1992), 'An Analysis of Private Loan Guarantees', (1992) 6 Journal of Financial Services Research 223–48.

We compute the value of debt for each entity using contingent claims pricing. For the bank, we consider both the standalone value and the value if there is a guarantee from the sovereign. For simplicity, we consider a one-period model in which debt is issued at time 0 and matures at time 1. The assets of the bank and the sovereign evolve as a bivariate continuous-time Wiener process, which is a direct extension of the Merton model. The distribution of time 1 assets is bivariate lognormal, which leads to straightforward numerical calculations, though not in general to closed-form solutions.

For standalone bank debt, the payoff at time 1 is

$$R_B = \begin{cases} L_B & \text{if } A_B \geq L_B \\ A_B & \text{if } A_B < L_B \end{cases}, \tag{12.1}$$

where A_B and L_B are the assets and liabilities (face value of debt) of the bank. The payoff may also be expressed as

$$R_B = L_B - \begin{cases} 0 & \text{if } A_B \geq L_B \\ L_B - A_B & \text{if } A_B < L_B \end{cases}, \tag{12.2}$$

where the second term is equivalent to a put option on the bank's assets with strike price equal to its debt.

In some earlier analyses of sovereign debt guarantees, the sovereign is assumed to be risk free. Here we follow, for example, the theoretical discussion in Gray, Merton, and Bodie and assume that the sovereign's assets are also subject to risk and that its debt is therefore risky. By analogy to the bank case, the payoff of sovereign debt is

$$R_s = \begin{cases} L_s & \text{if } A_s \geq L_s \\ A_s & \text{if } A_s < L_s \end{cases}, \tag{12.3}$$

and it also has a put option interpretation corresponding to (12.2). Gray, Merton and Bodie suggest that we can think of sovereign assets as foreign reserves, net fiscal assets, and other public assets, and that sovereign liabilities may include foreign-currency debt, local-currency debt, base money, and guarantees.

In addition to its direct liabilities, the sovereign may also provide a guarantee on the debt of the bank. In this case, sovereign assets at the end of the period, if they exceed sovereign liabilities, may be used to cover any shortfall of bank assets in covering the face value of bank debt. As noted earlier, we assume that the sovereign's own debt is senior to the bank guarantee. Thus, the payoff for guaranteed bank debt is as summarized in the following table.

Table 12.1 Conditional payoffs for bank debt guaranteed by the sovereign

Case	Payoff R_G is	If
1	L_B	$A_B \geq L_B$
2	L_B	$A_B < L_B$ *and* $A_S \geq L_S + L_B - A_B$
3	$A_B + A_S - L_S$	$A_B < L_B$ *and* $L_S \leq A_S < L_S + L_B - A_B$
4	A_B	$A_B < L_B$ *and* $A_S < L_S$

If the bank has sufficient assets at the end of the period to pay off all its debt, the assets of the sovereign are not relevant for the repayment of bank debt. If the bank has insufficient assets to cover its debt, the sovereign guarantee essentially provides a collar whereby the investor receives a payoff with a floor of A_B and a ceiling of L_B.

We price the bank and sovereign debt using the extended Merton methodology, making the following assumptions.

1. Both the bank and the sovereign have debt outstanding (in contrast to earlier work in which the sovereign is frequently assumed to have no debt).
2. Sovereign debt is senior to the bank guarantee.
3. Bank and sovereign assets follow a bivariate Wiener process and their values are jointly lognormal (in contrast to some earlier work that assumes the sovereign is risk-free).
4. A closed-form solution for guaranteed debt is not feasible since it involves the sum of lognormal variables. We therefore use numerical integration of the exact bivariate lognormal density.
5. We apply risk-neutral valuation as in Merton.[9]

The mathematical details and final valuation formulae are explained in the Appendix.

C. Sensitivity of Bank Debt Guaranteed by the Sovereign to Changes in Variable or Parameter Values

To analyse the characteristics of the proposed model and examine its implications for debt guarantees, we provide numerical results based on the following calibration of model parameters. Parameters in the illustrations assume the following base case values unless otherwise noted. We

[9] Merton, above, n. 3.

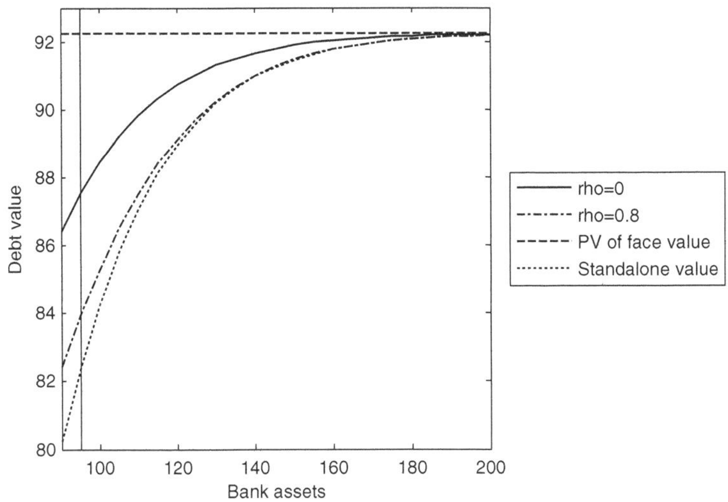

Figure 12.1 Sensitivity of bank debt value to changes in initial bank assets

take the time period loosely to represent one year and the riskless interest rate to be 3 per cent on a per-period compounded basis. The value of bank assets is 100 at time 0 and the face value of bank liabilities, payable at time 1, is 95. Although these values seem to indicate that the bank has formally a 5 per cent capital ratio, when discounting and risk are taken into account, the true value of the capital ratio is closer to 12 per cent.

We take time 0 sovereign assets to be 200 and the face value of sovereign liabilities to be 180. The volatility of asset returns is 0.3 for both the bank and the sovereign. For the correlation of bank and sovereign asset returns, which we denote as 'rho', we look at two cases, zero and 0.8. A higher correlation tends to undercut the value of the sovereign's debt guarantee, since the sovereign's financial position would tend to be unfavourable when a potential bank default occurs.

Figure 12.1 shows the value of bank debt as a function of the initial value of bank assets, as the latter varies from 90 to 200, with all other parameter values fixed at the base case levels. The vertical dotted line indicates the base case face value of liabilities. Debt values are presented under four different sets of assumptions. An upper bound is given by the present value (PV) of face value, which corresponds to the assumption that the debt is riskless (dashed line). This value is independent of initial bank assets. A lower bound is provided by the standalone value of the debt, which assumes that there is no guarantee from the sovereign or any other source (dotted line).

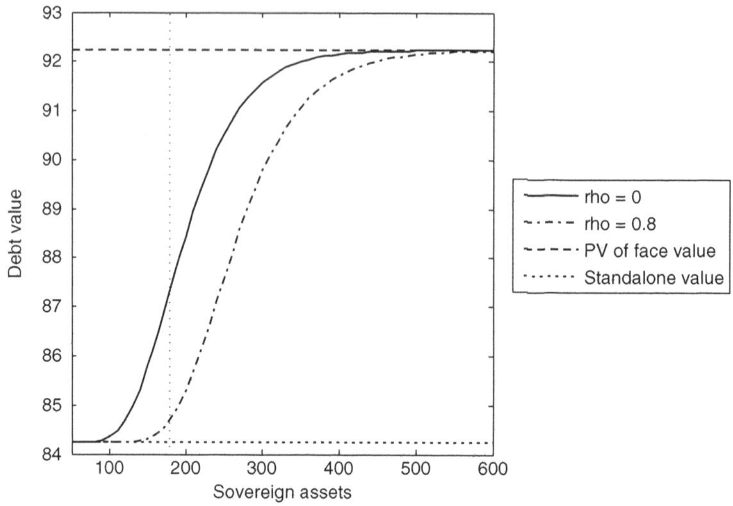

Figure 12.2 Sensitivity of bank debt value to changes in initial sovereign assets

When there is a guarantee from the sovereign, the value of the guarantee depends on the correlation between bank and sovereign assets, as noted earlier. When the correlation is high (rho = 0.8), the uplift in bank debt value provided by the guarantee is very modest, as indicated by a comparison of the standalone value and the guaranteed value (dash-dot line). A much more substantial effect on the value of the guarantee occurs when the correlation is zero, in which case the financial state of the guarantor is independent from that of the bank and the sovereign may be in good shape to cover the payment of bank debt when the bank is in a default state.

It was observed that, in all but the riskless case, the sensitivity of the value of debt to bank asset value (the bank asset 'delta') is substantially larger for lower asset values. This sensitivity approaches zero as the initial value of bank assets grows well beyond the base case value of 100. This non-linearity means that the value of debt becomes more volatile as the condition of the bank deteriorates.

We next perform a similar exercise by letting the initial value of sovereign assets vary from 50 to 600, with the value of bank assets and all other parameters at their base case levels. Results appear in Figure 12.2. Once again we show the upper and lower bounds given by the present value of face value and the standalone value, respectively, which in this case are both independent of sovereign asset value and appear as horizontal lines. The vertical dotted line represents the base case face value of sovereign liabilities.

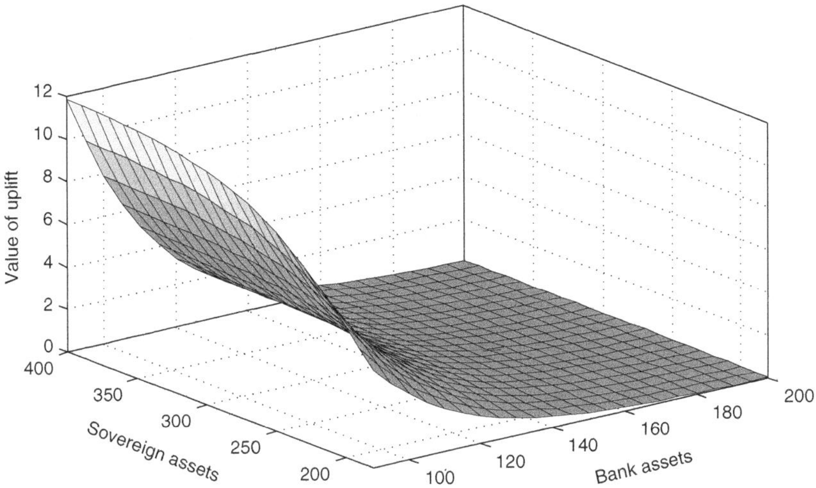

Figure 12.3 Sensitivity of value of uplift to changes in initial bank and sovereign assets

As in the case of the sensitivity to bank assets, sensitivity to sovereign assets grows non-linearly from the lower to the upper bound. However, the non-linearity in this case is different in that bank debt value is less sensitive when sovereign assets are low as well as high. Sensitivity is much higher in an intermediate range of sovereign asset values. In practical terms, this means that changes in the financial condition of the sovereign have little import for bank debt both when the sovereign's financial condition is very strong (the guarantee makes bank debt close to riskless) and very weak (the guarantee is close to worthless). In the intermediate range, it is clear again that the uplift provided by the sovereign is less if the assets of the two agents are more highly correlated.

From a real-world empirical point of view, we are very interested in the uplift that a sovereign guarantee can provide for bank debt, which we examine in Figure 12.3. This three-dimensional figure shows the uplift in the value of bank debt, that is, the difference between the guaranteed and standalone values as a function of both bank and sovereign assets. The correlation is zero in the figure. The shape of the function is qualitatively the same if the correlation is higher (for example, 0.8), but the numerical values of the uplift are lower.

Figures 12.1 and 12.2 show that the value of guaranteed bank debt is positively related to the values of both bank and sovereign assets. In contrast, we see in Figure 12.3 that while the uplift is also positively related to sovereign assets, it is negatively related to bank assets. Intuitively, a sovereign in better financial condition is better able to support bank debt, whereas a bank in worse financial condition stands to gain more from a guarantee than one in better shape. We see in Section III that this type of relationship holds empirically when debt values are proxied by ratings from the credit rating agencies.

The sensitivities of bank debt to other parameters of the model are largely straightforward. For instance, the value of guaranteed bank debt responds positively to increases in the scale of the sovereign if the financial condition of the sovereign (ratio of assets to liabilities) is held fixed. That is, a large country can take better care of a small bank than when the sizes are reversed.

Higher volatility of sovereign assets means that the guarantee is riskier, decreasing the value of bank debt correspondingly. Higher volatility of bank assets also has in general a negative effect on the value of bank debt, but non-monotonic relationships have been observed by, for example, Stulz and Johnson and Lai when the asset return correlation is close to −1 or when the ratio of bank to sovereign volatility is either very large or very small. We find limited evidence of these results if we start from our base case calibration.

The effect of changes in asset correlation is generally as indicated in Figures 12.1 and 12.2 and discussed earlier, even if the correlation is negative. Lower correlation provides a kind of diversification effect and enhances the value of the guarantee and the value of bank debt.

We conclude this section by examining the possible consequences of allowing the distribution of asset returns to be more leptokurtic, which some of the empirical literature on asset returns suggests is the case in practice. Figure 12.4 has essentially the same format as Figure 12.2, but in this case we show results for both the bivariate lognormal distribution (entries labelled 'n') and the bivariate log-*t* distribution with 4 degrees of freedom in both dimensions (entries labelled 't').

We readily see that results using the *t* distribution are qualitatively the same as those using the normal distribution. For example, the value of guaranteed bank debt is non-linearly increasing with sovereign assets, with decreased sensitivity at both ends of the scale. The main difference is that leptokurtosis or fatter tails implies more risk of extreme events. Since the upside potential of debt is limited to full payment of the face value, the fat tail on the negative side is more important for debt valuation. Thus, fatter tails are associated with lower debt values for every pair of corresponding curves in Figure 12.4.

A distribution with an appropriate level of leptokurtosis would be very helpful in modelling debt values observed in practice. From our theoretical perspective, which is largely qualitative, the straightforward extension of the standard Merton model is generally sufficient.

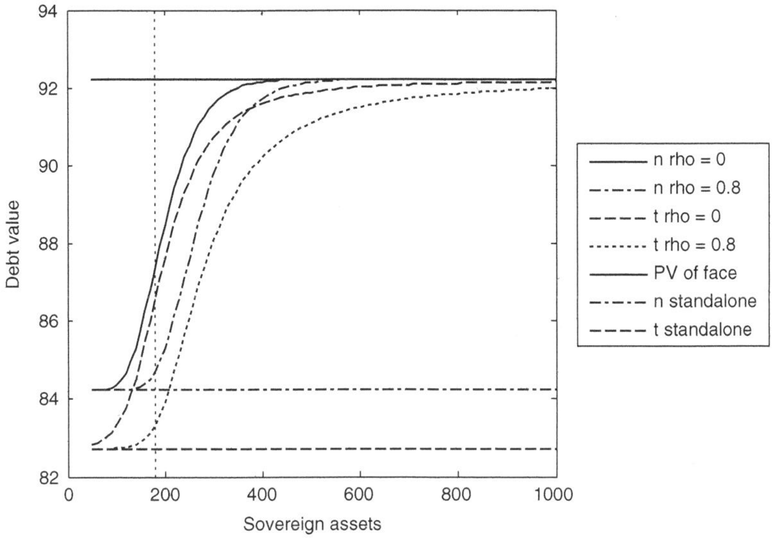

Figure 12.4 Sensitivity of bank debt value to changes in initial sovereign assets, bivariate normal distribution and bivariate t distribution with (4,4) degrees of freedom

III. EMPIRICAL ANALYSIS: IMPLICIT SOVEREIGN SUPPORT FOR LARGE EUROPEAN BANKS

A. Data

The model described in the previous section implies that the uplift in the value of bank debt due to a sovereign guarantee is a positive function of the level of sovereign assets and a negative function of the level of bank assets. Conceptually, this implication applies regardless of whether the guarantee is explicit or implicit, as long as the latter is known. We test these implications using data on the assumed external support for a sample of 100 large European banks. In particular, our data consist of Standard & Poor's estimates of the 100 largest European banks rated by that agency of the standalone credit profile (SACP) and issuer credit rating (ICR), as published in April 2011.[10] The ICR factors in the possibility and

[10] Standard & Poor's, Global Credit Portal, RatingsDirect, 'Ratings for Europe's Largest 100 Banks Show the Widest Range in Creditworthiness in 30 Years', 18 April 2011.

likelihood of external support that the bank under consideration receives from its parent or public authorities, when needed. The SACP abstracts from such support. The difference between the two types of ratings is referred to here as UPLIFT. Thus,

Standalone credit rating (SACP) + credit rating uplift (UPLIFT) = issuer credit rating (ICR).

In our sample, the difference between these two ratings, that is, the credit rating UPLIFT, is typically either zero or positive, but it can also be negative. Out of 100 banks, 46 enjoy a positive UPLIFT. Two banks, both from the United Kingdom, are characterised by a negative UPLIFT.[11] Note that standalone ratings abstract not just from sovereign guarantees but also from other external effects, such as guarantees and drags from a parent company.

A positive UPLIFT reflects the existence of explicit or perceived implicit support from either the parent or the government, or other favourable factors such as access to central bank liquidity and emergency liquidity support. Whatever the specific form that the external support might take, it effectively facilitates the issuer's servicing of its debt, and is thus functionally equivalent to an implicit guarantee for that debt. By far the most important element is the assumed support from the government and, therefore, this difference is now commonly used as an empirical measure of the extent of explicit or implicit support from the government.[12]

In our sample, the average issuer SACP in numerical values[13] is 13.70,

---

[11] One is the FCE Bank, which is a captive finance subsidiary of Ford Motor Co, with the subsidiary having a stronger rating than its parent. The FCE Bank is a regulated entity, where the regulatory and legal framework limits the parental influence or the extension of bankruptcy proceedings from the parent to the subsidiary. The subsidiary's business franchise is nonetheless inextricably linked to the fortunes of its (weaker) parent and Standard & Poor's expect that, were the parent to experience severe stress, it would inevitably have an adverse effect on the activity and asset quality of the captive, including through parent-related credit exposures. The other bank with a negative UPLIFT is HSBC Holding Plc, which is a holding company, with its banks being operating subsidiaries. Claims on the holding company are subordinated compared to claims on the operating bank subsidiaries and, therefore, the holding company's ICR is not considered as strong as its SACP.

[12] See Committee on the Global Financial System, 'The Impact of Sovereign Credit Risk on Bank Funding Conditions', Report by a Study Group established by the CGFS and chaired by Fabio Panetta of the Banca d'Italia, CGFS Papers No. 43, July 2011; and F. Packer and N. Tarashev, 'Rating Methodologies for Banks', BIS Quarterly Review, June 2011.

[13] The mapping is as follows: AAA is equivalent to 20, AA+ is equivalent to

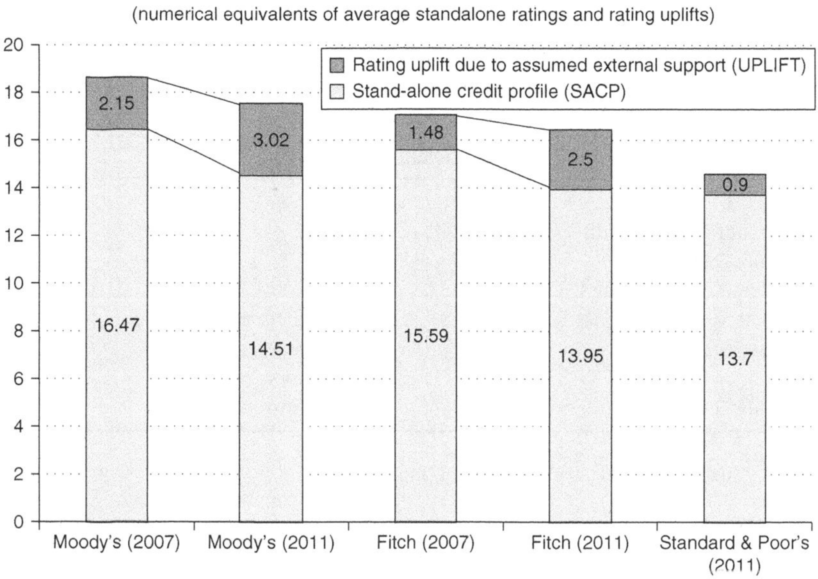

Notes: The figure provides numerical approximations of standalone credit profiles and credit rating uplifts due to assumed external support, according to estimates by credit rating agencies. Credit ratings are translated into numbers, with AAA or Aaa equal to 20, AA+ or Aa1 equal to 19, and so forth. The data shown for Moody's and Fitch (obtained from Packer and Tarashev, 2011) are equally-weighted averages of individual country averages for six European countries (Germany, France, Italy, Spain, Switzerland, United Kingdom) and four non-European countries (Australia, Canada, Japan, United States). The data shown for Standard & Poor's (2011) are averages of individual bank standalone credit profiles and rating uplifts for a sample of the 100 largest banks rated by that agency.

Sources: Authors' estimates based on Standard & Poor's (2011), Global Credit Portal, RatingsDirect, 'Ratings for Europe's Largest 100 Banks Show the Widest Range in Creditworthiness in 30 Years', 18 April; and F. Packer and N. Tarashev, 'Rating Methodologies for Banks', BIS Quarterly Review, June 2011.

Figure 12.5 Changes in standalone and all-in ratings of large international banks

while the average UPLIFT is 0.90. Thus, the average ICR is 14.60. The data are shown in Figure 12.5, together with broadly similar data from Moody's and Fitch for 2007 and 2011 (see notes to the Table). Given the differences in samples and methods used, the estimates are not strictly comparable across agencies. They show nonetheless that, over time,

---

19, and so forth. Each change from one to the adjacent credit rating category is henceforth referred to as one 'notch'.

Table 12.2 Regression of UPLIFT on standalone credit ratings and sovereign ratings

(Ordinary Least Squares)				
Variable	Coefficient	Std. error	t-Statistic	Probability
Constant	0.01	0.62	0.01	0.99
Issuer standalone credit rating (SACP)	−0.24*	0.04	−5.52	0.00
Sovereign credit rating (SCR)	0.23*	0.04	5.55	0.00
R-squared	0.28	Mean dependent variable		0.90
Adjusted R-squared	0.27	Standard error of dependent variable		1.22
Standard error of regression	1.04	Log likelihood		−144.67

Note: * denotes significance at the 1 per cent level.

UPLIFT is negatively related to SACP, which is consistent with our model.

B. Results

The relationship between the uplift on the one hand and the quality of banks and sovereigns on the other is further analysed using the sample of 100 cross-section observations of our sample. Among other things,[14] we estimate a linear regression of UPLIFT on SACP and SCR. The results are shown in Table 12.2.

As regards the intrinsic strength of banks, SACP, the estimated coefficient is negative as suggested by the model described in Section II. The estimated coefficient is also highly significant: relatively weaker banks tend to benefit from a greater UPLIFT than do relatively stronger banks.

As regards the role of the sovereign strength, the UPLIFT tends to be greater, the better the sovereign credit rating. This finding is also consistent with the model implications. Both variables are significant at the 1 per cent level. They explain close to 30 per cent of the variation in the dependent variable, which appears considerable given the simplicity of the empirical model.[15]

---

[14] The discussion here presents selected results; further results and more details are contained in Estrella and Schich, above, n. 1.

[15] To check whether that result holds even when controlling for country

This observation is noteworthy given that neither the standalone credit profiles nor the issuer credit ratings are the direct outcome of quantitative models, even if the latter do certainly influence the ratings. In fact, Packer and Tarashev explain that 'ratings are opinions about the creditworthiness of a rated entity, be it a sovereign or an institution. They reflect both quantitative assessments of credit risk and the expert judgment of a ratings committee. Thus, no rating can be unequivocally explained by a particular set of data inputs and formal rules.'[16] Against the background of this assessment, it is remarkable that a simple empirical model explains a considerable amount of the variation in the credit rating uplift due to assumed external support.

Quantitatively, the influences of the standalone bank rating, SACP, and the sovereign rating, SCR, on the credit rating uplift are statistically significant but economically somewhat modest in size.[17] For each of the variables, a difference in rating of four notches corresponds to a difference in UPLIFT of a single notch, positive for SCR and negative for SACP.

IV. POLICY IMPLICATIONS: PRICING SOVEREIGN GUARANTEES FOR BANK DEBT

For a given bank debt issuer, the value of a government debt guarantee depends not only on the relationship between the banks' own assets and liabilities, but also on the relationship between the assets and liabilities of the guarantor. The value of a guarantee is given as the difference between V_G and V_B, as defined in equations (12.10) and (12.8) in the appendix to this chapter. Thus, the value of a sovereign bank guarantee depends on the riskiness of the bank and that of the sovereign: the value of a guarantee is higher the stronger the sovereign.

effects, we estimated a similar equation introducing country dummy variables and the effect of SACP was very similar to Table 12.2.

16 Packer and Tarashev, above, n. 12.

17 One potential issue with the above specification is that the sovereign rating, SCR, might be determined simultaneously with the credit rating uplift, UPLIFT. To address the issue, we apply the Generalised Method of Moments and use a sovereigns' gross debt (the logarithm of 'general government gross financial liabilities, as a percentage of GDP' from the OECD's Economic Outlook Database) as an instrument for the sovereign credit rating. The estimated coefficients of the marginal effect of SACP and SCR are larger in absolute values and continue to be highly significant. In this case, the coefficients are closer to a 2 to 1 relationship between the standalone and sovereign ratings and the UPLIFT effect. The results are available in Estrella and Schich, above, n. 1.

Under those circumstances, to avoid competitive distortions in a situation where different sovereigns individually provide guarantees for their banks and banking sectors,[18] the fees charged in exchange need to reflect the sovereigns' own creditworthiness. Stronger sovereigns with more limited own debt need to charge higher fees to their domestic banks than weaker sovereigns to their banks if the aim is to avoid distortions to competition and incentives.[19]

There are alternatives to providing sovereign bank debt guarantees while reducing the potential competitive distortions that could arise from the inadequate pricing of such guarantees in the presence of differences in the quality of sovereigns. One alternative is that any sovereign could provide guarantees not just for their own domestic banks but for any international bank. Obviously, only stronger sovereigns would be in a position to provide such guarantees, while the guarantees that weaker sovereigns could provide would not necessarily add much value to bank debt. The feasibility of such arrangements is also questionable, especially as political and legal issues might prevent sovereigns from guaranteeing the debt of other countries' banking sectors.

Another approach is for guarantees to be provided jointly by several sovereigns or by specific international institutions or facilities. Such solutions would be helpful to overcome the issue that the credit quality of some weak sovereigns alone is such that investors in bank debt would not be sufficiently reassured. The desirability of such arrangements has been questioned given that their availability may influence incentives on the part of weaker sovereigns to address their own problems and, again, political and legal issues might arise.

While a discussion of these proposals is beyond the scope of this

---

[18] The design of bank debt guarantees provided by individual sovereigns in a large number of OECD countries between 2008 and 2010 is discussed in A. Levy and S. Schich, 'The design of government guarantees for bank bonds: Lessons from the recent financial crisis', (2010) 2 OECD Financial Market Trends, July (available at http://www.oecd.org/dataoecd/46/47/45636972.pdf (last accessed 25 September 2012)); G. Grande, A. Levy, F. Panetta and A. Zaghini, 'Public Guarantees on Bank Bonds: Effectiveness and distortions', (2011) OECD Journal: Financial Market Trends, October, (available at http://www.oecd.org/dataoecd/1/55/49200208.pdf (last accessed 25 September 2012)); and in F. Panetta, T. Faeh, G. Grande, C. Ho, M. King, A. Levy, F. M. Signoretti, M. Taboga and A. Zaghini, 'An assessment of financial sector rescue programmes', BIS Papers, No.48, 2009.

[19] See A. Levy and S. Schich, 'The design of government guarantees for bank bonds: lessons from the recent financial crisis', (2010) 1 OECD Journal: Financial Market Trends, No. 1.

chapter, it is noted here, however, that the choice of appropriate pricing remains an issue, regardless of whether the guarantees are provided across borders, individually or jointly by several sovereigns. Our conceptual approach, here developed in a single-country setting, can be extended to a multi-country context to address questions regarding the value (and pricing) of joint sovereign guarantees and the value of the individual sovereign marginal contributions to those values.

CONCLUDING REMARKS

Based on a contingent claims model to value sovereign guarantees of bank debt, this chapter demonstrates that the value of a guarantee of risky debt depends both on the characteristics of the borrower and the guarantor. For a given bank, the value of a government guarantee for its debt decreases with the bank's creditworthiness and increases with the sovereign's creditworthiness. These implications are consistent with our empirical findings. For a sample of 100 large European banks, we find that a measure of implicit sovereign support is higher, the lower the bank's own standalone creditworthiness and the higher the sovereign's creditworthiness.

These results have implications for the pricing of sovereign guarantees for bank debt. In a situation where such guarantees are provided separately by each sovereign to its domestic banks, to avoid creating additional competitive distortions, the fees each sovereign charges its domestic banks for debt guarantees need to reflect the sovereign's own creditworthiness. Stronger sovereigns need to charge higher fees than weaker sovereigns. In a situation where bank debt guarantees are provided jointly by several sovereigns, the allotment of premium income among the participating sovereigns should reflect each sovereigns' creditworthiness. Stronger sovereigns should receive higher shares of premium incomes than weaker sovereigns even for identical amounts of committed or used guarantees.

APPENDIX: MATHEMATICAL DETAILS OF THE MODEL

This appendix provides technical details of the valuation method. The dynamics of the assets are assumed to follow a bivariate Wiener process

$$\begin{bmatrix} dx/x \\ dy/y \end{bmatrix} = \begin{bmatrix} r - \frac{1}{2}\sigma_B^2 \\ r - \frac{1}{2}\sigma_S^2 \end{bmatrix} dt + \Sigma dW \tag{12.4}$$

where x and y correspond to bank and sovereign assets, respectively, dW is two-dimensional standard Brownian motion, and

$$\Sigma\Sigma' = \begin{bmatrix} \sigma_B^2 & \rho\sigma_B\sigma_S \\ \rho\sigma_B\sigma_S & \sigma_S^2 \end{bmatrix} \tag{12.5}$$

For example, Σ could be the Cholesky decomposition of $\Sigma\Sigma'$ in (12.5), that is,

$$\Sigma = \begin{bmatrix} \sigma_B & 0 \\ \rho\sigma_S & \sqrt{1-\rho^2}\sigma_S \end{bmatrix} \tag{12.6}$$

The joint lognormal density function for asset values at time τ is then:

$$f(x,y) = \frac{1}{2\pi\sigma_B\sigma_S\tau\sqrt{1-\rho^2}}\frac{1}{xy}\exp\left(-\frac{u(x)^2+v(y)^2-2\rho u(x)v(y)}{2(1-\rho^2)}\right) \tag{12.7}$$

where

$$u(x) = (\log(x) - (r - \tfrac{1}{2}\sigma_B^2)\tau)/\sigma_B\sqrt{\tau}$$

$$\text{and } v(y) = (\log(y) - (r - \tfrac{1}{2}\sigma_S^2)\tau)/\sigma_S\sqrt{\tau}.$$

The payoff at time τ of standalone bank debt is given by (12.1) and its value is obtained from the marginal distribution $f_B(x) = \int_0^\infty f(x,y)\,dy$ implied by (12.7):

$$V_B = e^{-r}\left[\int_{L_B}^{\infty} L_B f_B(x)\,dx + \int_0^{L_B} x f_B(x)\,dx\right] \tag{12.8}$$

The payoff at time τ of sovereign debt is given by (12.3) and its value is similarly obtained from the marginal distribution $f_S(y) = \int_0^\infty f(x,y)\,dx$ implied by (12.7):

$$V_S = e^{-r}\left[\int_{L_B}^{\infty} L_S f_S(y)\,dy + \int_0^{L_S} y f_S(y)\,dy\right] \tag{12.9}$$

For bank debt guaranteed by the sovereign, the payoff at time τ is given by Table 12.1 in the main text and its value is obtained from the bivariate distribution (12.7) as

$$V_G = e^{-r}\left[\int_0^{\infty}\int_{L_B}^{\infty} L_B f(x,y)\,dx\,dy + \int_{L_B+L_S-x}^{\infty}\int_0^{L_B} L_B f(x,y)\,dx\,dy \right. \tag{12.10}$$

$$\left. + \int_{L_S}^{L_B+L_S-x}\int_0^{L_B} (x + y - L_s) f(x,y)\,dx\,dy + \int_0^{L_S}\int_0^{L_B} x f(x,y)\,dx\,dy\right]$$

The four double integrals in equation (12.10) of that box correspond to the respective four rows of Table 12.1.

13. An insurance approach for preventing financial crises

Michael Faure and Klaus Heine*

INTRODUCTION

With the financial crisis, the amount of subsidies provided by government has increased considerably. Governments also provide compensation in other types of crises, for example after a natural catastrophe. We argue in this chapter that the economic approach towards compensation of victims in case of natural catastrophes can also provide an important contribution to the interventions of a government during the financial crisis. That is, also for risks emerging from the financial crisis, insurance may provide an attractive solution. In a recent paper Michel-Kerjan[1] has programmatically pointed to this idea:

> [T]he matter of financing large-scale disasters has relevance for many other catastrophes: hurricanes, earthquakes, pandemics, terrorist attacks, technological accidents, and even *financial crises* [emphasis added]. In all of these settings, one fundamental question arises: Who will pay for the economic consequences of future catastrophes and how best to organize this payment? . . . Catastrophe economics, which seeks to shed light on these issues, is likely to become a more significant field of research in the coming years.

But not only in academia has the relevance of 'catastrophe economics'[2] been discovered for the regulation of financial catastrophes. In a recent

---

* This chapter builds in large parts on the article 'Insurance Against Financial Crises?', forthcoming in: New York University Journal of Law and Business, Vol. VII. We are grateful to the discussants at the Banking Law Symposium 2011 'Crisis Management and the Use of Government Guarantees' at the OECD, Paris. Special thanks go to the colleagues at the symposium dinner, who gave many extra comments for improving the paper.

[1] E.O. Michel-Kerjan, 'Catastrophe Economics: The National Flood Insurance Program' (2010) 24 Journal of Economic Perspectives 184.

[2] Michel-Kerjan, above, n. 1.

OECD publication[3] a subchapter has been titled 'New insurance mechanisms inspired by arrangements for catastrophic risks?'. However, neither in academia nor in practice have the design questions of insurance against financial crises yet been solved. Our chapter attempts to address these questions, even though a lot of future work will have to be done.

The remainder of our chapter is set up as follows: first, we simply ask the question: why insurance against financial crisis and we sketch out the conditions which would make it possible (Section I). Next, we sketch the insurance for catastrophes, including where government needs to intervene (Section II). Then, we present a proposal for a multi-layered insurance approach for tackling financial crisis (Section III). Finally, we end the contribution with a few concluding remarks.

I. INSURABILITY OF FINANCIAL CRISIS?

The traditional instrument to protect risk-averse individuals and enterprises against risk is insurance. Also corporations use insurance on a large scale and for a variety of reasons. Why would it be impossible, theoretically, to then insure against financial crisis?

A variety of reasons can be advanced which would make a financial crisis an uninsurable risk. The first problem that may arise is the predictability of the risk. Insurance, also for systemic risks, is possible to the extent that risks remain predictable.[4] It supposes that actuarially fair information is available (preferably via statistics) on which the insurer can base his calculation of the likelihood that the insured event will occur. Factual and legal uncertainties may endanger this *ex ante* predictability.[5] Financial crisis may for obvious reasons be problematic in that respect for the simple reason that reliable statistics to predict such a crisis may be lacking.

The second problem relates to the fact that the insured risk has to be exogenous in the sense that the insured himself cannot influence the risk. Endogeneity may be a serious problem to the extent that it will usually not be the financial crisis as such that will be the subject of insurance, but the

---

3 S. Schich and Byoung-Hwan Kim, 'Systemic Financial Crises: How to Fund Resolution' (2010) 2 OECD Financial Market Trends.

4 M. Faure and T. Hartlief, *Insurance and Expanding Systematic Risks* (OECD 2003), pp. 84–5.

5 Monti rightly points out that both factual and legal uncertainty could endanger predictability of risky events (A. Monti, 'Environmental Risk: A Comparative Law and Economics Approach to Liability and Insurance', (2001) European Review of Private Law 51–79).

risk that a financial institution will run into financial difficulties as a result of the crisis, for instance. The risk of endogeneity will hence pop up in case it is impossible to determine whether business failure (of the financial institution) occurred as a result of the crisis or rather because of other causes (such as risky investments or mismanagement). For that reason it was held that the enterprise risk itself is traditionally, in principle, not insurable. The main reason advanced for refusing to insure the enterprise risk would be that this risk would not be predictable and that hence an actuarially fair premium could not be calculated. The economic success of an enterprise could indeed be influenced by a lot of complex elements that may also mutually influence each other. Additionally, enterprise risks could be related to general characteristics of business cycles, as a result of which there would not be an independent risk.[6] From a societal perspective full insurance of the enterprise risk may also have the disadvantage that (as a result of control exercised by the insurer) risky innovations would potentially not take place.

However, the main reason why insuring enterprise risk is considered problematic is of course linked to the well-known problems of moral hazard and adverse selection. Not only will insurance increase the demand for risky activities; insurance will be particularly attractive for those who need it most. That is of course precisely the problem of adverse selection.[7] The main problem both with moral hazard and adverse selection is the information asymmetry between the insurer and the enterprise.[8] If insurers would not be able to distinguish whether the enterprise risk would be exogenous (caused by a financial crisis) or endogenous (for example, caused by mismanagement) incurable moral hazard would make the risk uninsurable.[9]

The final reason why damage resulting from a financial crisis may not be insurable is simply that the damage resulting from a financial crisis

---

[6] See the interesting contribution of A. Gosner, 'Gibt es neue unversicherbare Risiken?' in *Der Umgang mit den Risiken im Grenzbereich der Versicherbarkeit*. Documentation about a Symposium on 18–20 October 2001 in Marbach Castle, Böhningen, Karlsruhe 5-10 (2002) from before the financial crisis.

[7] K.J. Arrow, 'Uncertainty and the Welfare Economics of Medical Care' (1963) 53 American Economic Review 941–73.

[8] Compare G.A. Akerlof, 'The Market for "Lemons": Quality, Uncertainty and the Market Mechanism' (1970) 84 Quarterly Journal of Economics 488–500.

[9] See further on moral hazard R.A. Winter, 'Optimal Insurance under Moral Hazard' in Georges Dionne (ed.), *Handbook of Insurance* (Springer, Norwell, MA, USA 2000), pp. 155–83 and on adverse selection G. Dionne, N. Doherty and N. Fombaron, 'Adverse Selection in Insurance Markets', in G. Dionne (ed.), op. cit., pp. 185–243.

may largely outweigh the possibilities of commercial insurers and even reinsurers. Hence, capacity may simply be lacking to cover this type of catastrophic financial risk.[10]

We underscore these problems. There are, however, remedies available as a result of which they are not necessarily incurable. As a starting point we should state that using insurance to cope with risks caused by a financial crisis may not be as odd as perhaps first thought. After all, in recent years insurance companies have become very inventive in order to insure a variety of risks which are also part of the enterprise risk. Moreover, within this process insurance companies themselves have increasingly used financial instruments to cope with particular risks. Typical in this respect is the increasing use of capital markets to cover insured risks, also referred to as securitisation or alternative risk transfer.[11]

The use of these financial instruments by insurance companies was praised (before the financial crisis) *inter alia* because these alternative risk financing instruments would have more flexibility and would minimise the total risk costs.[12] Interestingly empirical evidence shows that, contrary to what one would think, the financial instruments used as means of alternative risk transfer have not done badly during the financial crisis and hence the use of these instruments has not been reduced.[13] This shows that financial instruments are also used as tools for insurance. As a result the border between insurance and financial instruments has become less clear. In fact the question we would like to address is the reverse of using financial instruments for insurance, but rather looking at the possibilities

---

[10] See on capacity as a condition for insurability of systemic risks Faure and Hartlief, above, n. 4, at 88–106.

[11] See on this securitisation E. Müller, 'Möglichkeiten des Kapitalmarktes zur Aufnahme von Versicherungsrisiken (Securitisation)' in *Der Umgang mit den Risiken im Grenzbereich der Versicherbarkeit*. Documentation about a Symbosium on 18–20 October 2001 in Marbach Castle, Böhningen, Karlsruhe 43–46 (2002) and see on alternative risk transfer F. Wagner, 'Risk Securitisation. An Alternative Risk Transfer of Insurance Companies', (1998) Geneva Papers on Risk and Insurance 540–607 and R.E. Smith, E.A. Canelo and Anthony M. Di Dio, 'Reinventing Reinsurance using the Capital Markets' (1997) 22 Geneva Papers on Risk and Insurance 26–37 as well as J. Zech, 'Will the International Financial Markets Replace Traditional Insurance Products' (1998) 23 Geneva Papers on Risk and Insurance 490–95.

[12] Jürgen Zech, 'Rethinking Risk Management: the Combination of Financial and Industrial Risk' (2001) 26 Geneva Papers on Risk and Insurance 71–5.

[13] V. Bruggeman, 'Capital Market Instruments for Natural Catastrophe and Terrorism Risks: A Bright Future?' (2010) 40(2) Environmental Law Reporter, News & Analysis 10136–53.

of using insurance for financial institutions. We believe that notwithstanding the problems mentioned above there are potential remedies as well.

Looking first at the issue of predictability: admittedly, financial crises may technically be difficult to predict. However, the 2008 crisis was certainly not the first global financial crisis. In addition, with the emergence of this crisis additional information has become available to make better estimates of the likelihood of future financial crises. Moreover, the literature has equally indicated that a lack of reliable statistics does not necessarily make a risk uninsurable. Insurers can respond to this so-called 'insurer ambiguity' by charging a risk premium to account for the uncertainty following from the 'hard-to-predict' nature of an event.[14] Problems may only occur when insurers charge high additional risk premiums to deal with 'insurer ambiguity', whereas the enterprise would not recognise the uncertainty and hence have no willingness to pay the additional risk premium. The lack of information on the side of insured may result in an unwillingness to pay. This may, however, change, if more information on risks becomes available or an increasing awareness of risks becomes apparent.[15] In that respect the recent financial crisis in fact only adds to the insurability of the risk by providing more actuarial information to both insurers and potential insured.

The main issue is indeed the moral hazard problem. From the literature various tools are known to remedy the moral hazard problem.[16] If moral hazard can be adequately controlled, the insured in fact behaves as if no insurance were available. The crucial question is hence whether more information can be made available to adequately control the moral hazard problem. Time and technologies to accurately assess risks are crucial in that respect. As far as financial crisis is concerned the key issue will of course be for insurers only to intervene when damage resulting from business failure was effectively caused by the financial crisis and not by causes which lay in the behaviour of the insured himself and hence could have been prevented (for example, mismanagement). To the extent insurers invest in risk classification and risk management they will also be able to obtain information on whether the business failure resulted from an insured risk (financial crisis) or from an endogenous factor.[17]

Another problem is the capacity issue. Although techniques such as

---

[14] H. Kunreuther, R. Hogarth and J. Mezaros, 'Insurer Ambiguity and Market Failure' (1993) Journal of Risk and Uncertainty 71–87.

[15] Faure and Hartlief, supra n. 4, at 86–7.

[16] See S. Shavell, 'On Moral Hazard and Insurance' (1979) 93 Quarterly Journal of Economics 541–62.

[17] See on the importance of risk differentiation and classification K.J. Crocker

pooling, co-insurance and reinsurance undoubtedly have increased the capacity of the traditional insurance market,[18] the traditional problem with the insurance of risks of a catastrophic nature is that insurance markets may lack the capacity to deal with those catastrophic risks.[19] At this point the question arises whether government could step in as a lender or reinsurer of last resort to support the functioning of insurance markets where they would otherwise, due to capacity problems, fail. We will now turn to a case where such a role for government already exists, being in insurance of catastrophes.

II. INSURANCE FOR CATASTROPHES

Many law and economics scholars favour insurance solutions for catastrophic risks, especially when compared to the alternative of government provided compensation:

(1) insurance better enables an adequate risk differentiation and risk spreading; and
(2) if insurance markets are competitive, insurers can be assumed to be better able to deal with classic insurance problems, such as moral hazard and adverse selection.[20]

The argument in favour of government intervention is that without government support insurance coverage for disasters would simply not have developed.[21]

Reinsurance by the state can then be considered as an adequate method

---

and A. Snow, 'The Theory of Risk Classification' in Georges Dionne (ed.), *Handbook of Insurance* (2000) (above, n. 9), pp. 245–76

[18] Faure and Hartlief, supra n. 4, at 88–90.

[19] K.A. Froot, *The Financing of Catastrophe Risk* (University of Chicago Press, Chicago 1999).

[20] R.A. Epstein, 'Catastrophic Responses to Catastrophic Risks' (1996) 12 Journal of Risk and Uncertainty 287–308; G.L. Priest, 'The Government, the Market and the Problem of Catastrophic Loss' (1996) 12 Journal of Risk and Uncertainty 219–37; L. Kaplow, 'Incentives and Government Relief for Risk' (1991) 4 Journal of Risk and Uncertainty 167–75.

[21] See H. Kunreuther, 'Mitigating Disaster Losses through Insurance' (1996) 12 Journal of Risk and Uncertainty 180–83; S.E. Harrington, 'Rethinking Disaster Policy' (2000) 23 Regulation – The Cato Review of Business and Government 40–46 and R. Schwarze and G.G. Wagner, 'In the Aftermath of Dresden. New Directions in German Flood Insurance' (2004) 29 Geneva Papers on Risk and Insurance 154–68.

to resolve the uninsurability problem. A condition is of course that the government charges an actuarially fair premium for its intervention.[22] This type of government intervention has, moreover, the advantage that *ex post* relief sponsored through the public purse can be avoided. Where the government acts as reinsurer, this at least has the advantage that a premium can be paid by those who actually cause or run the risk. It thus facilitates market solutions, still provides incentives for the prevention of disasters and avoids a negative redistribution from taxpayers to victims. Thus an intervention by the state as reinsurer may avoid 'catastrophic responses to catastrophic risks'.[23]

Recently, Kunreuther and Michel-Kerjan have also argued in favour of this type of government provided reinsurance. They argue that one advantage is that the government has the capacity to diversify the risks over the entire population and to spread past losses to future generations, thus creating a form of cross-time diversification which the private market could not achieve.[24] On the other hand, they argue that, especially as far as terrorism is concerned, government participation in insurance programmes is crucial since the risk of terrorist attacks is partly in the government's control and the government can have more information on ongoing terrorist groups' activities through intelligence services.[25]

There are many examples of governments intervening in the financing of catastrophe risks, whereby the government acts as reinsurer of last resort. A well-known example in the field of natural catastrophes is provided by the case of France. France introduced mandatory insurance against natural disasters and reinsurance is provided through the Caisse Centrale de Réassurance (CCR). This CCR provides reinsurance via the state and even provides for unlimited coverage for natural disasters and technological risks.[26] The French state provides an unlimited guarantee to

---

22 M.G. Faure, 'Financial Compensation for Victims of Catastrophes: A Law and Economics Perspective' (2007) 29 Law & Policy 358.

23 Epstein, above, n. 20. See in this respect also H. Kunreuther and M. Pauly, 'Rules rather than Discretion: Lessons from Hurricane Katrina' (2006) 33 Journal of Risk and Uncertainty 113, arguing that this government's role in assisting the supply side allows avoiding the inefficiencies and inequities associated with disaster assistance.

24 H. Kunreuther and E. Michel-Kerjan, 'Challenges for Terrorism Risk Insurance in the United States' (2004) 18 Journal of Economic Perspectives 210.

25 H. Kunreuther and E. Michel-Kerjan, 'Insurability of (Mega-) Terrorism Risk: Challenges and Perspectives', in *Terrorism Risk Insurance in OECD Countries* (OECD 2005), pp. 107–48.

26 For further information on this CCR, see http://www.ccr.fr (last accessed 25 September 2012).

the CCR, which could never be provided by an ordinary insurer.[27] Many other examples of the government acting as reinsurer of catastrophe risks exist; in many countries, since 9/11, the government also intervenes in the reinsurance of terrorism risk.[28]

Of course it is not difficult to point at many differences between natural disasters or terrorism on the one hand and a financial crisis on the other. For example, the absolute economic impact of a financial crisis can be huge because of the worldwide interrelatedness of banks, issuers of securities and industry. Natural and technological disasters can have widespread damage as well (with huge amounts of losses resulting from it), but the disasters are usually limited to a certain population and some part of the public budget may be possible for compensating victims. The predictability of the total amount of the loss in case of financial disasters can be more problematic.

A second difference is that the causes of natural disasters or terrorism can usually be easily defined. In a financial crisis it is not so easy to determine whether the economic failure of a firm traces back to the financial crisis or is induced by general mismanagement. Hence the endogeneity of the risk may be a much more serious problem in case of a financial crisis. Still there are a few lessons to be learned from the literature and the states' policy in the field of catastrophes.

First, in the field of catastrophes many scholars have pointed at the risk of the so-called 'charity hazard', suggesting that an *ex post* payment by government to victims of (natural) catastrophes may create a moral hazard problem on the side of the victims.[29] The same problem arises also in the case of bailouts after a financial crisis. Hence in both cases there may be reasons to avoid, in the words of Epstein[30] 'catastrophic responses to catastrophic risk'.[31]

Second, also in the case of natural catastrophes a structural solution may be warranted to avoid randomness and *ad hoc*-ism.

Third, the case of catastrophes shows that a multi-layered approach could be followed, whereby the advantages of insurance (with the

---

27 V. Bruggeman, M.G. Faure and K. Fiore, 'The Government as Reinsurer of Catastrophe Risks?' (2010) 35 Geneva Papers on Risk and Insurance 381.

28 For an overview see Bruggeman, Faure and Fiore, above, n. 27.

29 M.J. Browne and R.E. Hoyt, 'The Demand for Flood Insurance: Empirical Evidence' (2000) 20(3) Journal of Risk and Uncertainty 291–306; P.A. Rashky and H. Weck-Hanneman, 'Charity Hazard – a Real Hazard to Natural Disaster Insurance?' (2007) 7 Environmental Hazard 321–9.

30 Epstein, above, n. 20.

31 Ibid.

possibilities of risk differentiation) are used to the full extent (thus providing incentives to the prevention of risks), whereby government only intervenes as reinsurer or lender of last resort to provide capacity where commercial (re)insurance markets would fail.[32]

Fourth, making compensation for victims of catastrophes the joint responsibility of insurers and government may provide for an optimal combination of incentives of all parties involved: insurers, specialised in risk differentiation can take preventive measures through risk classification and monitoring. The state, being exposed to the residual risk will also have incentives, for example in the case of natural catastrophes, to take preventive measures to avoid the catastrophe in the first place. Any economies of scope argument may also be valid here: government may be better placed to prevent terrorist attacks or to build dykes to prevent flooding, for instance. These arguments apply to a large extent *mutatis mutandis* to the case of financial crisis-risks as well.

III. MULTI-LAYERED INSURANCE APPROACH AGAINST FINANCIAL CRISES

A. General Outline

A multi-layered approach can be introduced whereby a first layer is typically borne by the financial institution itself. The second layer of losses is covered by private insurance companies and reinsurance. The third layer of losses is covered by the public budget whereby the government becomes a reinsurer of last resort. This model, so we propose, also has capacity to be applied to potential losses caused by a financial crisis.

While it is not likely that the economic risks of a financial crisis can be fully insured by private insurers, because insurers are highly intertwined with financial markets and because of the sheer amount of funds that are needed, the introduction of private insurance can reduce the risk of the public providing subsidies to firms, which are in trouble, even without financial crisis. More technically spoken, a multi-layered insurance programme can serve as a screening device that reduces the likelihood of granting non-eligible subsidies, when a public agency has to decide on a huge amount of applications for subsidies in a short time.

The *first* layer of a multi-layered insurance programme is typically

32 Schwarze and Wagner, above, n. 21.

the requirement that the insurance holder bears a part of the costs by himself.[33] This is an incentive for firms not to engage in moral hazard, but it may also help to overcome adverse selection. For example, the requirement to hold enough equity to compensate temporary losses may be understood as a sort of obligation for firms to self-insure a part of the losses in the event of a financial crisis. In addition, a firm may freely adopt Corporate Governance Codes, in order to signal insurers that the firm strives for high standards of management. This kind of self-selection may lead to a reduction of premiums for insurance and may also be a convincing argument for the public to speedily grant aid in the event of a financial crisis.

The *second* layer consists of private insurers that offer risk adjusted insurance contracts to firms, which will cover the risk of becoming illiquid and which will guarantee the maintenance of a firm's operations. Although in the case of a severe financial crisis, this private part of the financial safety net will often not be sufficient to rescue all firms, it will nevertheless contribute to financial stability. The most significant aspect of the second layer is that insurers will undertake investigations (due diligence and stress tests), in order to calculate the risk adjusted premiums for firms. By doing such investigations information about a firm's economic performance and financial stability will be uncovered. This information is of great importance, when a public agency has to decide quickly whether a subsidy is applicable. While in 'normal' times a public agency may have enough time and resources to undertake its own *ex post* investigations, whether a firm is eligible for benefit, in times of a financial crisis the public administration will be overburdened by applications for financial help and can hence refer to the information provided by insurance companies.

Again, there is a parallel to the insurance of natural catastrophes. For example, after introducing the National Flood Insurance Program (NFIP) in the US in 1968, it was responsible for developing flood maps and gathering all the information which is needed to calculate risk adjusted insurance premiums. Thereby systematically certain high-risk areas were detected, which have a flooding risk of 1 per cent per year. Also, the Community Rating System became installed which constantly monitors the efforts of communities to reduce the flooding risk. Those efforts to reduce the flooding risk result in turn in lower insurance premiums.[34]

We should add one note here: in our system, the *second* layer would

---

33 Kunreuther and Michel-Kerjan, above, n. 24.
34 Michel-Kerjan, above, n. 1.

consist of an intervention of private insurers. However, in practice, several alternatives have developed to deal with catastrophic risk as alternatives to insurance. One obvious example concerns the use of the financial market for catastrophes in so-called catastrophe bonds. Although it may seem a strange option to use financial instruments to deal with risks posed by financial institutions, this option should certainly not be ruled out. For example, catastrophe bonds as a means of reinsurance have the advantage that third parties (private financial investors) cover a part of the risk, while otherwise taxpayers would have to step in. One could also imagine that governments issue catastrophe bonds directly, in order to avoid using taxpayer's money in case of a catastrophe. For example, Mexico did so in collaboration with the World Bank in 2006 and 2009 in the form of a three-year maturity bond that covers hurricanes and earthquakes. And, it has been proposed to transfer this instrument to the US NFIP as well.[35]

At the *third* layer the public steps in as a 'reinsurer of last resort' and may grant subsidies. While at the second layer private insurance companies can only diversify risk horizontally between actual firms of a risk pool, government can diversify the risks over the entire population of firms and spread past losses to future taxpayers, which is a sort of cross-time diversification of risk which private insurance markets cannot achieve.[36] Again, because of the information which is generated by private insurance firms on the second layer and the signals that are freely given by firms on the first layer, public agencies can make timely decisions on subsidies with a considerably reduced failure rate.

B. Possible Problems

Admittedly, it is sufficient at this juncture, to point to the potential of insurance for dealing with financial crisis via a multi-layered insurance approach. However, we do realise that a lot of practical 'details' may still have to be answered which can be crucial for the effectiveness of the system. The first concern, is whether the multi-layered framework should be provided as a protection against financial crisis. Theoretically the system could be applicable both to financial intermediaries as well as to companies in the real economy. However, the bailing out, for which we precisely want to present an alternative, especially took place as far as financial intermediaries are concerned. Therefore, for simplicity, we

---

35 Michel-Kerjan, above, n. 1.

36 Kunreuther and Michel-Kerjan, above, n. 24.

explored the possibilities of our model first for financial institutions, although it could be applicable to the real economy as well.

A second issue is how one distinguishes whether losses are caused by a financial crisis. This problem is as such not new. It also appears in the insurance of natural catastrophes where, for example, in France specific insurance coverage is only provided when damage is caused by a natural catastrophe. Hence, in France it has to be determined whether an event can be classified as a natural catastrophe. Likewise in our case it will have to be determined whether a financial problem can be classified as a financial crisis, as a result of which the proposed system will be triggered. In the literature those decisions are associated with 'sorting costs'[37] and can as such be overcome as well. The example of France shows that the government will take an administrative decision declaring a particular event a natural catastrophe, as a result of which the system will be triggered.[38] A similar system could thus be used in our model as well to deal with the sorting costs: government could declare a particular stressful financial situation 'a financial crisis' as a result of which the multi-layered approach will be triggered. Thereby an advantage of the proposed approach is that the government can also refer to the specific information which insurers have already collected. However, the official declaration of financial crisis will of course not mean that all damages claimed by the insured companies will be paid by the system. It will obviously still have to be determined whether the business failure and resulting problems of the financial intermediaries were really caused by the financial crisis and not by endogenous factors such as mismanagement.

Third, we referred to government intervening as a reinsurer of last resort to grant financial aid. This assumes that the intervention of government in the *third* layer would amount to a subsidy. That should of course not necessarily be the case. It has been argued that an efficient reinsurance by the government would suppose that risk-based premiums should be charged in order to provide incentives to invest in cost effective loss prevention measures.[39] State provided reinsurance should thus in principle use risk-based

---

37 See S. Levmore and K.D. Logue, 'Insuring against Terrorism – and Crime' (2003) 102 Michigan Law Review 268–327.

38 O. Moreteau, 'Policing the Compensation of Victims of Catastrophes: Combining Solidarity and Self-responsibility, in Shifts in Compensation between Private and Public Systems' in W.H. van Boom and M.G. Faure (eds), *Shifts in Compensation between Private and Public Systems* (Springer, Vienna/New York 2007) and O. Moreteau, M. Cannarsa and F. Lafay, 'France in Financial Compensation for Victims of Catastrophes' in M.G. Faure and T. Hartlief (eds), *A Comparative Legal Approach* (Springer, Vienna/New York 2006) pp. 81–118.

39 A. Gron and A.O. Sykes, 'A Role for Government?' (2002) 25 Regulation 44–51.

premiums as far as possible to reflect actual risk.[40] Nevertheless, the intervention of government as reinsurer has been criticized because it would amount to a subsidy.[41] However, government reinsurance should of course not necessarily be provided at a reduced cost.[42] To the extent it is feasible the government should charge a price for the reinsurance it provides. To the extent this is possible the subsidy character of the government intervention is reduced.

A fourth and complicated issue is whether a multi-layered coverage system for financial crisis should be made mandatory. Here the parallel with natural catastrophes may not be that obvious. In the case of natural catastrophes the system is often made mandatory (like in France and Belgium) and the suggestions to come to comprehensive natural disaster insurance, repeatedly made by Kunreuther[43] also seem to be based on a mandatory system of insurance.[44] The arguments supporting compulsory insurance for natural disasters are that potential victims largely underestimate risks. Behavioural experiments also show that individuals do not take insurance against low probability high loss events, even if it would increase their utility.[45] Behavioural problems like bounded rationality cause individuals to take an 'it will not happen to me' attitude and hence not to purchase insurance coverage.[46] However, these behavioural arguments based on limited information and bounded rationality which support mandatory insurance in the case of natural catastrophes may not apply in the case of financial intermediaries who seek coverage against risks caused by a financial crisis. As a starting point the system should therefore be voluntary. The advantage is that a separating equilibrium is created to distinguish between the good and the bad risks. Those who would not seek insurance coverage (presumably the bad risks) would then also not be bailed out, in order to preserve the credibility of the system.

The problem is, however, that the starting point to create the system in the first place was that financial risks are systemic. In other words:

---

40 Bruggeman, Faure and Fiore, above, n. 27, at 377–8.

41 Levmore and Logue, above, n. 37, at 304.

42 Kunreuther and Michel-Kerjan, above, n. 24, at 204 and at 211.

43 For example, Kunreuther and Pauly, above, n. 23.

44 Kunreuther, above, n. 21.

45 Paul Slovic, Baruch Fischoff, Sarah Lichtenstein, Bernhard Corrigan and Barbara Combs, 'Preference for Insuring against Probable Small Losses: Insurance Implications' (1977) 44 The Journal of Risk and Insurance 60–61 and 70–71.

46 Kunreuther, above, n. 21, at 175; M.G. Faure and V. Bruggeman, 'Catastrophic Risks and First Party Insurance' (2008) 15 Connecticut Insurance Law Journal 21–7.

destabilisation of one financial intermediary (like Lehman Brothers) could lead to the destabilisation of the entire economy. If the system is supposed to prevent these kinds of systemic risks there may be an argument in making it mandatory. However, this may create the problem that there could be a pooling equilibrium in which it is no longer possible to distinguish between good and bad risks. Moreover, a system of mandatory insurance unavoidably always lead to a cross-subsidisation whereby good risks finance bad risks.[47] The question therefore arises whether it is possible, even under mandatory insurance, to attain a separating equilibrium; in other words, distinguishing between good and bad risks. Again, the example of natural catastrophes may be instructive. For example, in Belgium there is mandatory insurance against flooding, included in the fire insurance. However, premiums are not fixed and can hence be differentiated. Thus good risks, for example, protecting themselves with preventive measures against flooding, can, even in a mandatory insurance system, still be rewarded as a result of risk differentiation.

The problem remains, however, that insurers should still have sufficient information to punish the bad risks with higher premiums and reward the good risks with lower premiums. If that were not the case the risk would remain that a financial institution has incentives to behave as a gambler (counting to be protected by the system). As a general rule one could therefore hold that the system could be mandatory in order to prevent systemic risks, but this supposes that insurers charge risk-differentiated premiums and are able to monitor financial institutions adequately. But those issues have to be examined in more detail in further research.

CONCLUDING REMARKS

In this chapter we transfer insights from the theory and practice of insuring technological and natural disasters to the idea of insuring the financial risk of financial intermediaries in case of a financial crisis. Although technological and natural catastrophes are certainly different from financial crises in many respects, it is striking that both events have similar features with regard to the problems that an adequate insurance for both risks has to overcome. This implies that it is theoretically possible to insure financial intermediaries against the risk of financial crisis. More practically it is possible to borrow 'insurance technology' from the technique of insuring natural and technological disasters.

---

47 Faure, above, n. 22, at 349–50.

At the heart of our proposal is the idea of a multi-layered approach which comprises self-insurance, private insurance and the state as reinsurer of last resort. These three layers of insurance have to be well-matched, in order to overcome a pooling equilibrium, undue state intervention and coordination problems. While these are all serious problems, they are not specific to our proposal and can be tackled by employing insights from insurance theory, antitrust and public choice.

One major advantage of our proposal is that insurance companies can monitor financial institutions and hence contribute to the prevention of financial crises. Of course, the effectiveness of the system will to a large extent depend upon the ability (and willingness) of insurance companies to actively exercise this monitoring. Moreover, we of course do not claim that monitoring by insurers is the only remedy to prevent financial crises. Other instruments (not addressed in this chapter), like regulation and a reform of corporate governance in banks[48] may have a far more important role to play in that respect. Our focus was firstly on the role that insurance could play in preventing financial crises and secondly about intervening in case crises would arise. The main thrust of our paper is that the role of insurers in that respect can be far more promising than the current practice of bailing out of financial institutions.

Notwithstanding our optimistic stance, we are aware that our proposal is only a first step on the way to an insurance approach towards the avoidance and management of financial crises.

---

48 See M.F. Hellwig, 'Systemic Risk in the Financial Sector: An Analysis of the Subprime-Mortgage Financial Crisis' (2009) 157 *The Economist* 129–207.

14. Transforming bailouts into investments: A proposal for the creation of the Federal Government Investment Corporation

Jeffrey Manns

INTRODUCTION

The European debt crisis has reignited the spectre of fear consuming markets and the return of bailouts for the financial world. The problem is that the US is ill-prepared for extending another round of lifelines to the financial sector. American politicians missed an opportunity to institutionalise a framework for handling future bailouts as they assumed financial reforms would render bailouts unnecessary.

In spite of politicians' optimism (or hubris), future bailouts are a matter of inevitability as the question is when, rather than whether, government intervention may address future crises.[1] The institutional design challenge is how to create a lasting framework to ensure that bailouts both mitigate systemic risks and safeguard taxpayers' interests.

The danger of not having a plan in place is that political capture or panic will lead to *ad hoc* bailouts that serve primarily as wealth transfers from the public to private sector. The US government succumbed to this fate in its response to the depths of the crisis in 2008–09. The government pursued a 'break even' approach for its overall investments and failed to impose meaningful reforms on beneficiaries or to reap returns commensurate with the risk to taxpayers.[2]

---

[1] See, for example, M. Deryugina, 'Shaping Global Financial Reform' (2009) 28 Review of Banking and Financial Law 683, 707–08 (discussing the consensus that 'government bailouts of large systemically significant institutions are inevitable . . . to prevent systemic disruption').

[2] See L. Montgomery, 'TARP Expected to Cost US Only $25 Billion',

Instead, the US government should approach bailouts as long-term investments and institutionalise contingency plans for future crises. Aid should stabilise financial markets during crises, yet be tied to long-term returns, shared sacrifices by beneficiaries, and structural reforms to mitigate moral hazard. The key to reform would be the creation of an independent agency that can serve as an 'investor of last resort' without facing conflicting regulatory responsibilities or vulnerability to political pressures. The Federal Government Investment Corporation (FGIC) would seek to depoliticise bailouts by establishing clear contours and conditions for aid to ensure beneficiaries share risks and returns with the government.[3]

The FGIC would serve as the bailout complement to the Federal Deposit Insurance Corporation (FDIC). While the FDIC's function is to wind up insolvent banks and systemically important financial institutions,[4] no single government institution is in a position to address bailouts.[5] The FGIC would fill this gap by establishing express, *ex ante* conditions for receiving aid that temper corporate risk taking, protect taxpayers and establish clear contours for bailouts. First, aid would be contingent on managers, shareholders, and creditors of ben-

Washington Post, 30 November 2010 (discussing the federal government's 'break even' objective for overall TARP investments).

[3] A number of academics have recognised the significance of the government's emergency liquidity provider role in stabilising the economy during financial crises. See, for example, S. Fischer, 'On the Need for an International Lender of Last Resort' (1999) 13 Journal of Economic Perspectives 85–9 (calling for international cooperation to provide emergency liquidity for financial markets due to the limited financial capacities of individual governments); S.L. Schwarcz, 'Too Big to Fail?: Recasting the Financial Safety Net' in L. Mitchell and A. Wilmarth (eds), *The Panic of 2008: Causes, Consequences, and Implications for Reform* (Edward Elgar, Cheltenham, UK and Northampton, MA, USA 2010), pp. 10–11 (calling for the creation of an equivalent of the market maker liquidity provider role for individual stocks for debt markets as a whole to ensure liquidity for emergency sales of debt); R.M. Solow, 'On the Lender of Last Resort' in Charles P. Kindleberger et al. (eds), *Financial Crises: Theory, History, and Policy* (Cambridge University Press, Cambridge 1982) (laying out the government's indispensable role in providing emergency liquidity).

[4] See Helen A. Garten, 'A Political Analysis of Bank Failure Resolution' (1994) 74 Boston University Law Review 429, 472–5 (discussing the evolution of the FDIC's bank liquidation and alternative resolution procedures); S.V. Ragalevsky and S.J. Ricardi, 'Anatomy of a Bank Failure' (2009) 126 Banking Law Journal 867, 868–70 (discussing the role and workings of the FDIC).

[5] See S.L. Schwarcz, 'Regulating Complexity in Financial Markets' (2009) 87 Washington University Law Review 216 (discussing the shortcomings of not having the government provide market liquidity during a crisis).

eficiaries facing upfront reductions in their respective stakes (based on the scale of the FGIC's investment) to deter over-reliance on aid and excessive risk taking. Second, the FGIC would assume a proportional stake in beneficiaries and seek long-term returns. Third, beneficiaries would be required to implement corporate governance reforms, including the appointment of independent directors in proportion to the government's stake, and to adopt substantive reforms to target the roots of systemic risk.[6]

A significant challenge is how to avoid having FGIC investments cause government overstretch and excessive entanglement with the private sector. The conditions the FGIC imposes must be draconian enough to deter corporations from seeking FGIC funds except *in extremis*. The FGIC must also face limits on when it is able to make investments, the level and duration of those investments, and the degree of control it can exert over private companies.

The FGIC should be limited to investing in systemically significant institutions.[7] The FGIC would be required to establish capital requirement guidelines (analogous to capital requirements that financial institutions currently face) to ensure that bailout beneficiaries have a realistic prospect of repaying those investments.[8] These guidelines would serve to delineate the dividing line between the respective roles of the FGIC and FDIC in investing in and winding down systemically significant institutions.

---

[6] Under the Troubled Asset Relief Program, the Treasury Department has the right to appoint two government directors to beneficiaries' boards if they miss their payments for six consecutive quarters. See Office of the Special Inspector General for the Troubled Asset Relief Program, Quarterly Report to Congress, 21 July 2010, at 72, available at: http://sigtarp.gov/reports/congress/2010/July2010_Quarterly_Report_to_Congress.pdf (last accessed 25 September 2012).

[7] The Dodd-Frank Act designated commercial banking groups with assets of $50 billion or more as 'systemically important financial institutions' (SIFIs), and empowered the Financial Stability Oversight Council to designate non-bank financial institutions as SIFIs. See A.E. Wilmarth, Jr., 'The Dodd-Frank Act: A Flawed and Inadequate Response to the Too-Big-to-Fail Problem' (2011) 89 Oregon Law Review 993–6. SIFIs are subject to special prudential standards and exposed to potential Orderly Liquidation Authority (OLA) wind-ups. In contrast, this chapter views potential bailout beneficiaries as a broader pool of 'systemically significant' firms.

[8] See, for example, J.W. Verret, 'Treasury, Inc.: How the Bailout Reshapes Corporate Theory and Practice' (2010) 27 Yale Journal on Regulation 301 (discussing how financial regulators can shape a bank's business model by adjusting capital requirements); C.K. Whitehead, 'Reframing Financial Regulation' (2010) 90 Boston University Law Review 26–8 (arguing that the design of capital requirements is key for shaping banks' risk taking).

The FGIC would also face substantive limits in the amount and duration of its investments to prevent *de facto* nationalisation of private enterprises. Investments would need to be capped at a percentage of the market capitalisation of beneficiaries to ensure that the other stakeholders will still have significant skin in the game.[9] The duration of investments should also be limited to a period of five years, a time frame designed to be sufficient to last through a cyclical correction and rebound.

Sceptics would argue that there is no point in imposing limits on bailouts because if a crisis is large enough politicians and regulators will suspend the rules.[10] Nothing short of a constitutional amendment can fully constrain politicians' ability to dole out aid with few or no strings attached.[11] However, creating a clear, depoliticised process for bailouts would make it more difficult for politicians to short-circuit rules and engage in giveaways.[12]

I. BLUEPRINT FOR THE FEDERAL GOVERNMENT INVESTMENT CORPORATION

The Dodd-Frank Act 2010 left a 'bailout gap' by failing to create a comprehensive framework for government intervention in the (likely) event financial reforms fail to pre-empt future crises.[13] While the Act more clearly delineated the circumstances for liquidating financial companies,[14]

---

[9] See O.H. Dombalagian, 'Requiem for the Bulge Bracket? Revisiting Investment Bank Regulation' (2010) 85 Indiana Law Review 836 (discussing how the absence of a direct financial stake in securitisations skewed issuers' incentives).

[10] See K. Ayotte and D.A. Skeel, Jr., 'Bankruptcy or Bailouts?' (2010) 35 Journal of Corporate Law 472–3 (discussing how regulators routinely suspend prompt corrective action rules when systemically important companies stumble).

[11] See R.W. Adler, 'Unfunded Mandates and Fiscal Federalism: A Critique' (1997) 50 Vanderbilt Law Review 1209 (suggesting that only a constitutional amendment could impose limits on Congress's spending powers).

[12] See K.C. Kettering, 'Securitization and Its Discontents: The Dynamics of Financial Product Development' (2008) 29 Cardozo Law Review 1647 (discussing how the FDIC's institutional design makes bank wind-ups less politicised); S.A. Ramirez, 'Depoliticizing Financial Regulation', (2000) 41 William and Mary Law Review 511 (discussing how institutional design can mitigate the politicisation of financial regulators).

[13] See David Zaring, 'A Lack of Resolution' (2010) 60 Emory Law Journal 97, 105 (discussing how the Dodd-Frank Act sought to prevent future bailouts of financial institutions).

[14] See Dodd-Frank Wall Street Reform and Consumer Protection Act (Dodd-Frank Act), Public Law Number 111-203, § 204, 124 Stat. 1376, 1454

at best an *ad hoc* approach exists for dealing with otherwise solvent companies that need emergency financing. This uncertainty is an invitation to opportunism as companies have perverse incentives to take on larger size and risks, so that the government would have little choice but to bail them out. The price of filling this gap through last-minute fixes may be far too costly – either in leaving out firms that merit aid or in having desperation bailouts that fuel opportunism.[15]

The challenge is establishing a credible commitment to handle bailouts in a structured way. The goal of an investor of last resort role would be to depoliticise bailouts by creating an independent agency and clear requirements for investments in distressed companies.[16] The FGIC would seek to provide taxpayers with long-term returns commensurate with the risks assumed and to deter over-reliance on aid.

II. CRAFTING AN INVESTOR PARADIGM FOR THE FGIC

The virtue of a long-term investment approach is that it would balance firms' need for emergency funding with deterrence against dipping too early or too deeply into the government's well and transforming aid into a *de facto* hedge position. The government is uniquely positioned to act as a long-term investor because its taxing power allows it to borrow vast sums for long durations at below market terms.[17]

The dilemma is determining how to price and condition aid. Without a bailout framework in place, politicians will be tempted to give aid with few strings attached to stimulate the economy at any cost.[18] For this reason the goal of seeking to 'break even' on overall bailout investments may

(2010) (delineating the FDIC's criteria for winding up systemically important financial institutions).

[15] See A.J. Levitin, 'In Defense of Bailouts' (2011) 99 Georgetown Law Journal 499–500 (discussing the implications of false negatives and positives on the efficacy of bailouts).

[16] See L. Schultz Bressman and R.B. Thompson, 'The Future of Agency Independence' (2010) 63 Vanderbilt Law Review 611–16 (laying out the merits of independent agencies).

[17] See, for example, A. Gelpern, 'Building a Better Seating Chart for Sovereign Restructurings' (2004) 53 Emory Law Journal 1117–18 (discussing the advantages sovereign borrowers enjoy over private sector parties).

[18] See M. Boardman, 'Known Unknowns: The Illusion of Terrorism Insurance' (2005) 93 Georgetown Law Journal 784–5 (discussing politicians' temptations to federalise liabilities).

seem to be an alluring middle ground. By disavowing any motive other than stabilisation, the government may reassure markets that it does not intend to usurp private roles.[19] However, if the 'cost' of excessive risk taking is simply a loan on favourable terms, then banks have little to lose from pushing the envelope and leveraging the government's borrowing power.

In contrast, approaching bailouts as long-term investments recognises the need to temper moral hazard from bailouts. An investment approach allows the government to stabilise markets while deterring over-reliance on state financing. However, delineating the scope of long-term return objectives poses a challenge. The FGIC would be tantamount to a natural monopoly (since it would offer financing when markets are unable or unwilling to do so).[20] It would have leverage to impose draconian terms for its financing services.[21] The conventional solution to curb natural monopolies is rate regulation, in which monopolists are limited to regulatory-set rates of return rather than profit maximization.[22] Applying rate regulation to the FGIC would be difficult to administer and time-consuming and could politicise the process.[23] The investor of last resort would always be at the mercy of rate regulators and may face pressure to keep rates of return artificially low and/or to steer investments towards influential groups.

The limits of rate regulation suggest the virtue of establishing a clearer, easily administrable principle to shape investment decisions. The most straightforward way to temper the government's monopoly power, while securing an investment return, would be to implement a 'proportional share' principle for government investments in distressed companies. The FGIC would receive convertible preferred stock whose value is proportional to the distressed company's overall capitalisation.[24] In other

---

19 See, for example, 12 USC. § 1823(c)(4)(A) (2006); see also 12 C.F.R. ch. 3, pt. 360.1 (2010) (laying out the FDIC's break-even mandate).

20 See S. Ghosh, 'Decoding and Recoding Natural Monopoly, Deregulation, and Intellectual Property' (2008) University of Illinois Law Review 1138–9 (discussing how a natural monopoly exists when only one company can cost-effectively provide goods or services).

21 See S. Breyer, *Regulation and Its Reform* (Harvard University Press, Boston 1982), pp. 15–16.

22 See J. Rossi, 'Universal Service in Competitive Retail Electric Power Markets: Whither the Duty to Serve?' (2000) 21 Energy Law Journal 34–5 (laying out the rationale for rate regulation of natural monopolies).

23 See J.P. Tomain, 'The Past and Future of Electricity Regulation' (2002) 32 Environmental Law 450 (discussing how rate regulation is a 'politically charged' process).

24 This approach contrasts significantly with the TARP warrants cover-

words, if a company has a market capitalisation of USD50 billion and the investor of last resort invests USD25 billion, then the federal government should receive convertible preferred shares whose value is one-third of the outstanding stock. Convertible preferred stock would give the FGIC priority over ordinary shareholders for any distributions.[25]

The government would have a five-year time frame in which it alone would have the option of converting its preferred shares to common stock (and reaping the returns of an economic rebound). This approach would also seek to use interconnectedness for a productive purpose.[26] The time frame would give the FGIC flexibility to engage in gradual draw-downs of investments based on economic circumstances, while guarding against a permanent, creeping transformation of the economy. This period would give the FGIC leverage to impose limits and oversight on managers, as well as equity and debtholders who might otherwise be tempted to revert to their pre-crisis risk taking. To avoid excessive entanglement with the private sector, investments should be limited to 50 per cent of the equity value of any recipient. This approach would provide an easily administrable way to institutionalise an investment approach and limit dangers of favouritism in financing terms.

III. LINKING BAILOUTS TO SHARED SACRIFICES BY STAKEHOLDERS

An equally important challenge would be to delineate who will be potentially eligible for bailouts, to what degree, and with what consequences. The key to designing bailouts is deterrence to mitigate moral hazard and over-reliance on government funds. Bailouts must come with a significant

ing only 15 per cent of the value of the Treasury Department's preferred stock purchases. See Press Release, US Dep't of the Treasury, Treasury Announces Warrant Repurchase and Disposition Process for the Capital Purchase Program (26 June 2009), available at http://www.treasury.gov/press-center/press-releases/Pages/200962612255225533.aspx (last accessed 25 September 2012)

[25] See M.A. Woronoff and J.A. Rosen, 'Understanding Anti-Dilution Provisions in Convertible Securities' (2005) 74 Fordham Law Review 144 (discussing convertible preferred stock's priority in bankruptcy).

[26] Throughout the crisis financial interconnections have been blamed for magnifying systemic risks. See M. Brunnermeier et al., 'The Fundamental Principles of Financial Regulation' (2009) 11 Geneva Report on the World Economy 24. Interconnecting the financial fates of the FGIC and beneficiaries is designed to do the opposite by making it difficult for stabilised companies to revert to their wayward ways.

enough impact on all levels of stakeholders to make government intervention a last resort. For this reason, managers, shareholders and creditors must face reductions in their stakes as a *quid pro quo* for aid, so that no stakeholders would have an interest in prematurely pushing for bailout assistance.

Transforming bailouts into long-term investments would implicitly impact managers and shareholders by diluting their stakes in proportion to the government's investment, but creditors would not be directly affected. For this reason the sticking point to ensuring shared sacrifice would be reductions of creditors' stakes. Reductions to creditors' stakes could be accomplished through a number of different means. The simplest approach would be a direct reduction in their holdings, analogous to the bankruptcy treatment for creditors in which creditors would recoup a set percentage less of their investments as a condition for a bailout. Reductions could be accomplished through more indirect means such as postponement of payments to creditors (as they lose the time value of money). Alternatively, creditors' interests could be diluted, based on the scale of government investment and priority for government investments in bankruptcy. Imposing uniform reductions to all stakeholders' interests would provide a clear signal to corporate stakeholders of the tradeoffs for bailouts. However, it may make the most sense to give the FGIC discretion to condition the degree of reduction of creditors' interests to the speed, sustainability, and degree of recovery, so that stakeholders and the FGIC benefit from a swift and lasting rebound.

IV. TYING BAILOUTS TO CORPORATE GOVERNANCE AND SYSTEMIC RISK REFORM

Another facet of bailout reform would entail linking bailout aid to corporate governance and systemic risk reform. During the recent crisis government dollars swooped in to save the day, but the aid did little to change the underlying incentives to take destabilising risks (so long as institutions follow large enough herds). By serving as stabilisers, bailouts removed the sense of urgency for regulatory reform and empowered beneficiaries to leverage aid to lobby and stymie reform.[27]

Because bailouts undercut pressure for reform, the FGIC should make

[27] See B. Appelbaum, 'With Financial Overhaul Near, Lobbyists Focus on Regulators', *N.Y. Times*, 26 June 2010 (discussing how banks hired legions of lobbyists and lawyers to limit financial reforms).

substantive reforms an upfront condition of bailouts, the time when the government's leverage is at its peak. For example, it was clear before the bailouts that vast derivative liability exposure had magnified systemic risks in the financial sector.[28] The Dodd-Frank Act requires banks to relocate derivative trading outside of the FDIC-insured banking operations, but firms can keep derivatives trading within the parent bank holding company.[29] This fact means that bank holding companies can still indirectly leverage FDIC-guaranteed funds for their derivatives operations, which leaves great pressure on the government to intervene if a major participant faces a risk of default.[30]

The irony is that the government had leverage to tie bailouts to divestments of derivatives operations during the depths of the crisis (even if for the sake of stability the divestment date was delayed until after the crisis subsided). Economic crises generally do not sneak up out of nowhere and the current crisis was no exception, as numerous government and academic observers had documented the roots of systemic risks before the crisis's climax in late 2008 and early 2009.[31] Given the awareness of the problems, the FGIC would have been in an ideal position to impose systemic risk exposure changes as a *quid pro quo* for aid.

Another complementary condition would be to enhance internal monitoring of risk taking by requiring beneficiaries to seat truly independent directors on their boards. Many academics have documented the sham of independent directors being hand-selected by existing boards and failing to play any significant oversight role.[32] For this reason the FGIC could require beneficiaries to have independent directors selected by an outside body in proportion to the stake of the FGIC's investment. This approach would formally separate the government's financial and managerial roles and mitigate entanglement between the government and beneficiaries. But it would also ensure that beneficiaries face more meaningful internal

---

28 See C.M. Baker, 'Regulating the Invisible: The Case of Over the Counter Derivatives' (2010) 85 Notre Dame Law Review 1349–50.

29 See E. Wyatt, 'For Securities Industry, Finance Law Could Bring New Light to Derivatives', *N.Y. Times*, 15 July 2010.

30 See Dodd-Frank Act § 716.

31 See, for example, A. Ferrell and A. Saha, 'Securities Litigation and the Housing Market Downturn', (2009) 35 Journal of Corporate Law 97, 106–08 (providing an overview of when policy-makers began to recognise the root causes of the sub-prime mortgage crisis).

32 See, for example, V. Brudney, 'The Independent Director – Heavenly City or Potemkin Village? (1982) 95 Harvard Law Review 610–15; R. Gilson and R. Kraakman, 'Reinventing the Outside Director: An Agenda for Institutional Investors' (1991) 43 Stanford Law Review 874–7.

scrutiny to help reduce the likelihood of a repeat of their financial overstretch. This approach may be particularly significant for financial firms as true outsiders may be less likely to be drawn into the conventional wisdom of risk taking that enveloped the industry during the run up to the financial crisis.

V. BOOM-TIME ROLE FOR A CRISIS AGENCY

One legitimate question about the FGIC is what the agency would be doing during prosperous times when the need for bailouts was a distant prospect. The vice and virtue of the existing *ad hoc* system of bailouts has been that regulators could shift hats from their regulatory mode to focus on bailouts when crises arise. In theory agencies could leverage their regulatory expertise and make a more smooth and rapid transition to intervention to prop up the financial sector.[33]

The problem is that simultaneously wearing regulatory and bailout hats raises an inherent conflict of interest.[34] When enforcement of regulatory constraints may matter the most to mitigate the scope of financial overstretch, rules may end up marginalised by conflicting mandates. To avoid this conflict of interest the FGIC would not have a direct regulatory mandate that would potentially conflict with its bailout role. Overseeing long-term bailout investments would mean that a core staff would have ongoing responsibilities in monitoring bailout beneficiaries, even at the height of the economic cycle. If the FGIC were self-funded, its personnel would also manage the agency's investment portfolio to ensure the fund met its own liquidity guidelines. But even these roles would likely be insufficient to keep the skills of the FGIC's staff sharp, so that they would be ready for future bailouts.

For this reason it would be important for the FGIC staff to have a complementary function that would strengthen their understanding of financial markets without rising to the level of a conflicting regulatory role. One role the FGIC could play is to serve as a watchdog in monitoring both

---

[33] See, for example, E.R. Morrison, 'Is the Bankruptcy Code an Adequate Mechanism for Resolving the Distress of Systemically Important Institutions?' (2010) 82 Temple Law Review 462–3 (discussing the virtue of integrating regulators' monitoring role with the ability to intervene to support faltering companies).

[34] Regulators may wish to avoid admitting regulatory failure and not intervene until the cost to taxpayers is much higher. See J.C. Coffee, Jr., 'Systemic Risk After Dodd-Frank: Contingent Capital and the Need for Regulatory Strategies Beyond Oversight' (2011) 111 Columbia Law Review 822.

industry and regulators. The FGIC could assess the health of the financial sector, identify weaknesses and stressors, and make recommendations to regulators about how to address gaps in the system.[35] The FGIC would generate the type of information it would need to have to be in a position to make informed decisions about bailouts on short notice. By serving as both a watchdog and policy incubator, the FGIC would also ensure that reform ideas would be considered at an earlier point and be ready for implementation when crises arise.[36]

One related problem is how FGIC staffing would work as it would likely need to grow quickly in the midst of future economic crises. The FDIC offers an example of how accordion-like an agency can be in having a core staff expand to meet greater need for its services. For example, FDIC employment grew 80 per cent from 2007 to 2010 in response to their expanded crisis role from approximately 4,500 employees in 2007 to 8,150 employees in 2010.[37] The FGIC could similarly grow from a smaller core staff in response to greater staffing needs for dealing with future crises. While crises frequently hit a peak during a rapid period of strain to the financial system, the gathering storm of risk factors often takes much longer time to coalesce, which would give the FGIC time to gradually build its staffing strength.

VI. THE NEED TO IMPOSE LIMITS ON THE FGIC

A significant concern with the FGIC would be how to guard against government overstretch.[38] Creating too expansive a role for the FGIC may cause the FGIC to overextend itself by propping up uncompetitive companies or by taking on so many investments that it cannot effectively screen applicants' investment-worthiness.

One way to temper the FGIC's reach is to require the agency to justify

---

[35] This role would complement the vision for the Financial Services Oversight Council ('FSOC') and provide another set of eyes within the government examining and making recommendations about potential systemic risk concerns. See Bressman and Thompson, above, n. 16, at 627–9 (discussing the role of collaborative relationships under the plan for the FSOC).

[36] See, for example, B. Appelbaum, 'On Finance Bill, Lobbying Shifts to Regulations', *N.Y. Times*, 27 June 2010 (discussing the efficacy of lobbying to undercut the Dodd-Frank Act and its implementation).

[37] See FDIC Statistics at a Glance, available at: http://www.fdic.gov/bank/statistical/stats/2011mar/fdic.html (last accessed 25 September 2012).

[38] See Dombalagian, above, n. 9, at 835–6 (discussing the danger of ad hoc oversight and limits becoming 'window dressing').

investments by certifying that the danger of a beneficiaries' potential default raises systemic risks.[39] This approach would balance limits on the FGIC with recognition of the need for flexibility since what falls within the parameters of having 'serious adverse effects on financial stability or economic conditions' may vary from crisis to crisis.[40] The dividing line between too big or too interconnected to fail and less significant companies would be hotly contested. However, it is worth keeping in mind that the myriad of smaller companies and individuals would still have recourse to the political process to seek aid. This approach recognises both the need to limit the FGIC's scope and the political reality that Congress may face overwhelming pressure to offer relief for smaller entities and individuals if the crisis is large enough.

Another concern is the level of investment risk that the FGIC could assume. One danger is that the FGIC may face perverse incentives to send bad money after good money in an effort to justify and/or preserve initial bailout investments.[41] For this reason it would be desirable to establish minimum capital requirement guidelines for beneficiaries to ensure that the FGIC could have a reasonable prospect to recoup investments. This approach would be analogous to the capital requirements that banks must meet to avoid falling into receivership by the FDIC and being liquidated.[42] Capital requirements would likely be much lower (as corporations do not face the same risks banks face of 'a run on the bank').[43] However, the underlying principle would be similar: to delineate between companies that could remain solvent with FGIC investments and those on the brink of insolvency. Capital requirements, coupled with a cap limiting the FGIC

---

39 The Dodd-Frank Act defines systemic risk as 'a default' or 'a danger of default' that 'would have serious adverse effects on financial stability or economic conditions in the United States'. Dodd-Frank Act § 203(b). The Federal Reserve Board must certify that a firm's potential default raises this concern for the FDIC to assume receivership over a systemically important financial institution. Ibid.

40 Ibid at § 1603(b).

41 See Richard W. Painter, 'Bailouts: An Essay on Conflicts of Interest and Ethics When Government Pays the Tab' (2009) 41 McGeorge Law Review 159 (discussing the problem of the government trying to 'bail' itself out of poor bailout decisions).

42 See J. Hilsenrath, D. Paletta and A. Lucchetti, 'Goldman, Morgan Scrap Wall Street Model, Become Banks in Bid to Ride Out Crisis – End of Traditional Investment Banking, as Storied Firms Face Closer Supervision and Stringent New Capital Requirements', *Wall St. J.*, 22 September 2008, at A1.

43 See, for example, FDIC Board Adopts Final Rule on Investments in Non-Financial Firms (2011) 77 BNA Banking Report 959 (17 December) (discussing the FDIC's lower capital requirements for banks' equity investments in non-financial companies).

to no more than 50 per cent of the capitalisation of any given company, would limit the degree of the FGIC's risk exposure to any individual company.

VII. THE CHALLENGE OF SUSTAINING FGIC INDEPENDENCE

Critics may recognise that sustaining FGIC independence is an admirable goal, but argue that the temptation and opportunity for political and private actors to capture, politicise, or distort the FGIC's agenda will prove too overwhelming.[44] Politicians revel in directing funds to their corporate supporters to save jobs or bolster their district's economy,[45] and private companies are always eager to outsource their liabilities to the federal government.

A similar concern exists concerning the revolving door between the FGIC and Wall Street firms (and their legal and accounting service providers).[46] Many of the crucial political appointees who were asleep at the wheel during the recent crisis were from Wall Street or soon headed in that direction once their term in government service ended.[47] For the FGIC to work it would need financial acumen, but there is a genuine dilemma about to whom these actors would be beholden (either *ex ante* in terms of their connections or *ex post* when they are looking to cash in from their experience at the FGIC). The FGIC may need the talent to understand the complexities of its investment targets, but this expertise may come at a high price if FGIC employees engage in favouritism towards beneficiaries.

There is not an easy solution to the private capture problem or to the

---

[44] See, for example, N. Devins and D.E. Lewis, 'Not-So Independent Agencies: Party Polarization and the Limits of Institutional Design' (2008) 88 Boston University Law Review 479–88 (discussing the increase in political capture of ostensibly independent agencies over the last generation); R.E. Barkow, 'Insulating Agencies: Avoiding Capture Through Institutional Design' (2010) 89 Texas Law Review 19–41.

[45] See, for example, J. Zeleny, 'Rougher Road for Democrats Without Obama Atop Ticket', *N.Y. Times*, 4 July 2010 (discussing Democrats' efforts to localise campaigns by emphasising the positive impact of stimulus initiatives).

[46] See Barkow, above, n. 44, at 23.

[47] See Z.A. Goldfarb, 'Regulators are Finding Opportunities at Firms Looking for Government Experience', *Washington Post*, 30 December 2010 (discussing the revolving door of White House, Justice Department, SEC, and banking regulators to Wall Street and law firms).

overall challenges to the FDIC's independence.[48] One way to temper politicisation pressures is to impose limits on the nature and scope of the FGIC's investments. These limits may give the FGIC the ability to push back at politicians who are clamouring for their states' prospective beneficiaries to receive aid by pointing at the constraints the FGIC faces. For example, the FGIC could potentially point to its capital requirement guidelines to justify not investing in a company whose balance sheet is under water.

Another way to seek to preserve the FGIC's independence is to have self-financing of operations through existing investments.[49] This approach would insulate the FGIC from the need for further Congressional or Executive branch grants of money (and the related political strings that may come with that funding), except in exceptional circumstances. These monies could be invested in treasuries or other short-term instruments during times when they are not invested in bailout beneficiaries.

The challenge of private capture is more difficult to overcome.[50] One way to mitigate the concern of private capture would be to give FGIC employees higher salaries to woo and retain their expertise, but to impose a *quid pro quo* of sharper bars on joining firms that benefit from bailouts or their service providers (for example, law or accounting firms).[51] Most federal agencies currently have modest bars limiting their employees from dealing with their own former agency for one year.[52] To justify the higher salaries and deter private capture, both the duration and nature of the ban on working for beneficiaries should be more expansive for FGIC employees.[53]

---

[48] See Painter, above, n. 41, at 149–50 (discussing how 'the corrupting influence from private employment prospects is difficult to mitigate with regulation').

[49] The virtue of self-funding is that it would liberate the FGIC from political meddling or under-financing that could compromise its ability to fulfil its mandate. See, for example, J. Seligman, 'Self-Funding for the Securities and Exchange Commission' 28 Nova Law Review 238–9 (discussing how self-funding could free the SEC from political constraints and allow it to more adequately fulfil its mandate).

[50] For an overview of public choice theory, see D.A. Farber and P.P. Frickey, *Law and Public Choice: A Critical Introduction* (Chicago University Press, Chicago 1991); J.L. Mashaw, *Greed, Chaos, and Governance* (Yale University Press, New Haven 1997).

[51] See, for example, Painter, above, n. 41, at 154–7 (suggesting that government employees should face a one to two-year bar on receiving compensation from bailout beneficiaries).

[52] See 18 USC. § 207 (delineating the limits that former government officials face in dealing with their former agencies).

[53] Senior officials and elected representatives face greater restrictions on

A related concern is that creating the FGIC and entrusting the agency with a bailout fund would create incentives for the FGIC to make investments simply to justify its own existence and payroll. Bureaucracies are always tempted to work to spend their budget to justify future allocations and to produce results for congressional overseers and the public.[54] But the incentives to expand the mandate may be even sharper for the FGIC as its investor focus may mean that its internal and external benchmark for success will be the return on its investments. The irony is the FGIC's investments will be counter-cyclical as its moments of greatest passivity will likely be the peak of the investment cycle when market actors are reaping the highest returns. The FGIC may therefore be tempted by the same herding effects that distort market investing in the effort to chase higher returns.[55]

Overly aggressive investing by the FGIC may blur the line between investments in systemically significant companies facing liquidity problems and purely speculative investments. This concern is particularly important given the function of the FGIC. This approach would not only lock up investment funds that would be needed in an emergency, but also would raise concerns about excessive entanglement between the private and public sector. The ability to turn on bailouts when needed and turn them off when they are not needed is a tricky challenge that does not have an easy answer.

The best way to temper FGIC overstretch may be to deter prospective beneficiaries from seeking and accepting bailout investments. Investments by the FGIC must have significant enough consequences for managers, shareholders, and creditors of beneficiaries to make the appeal of FGIC investments truly a last resort. This approach would serve as a check not only on private sector companies but also on the FGIC by creating incentives to resist FGIC investment offers.

---

dealing with matters under their supervision, which would form a precedent for imposing more onerous restrictions on former FGIC officials. See 18 USC. § 207(d)–(e).

[54] See W.A. Niskanen, Jr., *Bureaucracy and Representative Government* (Transaction Publishers, New Brunswick 1971), pp. 12–14 (discussing how bureaucracies try to spend annual budgets to secure equal or higher budgets in the future).

[55] See T.J. Fitzpatrick, IV and C. Sagers, 'Faith-Based Financial Regulation: A Primer on Oversight of Credit Rating Organizations' (2009) 61 Administrative Law Review 590 (discussing growing empirical evidence of herding effects in financial markets).

CONCLUSION

Institutionalising an investor of last resort and delineating contours and conditions for future bailouts would help to stabilise markets by putting all parties on notice about the scope of potential intervention. At the same time, FGIC conditions of having managers, shareholders and creditors facing cuts to their stakes, proportional sharing of returns with the FGIC over a multi-year time horizon, and corporate governance reforms would provide disincentives for corporations to receive or rely excessively on FGIC funds. Sceptics may argue that any bailout framework would be swept aside by politicians in a crisis or serve as an opening bid for haggling with beneficiaries. But by establishing a bailout framework, this approach would raise the political costs of deviating from this process and giving sweetheart deals to Wall Street. This proposal would face political hurdles, yet it offers a practical pathway for addressing and defusing future financial crises and protecting taxpayers in the process.

PART IV

Sovereign debt issues

15. The treatment of contingent liabilities in a sovereign debt restructuring

Lee C. Buchheit and Mitu Gulati[1]

INTRODUCTION

The question of how should the contingent liabilities of sovereigns[2] be treated in a general restructuring of the debt of that sovereign has played only a minor role in the sovereign debt restructurings of the last 30 years. Probably the reason is because the aggregate size of such contingent liabilities – in comparison to the overall debt stocks – has in most cases been very small. Slathering government guarantees on third party debts, however, has recently become the tool of choice for many countries in their efforts to quell an incipient panic in their financial markets. Inevitably, some of those sovereigns will need to restructure their own debts one day and this component of their balance sheets, or perhaps better said, their off-balance sheets, will need to be addressed.

I. THE CHALLENGE

The central problem with contingent liabilities of this kind is the fact that they are contingent. Neither the beneficiary of the guarantee (the creditor) nor the sovereign guarantor can know at the outset whether the primary obligor (the borrower) will be able to repay the debt on its own.

Therein lies the challenge for the sovereign debt restructurer. If one forces the beneficiary to call on the sovereign guarantee as a means of bringing the liability into the main restructuring in order to treat it in a

[1] The authors wish to thank Anna Gelpern and Rodrigo Olivares-Caminal for their helpful comments on an earlier version of this chapter.

[2] For example government guarantees of the debts of state-owned enterprises or even private sector entities.

manner identical to other debts, the sovereign may be taking on its own shoulders a liability that, left on its own, would never have emerged from the cocoon of contingency. Why? Because the primary obligor may have paid it at maturity without government assistance.

Leaving large contingent liabilities out of the main debt restructuring, however, may plant a land mine on the road to debt sustainability once the restructuring closes. Is the restructurer to assume that (a) some (b) all or (c) none of those contingent liabilities will eventually wind up as direct claims against the sovereign? The answer to that question may dramatically affect whether the plenary debt restructuring will achieve its primary aim of returning the country to a sustainable debt position.

The creditor/beneficiary of a state guarantee has a right to feel more aggrieved about being dragged into a sovereign debt restructuring than does a direct creditor of the State. The beneficiary of such a guarantee by definition holds 'two name paper'; the beneficiary enjoys the credit of both the state and the primary obligor. By roping the beneficiary of a state guarantee into a debt workout, the additional credit protection resulting from the independent obligation of the primary obligor to pay the debt is lost.

II. THE OPTIONS

There are three possible ways of treating these contingent liabilities in a debt restructuring:

(a) *Ignore them.* Under this approach, the sovereign deals only with guarantees that are actually called by the beneficiary before the debt restructuring closes. No pressure is put on beneficiaries to call the guarantees.

(b) *Force the beneficiaries to call.* Careening to the other extreme, the sovereign debtor could attempt to force the beneficiaries to call on their state guarantees in order to bring the resulting – now actual, no longer contingent – liabilities into the sovereign's debt restructuring. Presumably, this could only be done by threatening to repudiate any post-closing call of the guarantee.

(c) *Call or do not call; you will receive the same consideration.* The third option is to tell beneficiaries that they are free to call or not as they choose, but if they elect to call on the state guarantee after the debt restructuring closes, the sovereign will honour it by delivering consideration having a net present value equal to what the creditor would have received had the claim been brought into the main restructuring.

III. THE PROBLEMS

Each of these options has its own set of problems.

Leaving the guarantees out of a restructuring altogether (Option (a) above) places the sovereign at risk that the financial predicates underlying the debt restructuring could be undone. A large slug of liabilities coming onto the balance sheet of the sovereign unexpectedly in the future could render obsolete the debt sustainability analysis upon which the financial terms of the main restructuring was based. This is a risk both to the sovereign debtor and to the other creditors that joined the restructuring.

But forcing the beneficiaries to call on the guarantees (Option (b) above), even if legally possible (which it probably would not be), compels the beneficiaries to give up their claims on the primary obligors. As noted above, this works a special hardship on guaranteed creditors in comparison with their direct creditor counterparts.

Finally, telling beneficiaries that they will receive the same consideration in settlement of their guarantees regardless of when they may call on those guarantees (Option (c) above) may not be a credible threat. If things begin to improve in the debtor country after the restructuring closes, will the government really be eager to default on an item of guaranteed debt soon thereafter? Probably not.

IV. THE PRACTICE

There has been no consistent practice in previous sovereign debt restructurings on this issue. The workouts of commercial bank sovereign loans in the 1980s generally followed Option (a) above. Beneficiaries were not required, nor even encouraged, to call on their sovereign guarantees.[3]

When the Highly Indebted Poor Country initiative got under way in the mid-1990s, the HIPC rules required that all contingent liabilities of the debtor countries be brought into the settlement.[4] To our knowledge,

---

[3] The telex sent by Mexico addressed to 'The International Banking Community' on 8 December 1982 (at the very beginning of the global debt crisis of the 1980s) contained draft 'Restructure Principles'. The debt subject to the restructuring referred to principal maturities falling due within a specified time period, 'but, in the case of any Debt which arises from a guarantee, endorsement, aval or similar instrument, only such payment obligations which are invoked and payable' during that time period. This practice appears to have been followed by the other sovereign debt restructurings of that era.

[4] See *The HIPC Debt Initiative – Elaboration of Key Features and Proposed*

however, the HIPC rules did not confide to the sovereign debtors how they were to achieve this if a creditor/beneficiary simply declined the offer.

At least one country has chosen Option (c) above (promise equal treatment of the creditor whenever the guarantee may be called). Grenada, in its debt restructuring of 2005, had outstanding government guarantees in an amount equal to 10 per cent of the country's total stock of debt. Grenada could not legally force the beneficiaries to call on the guarantees, but it did expressly warn the beneficiaries that they should expect no better treatment if they elected to stay out of the restructuring and call on the guarantee after the restructuring closed. As described in a 2006 article:

> Grenada's solution to this dilemma had three elements:
>
> - Beneficiaries of all government guarantees were given the option to call upon their guarantees at any time prior to the expiration date of the offer. The face amount of any guarantee called by a beneficiary would then be exchanged, at par, for the new bonds being issued in the exchange.
> - A beneficiary calling a guarantee in these circumstances was required to subrogate the Government to all of the beneficiary's claims against the primary obligor and any collateral securing the debt of the underlying project.
> - If a beneficiary elected *not* to call on a government guarantee during the offer period, however, the disclosure document for the exchange warned that any subsequent call on the guarantee would be discharged by the delivery to the beneficiary on the same bonds being issued in the exchange on terms comparable to those reflected in the exchange offer (or, at the Government's option, by delivery of other consideration having an equivalent value).[5]

V. THE SOLUTIONS

There are two things a sovereign could do to deal with this problem. One obvious measure would be for the sovereign to insert into its standard form of guarantee a contractual provision to the effect that the guarantee will be deemed automatically called (or will be callable at the option of the sovereign guarantor) in the event of the announcement of a generalized debt restructuring by the sovereign. We have never seen such a provision,

---

Procedures, Box 3, p. 11, 26 August 1996) (defining the debt covered by the HIPC initiative).

[5] L. Buchheit and E. Karpinski, 'Grenada's Innovations' (2006) 4 Journal of International Banking and Regulation 227, 231 (footnote omitted).

however, and we doubt whether it would be well received by prospective beneficiaries of the guarantees.

Alternatively, a sovereign could attempt to preserve the economics of 'two-name paper' by telling a beneficiary who joins the sovereign's debt restructuring that if the exercise of any subrogation rights against the primary obligor produce a recovery after the restructuring closes, the proceeds of that recovery will be paid first to the beneficiary up to the amount of the financial loss it realized by joining the restructuring, and thereafter to the sovereign. The exercise of these subrogation rights ought logically to be placed in the hands of a third party such as a trustee. The sovereign cannot be trusted to pursue the primary obligor aggressively (particularly if it is a state-owned enterprise), while the beneficiary would have no economic incentive to pursue a primary obligor to recover anything more than the beneficiary itself could claim is its make-whole amount.

16. The European Stability Mechanism: Some notes on a new EU institution designed to avert financial crises

Rodrigo Olivares-Caminal

INTRODUCTION

The severe international financial crisis and economic downturn that was sparked by problems in the US sub-prime mortgage market and compounded by the failure of Lehman Brothers led to a widening in budget deficits and higher public debt to GDP ratios in many countries. This reflected not only lower public sector revenues and increased expenditures to shore up aggregate demand, but it also led to a need to lend support to troubled financial institutions and create measures to check the risk of financial panic.

As the financial and economic situation worsened, investors became increasingly risk averse and risk-evaluation became very difficult. In a number of countries the turmoil in the banking sector seems to have only been tempered by large infusions of government financial intervention that, in turn, aggravated the sovereign debt picture. For some European countries the deterioration in borrowing conditions seemed to go beyond what underlying economic fundamentals might have called for in more normal times.

The Euro Area Member States (EAMSs) are of particular interest as they have been at the epicentre of the sovereign debt crisis and there have been important spillover effects from one euro area member state (EAMS) to another, to the point that the stability of the euro area as a whole has been called into question. Greece, Ireland and Portugal, for example, have had to seek financial assistance from the European Union (EU), other EAMSs, the IMF, the European Central Bank and non-EAMS countries in attempts to rectify public sector finances and to reduce their debt burden in an orderly manner.

The introduction of the euro was accompanied by increased intra Eurozone financial interdependence and, as it has turned out, some financial fragilities and risks that have only become apparent under crisis conditions. Thus a euro area specific issue seems to have emerged as a component of the broader evolving international state of affairs.

Accordingly this chapter deals with the EU institutional reaction to recent European financial stresses. In particular it focuses on providing a critical analysis of the Treaty that created the European Stability Mechanism (ESM), an intergovernmental organization under international public law. This chapter concludes with some suggestions regarding the challenges going forward.

I. INITIAL RESPONSES

In early May 2010, Greece and the EC (acting on behalf of the EAMSs) entered into a Memorandum of Understanding (MoU) for a programme to correct fiscal and external imbalances and restore confidence.[1] The programme's financing requirements would be covered by the EAMSs and the IMF to facilitate Greece's re-access to capital markets. The estimated 'public financing gap' for the entire length of the programme was EUR110 billion,[2] with this to be covered through: (i) an intergovernmental framework involving pooled matching bilateral loans provided by the EAMSs in the amount of EUR80 billion[3] and, (ii) an IMF Stand-by

---

1 See Section 5 of the MoU between the European Commission, acting on behalf of the EAMSs and the Hellenic Republic, dated 3 May 2010 (unpublished, on file with the author).

2 See Section 23 of the MoU between the European Commission, acting on behalf of the EAMSs and the Hellenic Republic, dated 3 May 2010 (unpublished, on file with the author).

3 The Loan Facility Agreement was entered into on 8 May 2010 by the Kingdom of Belgium, Ireland, Kingdom of Spain, French Republic, Italian Republic, Republic of Cyprus, Grand Duchy Of Luxembourg, Republic of Malta, Kingdom of The Netherlands, Republic of Austria, Portuguese Republic, Republic of Slovenia, Slovak Republic, Republic of Finland and KfW (acting on behalf of the Federal Republic of Germany), as lenders; and, the Hellenic Republic as borrower (and the bank of Greece as the agent of the borrower). The lenders in all their functions, rights and obligations under the Loan Facility Agreement act through and are represented by the EC and have agreed to act in a coordinated manner and to channel communications (to the EC) through the Euro Working Group Chairman. The release of subsequent loans is conditioned upon the EAMSs (except Greece) deciding favourably after consultation with the ECB on the basis of the findings of verification by the EC that the implementation of the economic

Arrangement in the amount of EUR30 billion.[4] Greece would draw on these resources throughout the programme period on an eight-to-three ratio for each disbursement.[5] The coordination and management procedures were set out in an Inter-creditor Agreement.[6]

Following the execution of these agreements, the Economic and Financial Affairs (Ecofin)[7] Council met to address the Greek situation, which had broader Eurozone implications. The Council decided to adopt a comprehensive package of measures directed at preserving financial stability in Europe.[8] These measures included the establishment of two additional sources of financial assistance to complement the initial *ad hoc* loan facility agreed to with Greece. These two new sources of financial aid were:

(a) The European Financial Stabilisation Mechanism (EFSM) which is a mechanism based on Article 122(2) of the Treaty on the Functioning of the European Union (TFEU) that foresees financial support for

---

policy of Greece accords with the adjustment programme or any other conditions laid down in the Council decision on the basis of Articles 126(9) (EU Council recommendations in re budget deficits) and 136 (specific provisions for member states whose currency is the euro) TFEU and the MoU.

4 Greece requested a Stand-by Arrangement in an amount equivalent to SDR26,432.9 million (EUR30 billion) for a period from 9 May 2010 through 8 May 2013 which was approved on 9 May 2010.

5 See above, n. 2. The eight-to-three ratio has to do with the contribution ratio of the programme where the EAMSs contributed EUR80 billion and the IMF EUR30 billion.

6 The Inter-creditor Agreement was entered on 8 May 2010 between the Kingdom of Belgium, Federal Republic of Germany, Ireland, Kingdom of Spain, French Republic, Italian Republic, Republic of Cyprus, Grand Duchy of Luxembourg, Republic of Malta, Kingdom of The Netherlands, Republic of Austria, Portuguese Republic, Republic of Slovenia, Slovak Republic, and Republic of Finland (unpublished, on file with the author).

7 The Economic and Financial Affairs Council is commonly known as Ecofin and is composed of the Economics and Finance Ministers of the EU member states, as well as Budget Ministers when budgetary issues are discussed. It meets once a month and covers EU policy in areas such as economic policy coordination, economic surveillance, monitoring of EU member states' budgetary policy and public finances, the euro (legal, practical and international aspects), financial markets and capital movements and economic relations with third countries. One of the most important tasks of Ecofin (jointly with the European Parliament) is to prepare and adopt the budget of the European Union on a yearly basis. See http://www.consilium.europa.eu/policies/council-configurations/economic-and-financial-affairs?lang=en (last accessed 25 September 2012).

8 See Council of the European Union, Extraordinary Council Meeting, 9–10 May 2010, Press Release No. 9596/10 (Presse 108).

member states in difficulty due to factors beyond their control.[9] It consists of an intergovernmental agreement to provide financial assistance of up to EUR60 billion, subject to terms and conditions similar to those mandated by the IMF in the context of a joint EU and IMF support package. The EFSM was to operate independently of the facility providing medium-term financial assistance for non-euro EAMSs balance of payments disequilibria.

(b) The European Financial Stability Facility (EFSF) is a temporary credit-enhanced special purpose vehicle, with minimal capitalization, created to raise funds from capital markets on its investment grade rating, with the objective of providing financial assistance to distressed EAMSs at lower interest rates than otherwise would be available to them. On 26 October 2011, Heads of State or Government of EAMSs agreed on maximizing the capacity of the EFSF to enlarge the capacity of the EFSF based on two approaches: (i) partial credit enhancement to primary sovereign bonds issued by an EAMS; and (ii) the creation of one or more Co-Investment Funds (CIFs) to allow the combination of public and private funding to enlarge the resources available to the EFSF's financial assistance instruments.[10] Financial support to EAMSs through the EFSF would be on comparable terms to the stability support loans that were advanced by EAMSs to Greece.

In October 2010 (after financial assistance had been provided to Greece and while economic and financial conditions continued to deteriorate there), the EU Council agreed on the need for a permanent crisis prevention mechanism to help safeguard the financial stability of the euro area as a whole.[11] It was resolved that consultations should be undertaken towards a limited Treaty change for this purpose, but not for modifying the so-called 'no bail-out' clause included in Article 125 of the TFEU.[12] In December 2010 the EU Council agreed that there was a need for EAMSs to establish a permanent stability mechanism, that is, the ESM.

---

[9] As noted in Council Regulation (EU) No. 407/2010, these difficulties may be caused by a serious deterioration in the international economic and financial environment. See Council Regulation (EU) No. 407/2010 (OJ L 118/1).

[10] See Euro Summit statement dated 26 October 2011, p.6, para. 19, available at http://www.consilium.europa.eu/uedocs/cms_data/docs/pressdata/en/ec/125644.pdf (last accessed 25 September 2012).

[11] EU Council, 30 November 2010, EUCO 25/1/10 (REV 1), CO EUR 18 (CONCL 4).

[12] See above, n. 11.

The Conclusions of the European Council[13] and the EU Council Decision 2011/199/EU, amending Article 136 of the TFEU with regard to a stability mechanism for EAMSs,[14] were adopted on 25 March 2011. The next section analyses this new permanent stability mechanism.

II. THE EUROPEAN STABILITY MECHANISM (ESM)

The Treaty establishing the features of the ESM was finalised on 2 February 2012 and is still subject to ratification by its signatories. It is to come into force on the date when instruments of ratification approval or acceptance have been deposited by EAMSs signatories whose initial subscriptions represent no less than 90 per cent of the total capital subscriptions.[15]

The ESM is to be an international financial institution[16] based in Luxembourg.[17] It will mobilise funding and provide financial assistance, under strict economic policy conditionality, to its members, when they are threatened or experiencing severe financing problems.[18] Its underlying raison d'être is to help assure euro-area financial stability, in the context of macroeconomic adjustment programmes, taking into account the severity of the economic and financial imbalances of the EAMSs.[19]

The Treaty begins by restating the importance of the EU framework and its economic governance rules (for example, the Stability and Growth Pact; and, the macroeconomic imbalances framework and economic governance rules of Europe, including the Treaty on Stability, Coordination and Governance), whereby the ESM is to be seen as a back-stop mechanism to help safeguard the financial stability of the euro area as a whole.

Use of the ESM is to be limited to extreme circumstances; access to financial assistance is subject to strict economic policy conditionality,

---

13 EUCO 10/11 (D/11/3).

14 See 2011/199/EU (L 91/1). The following paragraph has been added to Article 136 of the TFEU: '[t]he Member States whose currency is the euro may establish a stability mechanism to be activated if indispensable to safeguard the stability of the euro area as a whole. The granting of any required financial assistance under the mechanism will be made subject to strict conditionality.'

15 See Article 48 of the ESM Treaty.

16 See Article 1(1) of the ESM Treaty.

17 See Article 31(1) of the ESM Treaty.

18 See Articles 3 and 12 of the ESM Treaty.

19 See Article 12 of the ESM Treaty.

accompanied by a macroeconomic adjustment programme, and a rigorous analysis of public debt sustainability is mandatory. Like the EFSM and EFSF, the ESM will call for active participation of the IMF on both technical and financial aspects. It is important to stress that one of the recitals of the Treaty states that financial assistance to the Treaty's contracting parties (ESM Members) will be limited to cases where regular access to market financing is impaired.[20] Thus lending is restricted to circumstances where no conventional party would be willing to lend,[21] that is to say the ESM would be acting as an international lender of last resort (ILOLR). The role of ILOLR is usually played by the IMF,[22] but the recital states that the ESM will enjoy preferred creditor status in a similar fashion to the IMF, while accepting preferred creditor status of the IMF over the ESM.[23] It is worth noticing that IMF creditor priority has not been formally established anywhere and is *de facto*. The Treaty is the first formal document where it has been officially acknowledged. The Treaty has created a second super-priority creditor, although one that is subordinate to the IMF.

The required funding is obtained either by: (i) issuing financial instruments; (ii) entering into financial or other agreements with third parties; and/or (iii) arrangements with ESM Members.[24] The ESM shall use risk management tools to minimise potential adverse outcomes.[25]

The ESM has an authorised capital stock of EUR700 billion[26] divided

---

20 See Recital 13 of the ESM Treaty.

21 It is worthy of note that theoretically speaking there could always be someone willing to lend if the associated risk is properly priced. So far, during the EU sovereign debt crisis, when financing rates have gone above a 7 per cent return (and have remained at such rate or increased) official financial assistance has been provided.

22 Regarding the ILOLR role of the IMF, see Jeffrey Sachs, 'Do We Need an International Lender of Last Resort', Frank D. Graham Lecture at Princeton University, 20 April 1995 (unpublished manuscript); Charles W. Calomiris, 'The IMF's Imprudent Role as Lender of Last Resort' (1998) 17(3) The Cato Journal 275–94; Stanley Fischer, 'On the Need for an International Lender of Last Resort' (1999) 13 Journal of Economic Perspectives 85–104; Adam Lerrick and Allan H. Meltzer, 'Blueprint For An International Lender Of Last Resort' (2003) 50 Journal of Monetary Economics 289–303; Giancarlo Corsetti, Bernardo Guimarães and Nouriel Roubini, 'The Tradeoff between an International Lender of Last Resort to Deal with Liquidity Crisis and Moral Hazard Distortions: A Model of the IMF's Catalytic Finance Approach', 2003, Mimeo, Yale University and New York University.

23 See Recital 13 of the ESM Treaty.

24 See Article 3 of the ESM Treaty.

25 See Article 21(3) of the ESM Treaty.

26 See Article 8(1) of the ESM Treaty.

into paid-in shares (EUR80 billion)[27] and callable shares[28] (EUR620 billion). If an ESM member fails to meet the required payment under a capital call[29] an appeal will be made to all other ESM members to cover the shortfall,[30] thereby ensuring that the ESM receives the total amount of required paid-in capital. Experience with the EFSF, which has required a capital increase and the use of leverage to increase its financing capacity as the crisis worsened, suggests that to reassure markets it would have been prudent to have provided the ESM with a more substantial capital base and/or allowed a more flexible approach.

The capital participation of ESM Members is based on their central banks' subscription to the ECB's capital, pursuant to Article 29 of Protocol (No. 4) of the Statute of the European System of Central Banks and the ECB.[31] As of July 2012[32] the ESM will assume tasks that would have been previously performed by the EFSM and EFSF.[33] Total lending outstanding will have an initial ceiling of EUR500 billion and given the ESM's limited capital, in order to increase the Eurozone's financial support capability, a temporary overlap between the ESM and EFSF has been agreed. In principle, between July 2012 and July 2013, the ESM, EFSM and EFSF will coexist. Although the total lending capacity has been limited to EUR500 billion, its firepower could go beyond that due to the EFSF's capacity maximisation resolved on 26 October 2011 (that is, partial credit enhancement and CIFs).

The governance structure of the ESM is complicated as it comprises a Board of Governors, a Board of Directors and also establishes the position of a Managing Director with specific tasks.[34] The Board of Governors is in charge of setting the guidelines and policies of the ESM, while the Board of Directors is entrusted with the day-to-day operations of the ESM in

---

27 See Article 8(2) of the ESM Treaty.

28 See Article 25(2) of the ESM Treaty.

29 See Articles 8(4) and 9 of the ESM Treaty.

30 See Article 25(2) of the ESM Treaty.

31 OJ C 115, 9/5/2008, p.230.

32 This is the envisaged date when the ESM will enter in force, subject to ratification by the different signatories of the Treaty.

33 There will be a transitional period from the establishment of the ESM until the phasing out of the EFSF. During this time, the consolidated ESM and EFSF lending shall not exceed EUR500 billion (see Article 39 of the ESM Treaty). Also, subject to the authorization of the Board of Governors in assuming the rights and obligations of the EFSF (Article 40 of the ESM Treaty).

34 For a detailed description of the responsibilities of the Boards of Governors and Directors and the required majorities to adopt decisions see Annex I.

accordance with the Treaty and its by-laws.[35] Considering the division of responsibilities, an analogy can be made with the governance structure of a company regarding shareholders' meetings and their role, as well as Board of Directors' meetings and their agenda. However, each ESM Member, irrespective of its percentage participation, only has one vote. Each ESM participant appoints one member to the Board of Governors[36] while, in turn, each Governor appoints a member to the Board of Directors;[37] Board appointments are revocable at any time.[38] Appointments to both Boards also include the appointments of alternates, in case of absence of the principal or impossibility to participate. Both the Board of Governors and the Board of Directors require a double threshold quorum of two-thirds of the members (number of ESM Members) with voting rights representing at least two-thirds of the voting rights (number of votes).[39] Decisions by the Board of Governors can be adopted either by mutual agreement (that is, unanimity, although abstentions do not prevent a mutual agreement decision)[40] or an 80 per cent qualified majority.[41] It is worth stressing that the Treaty contemplates an emergency voting proceeding for situations where the EU Commission and the ECB conclude that a failure to urgently adopt a decision to grant or implement financial assistance can threaten the economic and financial sustainability of the euro area. Although, in these cases (that is, under an emergency voting proceeding), the grant of financial assistance, the economic policy conditionality and the choice of instruments has to be adopted by unanimity meeting the requirement of a qualified majority of 85 per cent of the votes cast.[42]

Decisions of the Board of Directors can be adopted by mutual agreement, qualified majority and/or simple majority.[43]

Any ESM member who fails to comply with its financial obligations (for example, paid-in shares, calls of capital or reimbursement of the financial assistance) will not be able to exercise its voting rights until the situation is rectified.[44]

The Managing Director is the legal representative of the ESM and will

---

35 The ESM by-laws are going to be adopted by the Board of Governors (see Article 5(7)(c) of the ESM Treaty).

36 See Article 5(1) of the ESM Treaty.

37 See Article 6(1) of the ESM Treaty.

38 See Articles 5(1) and 6(1) of the ESM Treaty.

39 See Article 4(2) of the ESM Treaty.

40 See Article 4(3) of the ESM Treaty.

41 See Article 4(5) of the ESM Treaty.

42 See Article 4(4) of the ESM Treaty.

43 See Article 4(2) of the ESM Treaty.

44 See Article 4(8) of the ESM Treaty.

chair the meetings of the Board of Directors and shall participate in the meetings of the Board of Governors.[45]

There will be an Auditing Board comprised of five independent members not taking instructions from the ESM governing bodies, the ESM Members or any other public or private body.[46] The accounts will be subject to external audit.[47] The members of the Auditing Board are appointed by the Board of Governors and shall include two members from the supreme audit institutions of the ESM Members and one from the European Court of Auditors.[48]

ESM financial assistance for stability support can consist of: (i) precautionary financial assistance;[49] (ii) financial assistance for the recapitalisation of financial institutions of an ESM member;[50] (iii) loans;[51] (iv) primary market support facility;[52] and (v) secondary market support facility.[53] All these types of stability support are subject to strict conditionality which may range from a macroeconomic adjustment programme to a continuous respect of pre-established eligibility conditions.[54]

ESM members undertook an irrevocable and unconditional obligation to provide their respective contributions to the authorised capital stock,[55] which also is the limit of their liability.[56] The Board of Governors has the mandate to establish a reserve fund and, if required, other funds.[57] In the event of ESM losses, these shall be covered by (in order of priority): (i) the reserve fund; (ii) the paid-in capital; and (iii) the appropriate amount of the authorised unpaid capital, which shall be called in if needed[58] to cover a shortfall between the paid-in capital and the total subscribed capital.[59]

Any new member state adopting the euro will become an ESM member with full rights and obligations as from the entry into force of a decision

---

45 See Article 7 of the ESM Treaty.
46 See Articles 30(1) and 30(2) of the ESM Treaty.
47 See Article 29 of the ESM Treaty.
48 See Article 30(1) of the ESM Treaty.
49 See Article 14 of the ESM Treaty.
50 See Article 15 of the ESM Treaty.
51 See Article 16 of the ESM Treaty.
52 See Article 17 of the ESM Treaty.
53 See Article 18 of the ESM Treaty.
54 See Articles 12(1) and 13(3) of the ESM Treaty.
55 See Article 8(4) of the ESM Treaty.
56 See Article 8(5) of the ESM Treaty.
57 See Article 24(1) of the ESM Treaty.
58 See Article 25(1) of the ESM Treaty.
59 See Article 9(3) of the ESM Treaty.

of the EU Council taken in accordance with Article 140(2) TFEU.[60] New ESM members will be admitted on the same terms and conditions as existing ESM members[61] and shall receive shares in the ESM in exchange for their capital contributions.[62]

The Treaty encourages EU member states, EAMSs and non-EAMSs, to provide financial assistance on an *ad hoc* basis (for example Denmark, Sweden and the UK provided bilateral assistance to Ireland to complement the EFSM/EFSF/IMF programme).[63] In such cases, the EAMSs (that is, ESM members) will grant equivalent creditor status to those involved in bilateral lending alongside the ESM.[64] Recital 14 of the Treaty reads: '[EAMSs] will support equivalent creditor status of the ESM and that of other States lending bilaterally in coordination with the ESM'. The wording is not very clear and it can lead to conflicting views regarding the creditor status of other bilateral lenders. It can be understood that third parties (for example, a non-EAMS or, even a non-European state) lending on a bilateral basis can be equalled to the preferred creditor status of the ESM.

Non-EAMS countries providing financial assistance on an *ad hoc* basis will participate as observers in the ESM meetings when financial assistance and monitoring are discussed and will have access to all available information in this respect.[65]

The 27 EU member states authorized the EAMS to request the EU Commission and the ECB to perform the tasks required by the Treaty.[66] The EC and the EU Council are entrusted with post-programme surveillance within the framework established by Articles 121 and 136 of the TFEU.[67]

Any disputes concerning the interpretation and application of the Treaty arising among the ESM Members or between them and the ESM should be submitted to the Board of Governors.[68] If the decision of the Board of Governors is contested, the dispute shall be submitted to the jurisdiction of the EU Court of Justice, following the criteria set forth in Article 273 of the TFEU (EU Court of Justice Jurisdiction).[69]

---

60 See Article 2(1) of the ESM Treaty.
61 See Articles 2(2) and 44 of the ESM Treaty.
62 See Article 2(3) of the ESM Treaty.
63 See Recital 9 of the ESM Treaty.
64 See Recital 14 of the ESM Treaty.
65 See Articles 5(4), 6(3) and 38 of the ESM Treaty.
66 See Recital 10 of the ESM Treaty.
67 See Recital 17 of the ESM Treaty.
68 See Article 37(2) of the ESM Treaty.
69 See Article 37(3) of the ESM Treaty.

The procedure for the granting of the financial assistance is as follows:[70]

(a) A formal request for financial assistance to the Chairperson of the Board of Governors by an ESM member.
(b) Upon receipt of a request, the Chairperson of the Board of Governors will request the EC (in liaison with the ECB) to: (i) assess the existence of a risk to the financial stability of the euro area as a whole;[71] (ii) undertake (jointly with the IMF) an analysis of the debt sustainability of the ESM Member in distress;[72] and, (iii) assess the financing needs of the ESM Member[73] and the type of private sector involvement that is required (that is, maintenance of exposure or a re-profiling/restructuring).[74]
(c) Based on the European Commission's assessment, the Board of Governors may decide to grant – in principle – financial assistance to the ESM member.[75]
(d) If the decision of the Board of Governors is favourable, the EC (jointly with the IMF and in liaison with the ECB) will negotiate with the ESM member an MoU detailing the economic policy conditionality, contained in a macroeconomic adjustment programme, to be attached to the financial assistance.[76]
(e) The draft MoU will be considered by the Board of Governors and subject to its approval, the EC will sign the MoU on behalf of the ESM.[77]
(f) The Board of Directors will approve the financial assistance agreement drafted by the Managing Director, detailing the technical aspects of the financial assistance and the disbursement of the first tranche.[78]
(g) A warning system will be put in place by the ESM to ensure that it receives the repayments due under financial assistance in a timely manner.[79]
(h) The EC (jointly with the IMF and in liaison with the ECB) will be entrusted with monitoring the compliance with the economic policy conditionality attached to the financial assistance.[80] A mutual

---

70 See Article 13 of the ESM Treaty.
71 See Article 13(1)(a) of the ESM Treaty.
72 See Article 13(1)(b) of the ESM Treaty.
73 See Article 13(1)(c) of the ESM Treaty.
74 See Recital 12 of the ESM Treaty.
75 See Article 13(2) of the ESM Treaty.
76 See Article 13(3) of the ESM Treaty.
77 See Article 13(4) of the ESM Treaty.
78 See Articles 13(3) and 13(5) of the ESM Treaty.
79 See Article 13(6) of the ESM Treaty.
80 See Article 13(7) of the ESM Treaty.

agreement decision by the Board of Directors, based on the monitoring performed by the European Commission, is required prior to any further tranche disbursement in the case of financial assistance for re-capitalisation of financial institutions or loans.[81]

An additional feature, as a complementary measure to safeguard the stability of the euro, is the mandatory inclusion of standardised and identical Collective Action Clauses (CACs)[82] as of July 2013 in the terms and conditions of all new euro area government securities with maturities above one year.[83] It is ironic that a Treaty was required to do this, despite the April 2003 statement by EU member states of their intention to lead by example.[84] That same year the Ecofin Chairman (a former Minister of Economy and Finance of Greece) stated that '. . . EU Member States will no longer issue such bonds without any CACs'.[85] It may be that the Treaty is not the most suitable place for the inclusion of such a provision. The inclusion of CACs is something that the EU, as a whole, has been working on since 2003 and it may be that the requirement would be more appropriately included elsewhere where it would have broader application. Nevertheless, such an initiative should be welcomed, although extended to non-EAMSs.

---

81 See Articles 15(5) and 16(5) of the ESM Treaty.

82 CACs are clauses whereby, if they are included in the prospectuses of the bonds, the interaction of the bondholders is required. There are four different types of CACs. These are: (1) collective representation clauses; (2) majority action clauses; (3) sharing clauses; and (4) acceleration clauses. Within CACs, majority action clauses are the type that have been strongly pursued by the official sector and favoured by many academics, and they have been effectively incorporated in bond issuances. Majority action clauses enable the amendment of any of the terms and conditions of the bonds, including the payment terms, if the required majority therein established is obtained. So far, the required threshold to amend the terms of the bonds containing majority action clauses has been 75 per cent in aggregate principal amount of the outstanding bonds (for example, Egypt, Lebanon, Mexico, Qatar, Uruguay, and so on). Brazil and Belize have been the only cases where 85 per cent has been required.

83 See Article 12(3) of the ESM Treaty.

84 See ECFIN/CEFCPE(2004)REP/50483, 12 November 2004.

85 Statement by Mr. Christodoulakis, Minister of Economy and Finance of Greece, in his capacity as Chairman of the EU Council of Economic and Finance Ministers, to the International Monetary and Financial Committee, 12 April 2003. Ironically, perhaps, not all post-2003 Greek government bonds included a CAC.

III. CONCLUDING REMARKS

The ESM should be welcomed as the latest edifice in the international architecture to prevent and/or minimize the effects of financial crises. However, the analysis provided in the previous section suggests that considerable room for improvement remains. The new mechanism does not significantly change what the IMF could do except that it creates a European centred institution. The latest draft of the ESM Treaty has reduced the private sector involvement. In addition, the granting of preferred creditor status can produce a crowding-out effect. The ESM is another (small) step in strengthening the economic aspect of the union.

The financing capacity of the ESM clearly seems to be at odds with a realistic appraisal of potential requirements. The different pools of financial assistance that have been temporarily created until the ESM becomes operative collectively exceed the ESM's financing capacity. Additionally, some observers have estimated that in a scenario of distress involving countries like Italy or Spain, the EUR700 billion maximum capacity of the ESM would be insufficient to calm financial markets.[86] It has been suggested that at a least EUR1 trillion may be required.[87]

The ESM's scope for action may be too restrictive. The EFSF, the temporary SPV created to provide liquidity assistance potentially has greater capacity due to its maximising lending techniques (that is, partial credit enhancement to primary sovereign bonds issued by an EAMS and the creation of one or more CIFs). However, it is worthy of note that the Treaty authorises the Board of Governors to reassess and eventually increase the authorised capital stock.[88] Table 16.1 provides a comparison between the EFSF and ESM scopes.

It should also be kept in mind that extensive financial assistance from the ESM could inadvertently reduce the supply of funds from private lenders, since their claims would be subordinate to those of the ESM, as an 'international lender of last resort' (ILOLR). So far, the ILOLR role has been fulfilled by the IMF when other credit providers have not been willing to lend, as result of a country's deteriorated economic and

---

86 Adrian Blundell-Wignall, 'Solving the Financial and Sovereign Debt Crisis in Europe', (2011) 2 OECD Journal of Financial Market Trends, available at http://www.oecd.org/dataoecd/14/25/49481502.pdf (last accessed 25 September 2012).

87 John McDermott, 'China to Europe: that's sure a nice EFSF that you have there', *Financial Times Alphaville*, 28 October 2011.

88 See Article 10 of the ESM Treaty.

Table 16.1 Amendments to the EFSF and ESM

	EFSF I (old)	EFSF II (new)	ESM I (old)	ESM II (new)
Face Value	EUR 440bn	EUR 780bn	EUR 700 (EUR 80bn paid-in + EUR 620bn callable)	EUR 700 (EUR 80bn paid-in + EUR 620bn callable)
Effective Lending Capacity	EUR 255.5+/− bn	EUR 440bn	EUR 500bn	EUR 500bn
Over-guarantee	120%	165%	n.a.	n.a.
Lending capacity maximisation	n.a.	Partial guarantee on securities issuances by Member States + CIFs	n.a.	n.a.
Purpose	(1) Provide temporary financial assistance by the issuance of debt instruments. (2) In exceptional circumstances intervene in the debt primary market. (3) Not authorised to intervene in the secondary market. (4) Not able to provide precautionary credit lines	Financial assistance by way of: (1) loan disbursements; (2) precautionary facilities; (3) facilities to finance the recapitalisation of financial institutions in a EAMS through loans including non-programme countries; (4) facilities for the purchase of bonds in the primary and secondary markets	Financial assistance in the form of loans conditioned to strict economic policy conditionality under macroeconomic adjustment programme, a rigorous analysis of public debt sustainability and PSI.	Financial assistance by way of: (1) loan disbursements; (2) precautionary facilities; (3) facilities to finance the recapitalisation of financial institutions in a EAMS through loans including non-programme countries; (4) facilities for the purchase of bonds in the primary and secondary markets
In Force?	NO	YES	NO (amended before entering into force)	July 2012 (expected)

financial prospects.[89] On the other hand, bilateral and private creditors may see their positions enhanced, by virtue of the assistance provided by the ESM to the EAMSs and the associated policy conditionality. While the ESM will be providing ILOLR lending and therefore, should be granted priority, its priority will not be exempt from challenges in courts of law, since it is not pre-established but rather imposed by the Treaty. On a more practical note, to the extent that it diminishes perceived repayment prospects, the preferred creditor status assigned to the ESM (jointly, although inferior, to that of the IMF) may reduce the private sector demand for sovereign debt and thereby increase public sector financing costs. Since it is likely that the Treaty will be amended to broaden the financing capacity or 'firepower' of the ESM (and probably its scope as well), it may also be advisable to delete the reference to the preferred creditor status, which may offer little by way of protection and undermine support efforts.

The role of the ESM vis-à-vis that of the IMF raises some questions. The ESM has been designed to work very closely with the IMF. For example, upon the request for ESM stability support by a distressed EAMS, the EU Commission, together with the IMF and in liaison with the ECB, will assess the actual financing needs of the EAMS. Then, the EU Commission and the IMF (jointly with the ECB) will negotiate an MoU with the EAMS, outlining a macroeconomic adjustment programme. The EU Commission and the IMF (jointly with the ECB) will be responsible for monitoring compliance with policy conditionality. Thus there is a close relationship between the ESM (and the EU institutions) and the IMF. In common with the IMF, the ESM will be providing financial assistance in exchange for conditionality. In conclusion one might ask whether it is appropriate to create another international organization, under public international law with super-priority, which will replicate some of the functions of the IMF, but lack its experience, credibility, resources and long-established super-priority.

89 However, Bolton and Skeel Jr. contend that this de facto priority is partly an illusion because the IMF has generally agreed to roll over its loans when the sovereign is unable or unwilling to pay (See Patrick Bolton and David Skeel Jr., 'Redesigning the International Lender of Last Resort', (2005) 6 U. Chi. J. Int'l L. 177).

ANNEX GOVERNANCE STRUCTURE AND FUNCTIONING OF THE MAIN BODIES OF THE ESM

Majority Required	Board of Governors	Board of Directors
100 per cent abstentions do not prevent a mutual agreement decision	Issue new shares on terms other than at par (Art. 8(2))	Decide on the disbursement of the tranches of the financial assistance subsequent to the first tranche based on the report provided by the European Commission (jointly with the IMF and in liaison with the ECB) (Arts. 14(5) and 13(7)
	Capital calls (Art. 9(1))	Any decision delegated by the Board of Governors that requires mutual agreement (Art. 6(5))
	Change the authorised capital stock and adapt the maximum lending volume (Art. 10(1))	
	Updates of the subscription key (Art. 11(4) and 11(6))	
	Grant of financial assistance + economic policy conditionality included in the MoU (Art. 13(2) and 13(4)) and set the financial terms and conditions, and the choice of instruments (Arts. 14 to 18) * **meeting the requirement of a qualified majority of 85 per cent of the votes cast (Art. 4(4))**	
	Give mandate to the EU Commission to negotiate (jointly with ECB) the economic policy conditionality attached to each financial assistance (Art. 13(3)) * **meeting the requirement of a qualified majority of 85 per cent of the votes cast (Art. 4(4))**	
	Change the pricing structure/ policy for financial assistance (Art. 20)	

Majority Required	Board of Governors	Board of Directors
	Change the list of financial assistance instruments that may be used (Art. 19) Establish modalities of the transfer of EFSF support to the ESM (Art. 40) Approval of new members and any required adaptation to the Treaty (Art. 44) Delegations to the BoD (5(6)(l))	
80 per cent	Setting out the detailed technical terms of accession of a new member (Art. 44) Election of Chairperson and Vice-Chairperson (5(2)) Set the by-laws of the ESM and the rules of procedure applicable to the Board of Governors and Board of Directors (5(9)) Determine the list of Directors' incompatibilities (Art. 6(8)) Appointment and removal of the Managing Director (Art. 7) Establishment of other funds (Art. 24) Actions for debt recovery (Art. 25(2) and 25(3)) Approve annual accounts (Art. 27(1)) Appoint members of the Internal Auditing Board (Art.30(1)) Approve external auditors (Art. 29) Waive the immunity of the Chairperson of the Board of Governors, a Governor, alternate Governor, Director, alternate Director or the Managing Director (Art. 35(2)) Determine the taxation regime applicable to the ESM staff (Art. 36(5))	Any decision not listed above or below.

Majority Required	Board of Governors	Board of Directors
	on a dispute between an ESM Member and the ESM, or between ESM Members, in connection with the interpretation and application of the Treaty (Art. 37(2)) Any other necessary decision not contemplated (Art 5(7)(n))	
+50 per cent	n.a.	Call in authorised unpaid capital to restore the level of paid-in capital if the amount that the latter is reduced by the absorption of losses below the level established in Art. 8(2) (EUR 80bn), as may be amended by the Board of Governors following the procedure provided for in Art. 10, and set an appropriate period of time for its payment by the ESM Members (Art. 9(2)) Distribute a dividend to the ESM Members if the amount of paid-in capital and the reserve fund exceeds the level required to maintain the lending capacity of the ESM and proceeds from the investment are not required to avoid a payment shortfall to creditors (Art. 23(1))

17. Liquidity spillovers in credit markets during the Eurozone crisis

Giovanni Calice, Jing Chen and Julian Williams

INTRODUCTION

The theory of complete markets suggests that sovereign debt and credit default swap (CDS) credit spreads should track each other closely. In addition, liquidity risk should be priced into both instruments in such a way that buying exposure to the same default risk is identically priced, given appropriate collateral requirements for the hedging instruments and the payout structure in the CDS providing the desired recovery on the defaulting cash flow instrument. Therefore, we have developed an empirical model of the co-evolution of credit and liquidity spreads in sovereign bond and CDS markets to study the liquidity and credit interactions for Eurozone countries over the 1 January 2007 to 1 October 2010 period, a period commonly referred to as the Eurozone sovereign debt crisis.

During November 2009, shortly after the election of a new Greek government, the Greek public sector deficit was revised from 6 per cent to 12.7 per cent of GDP. This event initiated a sovereign debt crisis that has resulted in large financial interventions in financial markets and fiscal policies in Greece, Ireland and Portugal and is often referred to as the 'Eurozone sovereign debt crisis'.

Since the 'US subprime mortgage crisis' in August 2007, several interconnected crises occurred. In this chapter, we focus on the losses incurred by financial institutions on mortgage-backed securities and associated structured derivatives. We define 'credit crisis' and 'credit crunch' as the explosive growth in interbank lending rates, relative to policy rates, during early 2008. Finally, we refer to the 'Eurozone sovereign debt crisis' as the period of high growth in late 2009 of credit spreads on sovereign debt for several Eurozone countries. This event led to a sudden loss of confidence in sovereign debt markets, which revealed itself in the form of widening credit spreads between several euro area members and the Eurozone's largest economy, Germany. The response by Eurozone member states and international bodies such as the International Monetary Fund (IMF) and the European Union (EU) has been a suite of interventions led by the European Central Bank (ECB).[1]

Throughout 2010 the focus of the crisis was on Greece, Ireland and Portugal where there was a concern about the rising cost of financing government debt and the possibility of default on a sovereign debt issuance. On 2 May 2010, the Eurozone countries and the IMF agreed to a EUR110 billion loan for Greece, conditional on the implementation of a package of severe austerity measures. On 9 May 2010, the European Financial Stability Facility (EFSF) was established to collect funds and provide loans in conjunction with the IMF to preserve financial stability of Eurozone member states, subject to strict policy conditionality. The Greek bailout was followed by a EUR85 billion rescue package for Ireland in November 2010, and a EUR78 billion bailout for Portugal in May 2011.

The increases of sovereign debt in several countries notwithstanding, in May 2011, financial market concerns focused primarily on the refinancing of Greek public debts. The problems have been compounded by political instability in Greece. In late June 2011, the crisis situation was again brought under control with the Greek government managing to pass a package of new austerity measures and EU leaders pledging funds to support the country.[2]

In this chapter, we investigate the potential spillover effects between the credit and liquidity spreads in the Eurozone sovereign bond market and the sovereign credit default swap (CDS) market during the 2010 European sovereign debt crisis. We define two credit spreads, denoted by the suffix 'CS': (1) the difference in the required discount rate on Eurozone members benchmark sovereign debt issuance against a benchmark (in this case equivalent German benchmark bonds); (2) the difference between the CDS spread on benchmark sovereign debt against the equivalent German

[1] For brevity we use the term Eurozone to refer to the collection of countries in the euro area with monetary policy conducted by the ECB and operating under the rules of the euro system. Credit spreads, in this context, is the difference in yield between the sovereign bond issuance for a euro area member state and the equivalent maturity German government bond (bund).

[2] During the crisis, several commentators expressed concerns that manipulation of the CDS market by speculative investors was playing a crucial role in exacerbating the liquidity dry up in the market for Greek, Irish, Portuguese and Spanish sovereign debt. In particular, 'naked' CDS positions were blamed for driving bond yields on these countries' sovereign debt higher during the first half of 2010. In this context, Greece was suggested to have been a victim of short-term speculative short selling practices on its national debt and naked shorting practices in the CDS market.

sovereign debt. In equilibrium, both 'CS' spreads should co-move almost precisely.

We then use the bid-ask spread on the bond and CDS markets to proxy for market depth, transactions costs and market liquidity. This is denoted by the suffix 'LS', for liquidity spread.[3] As such, we build up a vector model containing these four variables. Several key results emerge from the analysis. First, we find that whilst the liquidity of the sovereign debt market dries up over the crisis period, the liquidity of the CDS market increases dramatically with spread bids and spreads asked approaching a one-to-one ratio. Second, the transmission effect from the credit spread in the sovereign CDS market to the credit spread on the sovereign bond market is, at times, large in magnitude and highly significant for Ireland, Spain, Greece and Portugal. Third, the significance of the interaction of the CDS liquidity spread and the credit spread on the bond market changes markedly over the sample period. This observation implies that the liquidity of the CDS market does impact the credit spreads and that this mechanism is higher during periods of high market stress, such as immediately after the Bear Stearns rescue and the Lehman Brothers default.

The remainder of the chapter is organised as follows: Section I provides background information on the Eurozone crisis and reviews the related literature on the pricing and liquidity of the bond and CDS market; Section II explains our empirical methodology; Section III examines the pre-processing of the data used in the study; and Section IV contains our analysis of the results followed by our concluding remarks and some ideas for follow-up studies.

I. BACKGROUND AND RELATED LITERATURE

In our analysis, we utilise a time varying vector autoregression (TV-VAR) model[4] to capture the changing relationship between the lagged credit and liquidity spreads for nine countries in the Eurozone. This VAR model is fully characterised by a matrix of coefficients and a covariance matrix that represents the spread of the random vector. Of key importance is that all variables are treated as evolving contemporaneously, therefore avoiding questions, such as having to decide *a priori* on what causes what. All

---

[3] For brevity we utilise the commonly understood equity/foreign exchange parlance bid-ask spread, to refer to the difference between the yield(spread) bid and the yield(spread) ask for the sovereign bond(CDS) market.

[4] A VAR model describes the evolution of multiple time series as a function of their joint histories and a vector (list) of random noise or information shocks.

variables are assumed endogenous so that we can then use diagnostic tests to infer causation.[5] The model is effectively:

Current credit spread AND current liquidity spread = weighted history of credit spreads + weighted history of liquidity spreads + some constant + noise

Therefore, in the VAR model, there are four equations: (1) the bond credit spread; (2) the CDS credit spread; (3) the bond liquidity spread; and (4) the CDS liquidity spread. Each equation makes up part of the 'vector process'. The transmission of information from the past to the present is defined via the magnitude of the coefficients that weight the histories of the VAR system. These are computed via an estimation method. In this study we explore a variety of methods for computing coefficients to achieve robustness.

The primary risk mechanism involved in triggering the Eurozone sovereign debt crisis is that each individual country, upon joining the Eurozone, gave up its ability to issue its own currency which meant that default risk on sovereign debt became a reality. Without an independent currency the central banks in Eurozone countries effectively lost their lender of last resort facilities and the lack of a mechanism to reassure financial markets. As such, financial sector liquidity problems could turn into solvency problems and then into fiscal problems. This implies that countries, in a manner identical to firms, could in theory completely default on sovereign debt issuances. Indeed, the collapse of Lehman Brothers in 2008 revealed that the so-called too-big-to-fail institutions could default on their debt; as a consequence credit spreads on corporate debt increased rapidly during the 2007–2010 period.

Earlier sovereign defaults, for instance Argentina in 2001, were caused by a similar ceding of seigniorage revenue[6] and a hard constraint on expansion of the monetary base. In this case, a currency board with the United States was fixed with supposedly 100 per cent US Dollar reserves. When the currency board was broken and the Argentinean peso devalued, several US Dollar backed sovereign debt issuances defaulted, with low recovery rates.

The reasons for the high levels of borrowing for certain members of the Eurozone in the aftermath of the financial crisis are not uniform.

[5] It should be emphasized that causation is strictly in a statistical sense.

[6] For instance in the debt ceiling stand-off in the United States during mid-2011, the concept of a USD 5 trillion coin was suggested to release Federal funds.

Table 17.1 Timeline of events during the Eurozone debt crisis

Date	Event
August 2007	BNP Paribas liquidates two funds heavily invested in mortgage-backed securities, sub-prime crisis effectively begins.
March 2008	Bear Stearns bought by JP Morgan with support from US Federal Reserve.
August 2008	Lehman Brothers enters Chapter 11 bankruptcy, global financial panic begins.
October 2008	Icelandic banking system nationalised, UK assets seized under anti-terrorism laws.
January/February 2009	Icelandic government collapses, first sovereign victim, Iceland applies to join European Union (EU).
November 2009	Greek government revises public sector deficit to 12.7% GDP from 6% originally stated.
December 2009	Greek credit rating cut by Fitch from A- to BBB.
April 2010	Greece applies for help from the EU and the International Monetary Fund (IMF).
May 2010	European Financial Stability Facility (EFSF) is set up with Euros 440 billion.
September 2010	Ireland announces it will need Euros 46 billion to bailout its crippled financial sector.
October 2010	End of CDS data provision by CMA for our sample.
April 2011	Portugal files for support from EFSF and IMF.
May 2011	Predicted total public debt for Greece, Ireland and Portugal forecast to be 166.1%, 117.9% and 107.4% of GDP respectively.

Countries such as Greece and Italy have consistently recorded high levels of government borrowing to ensure continuation of provision of public services and public sector pay and conditions settlements. The major issue for Ireland has been the provision of assurances for a large financial sector that has suffered great losses during the financial crisis.

During the crisis period we can observe a major change in many macroeconomic indicators for the Eurozone member countries. In Table 17.2, we present some of the background statistics that characterize the economic problems faced by selected Eurozone members during the 2007–2010 period and how it differs from the previous seven years following the formation of the common currency.

The most striking statistic is annual GDP growth. During 2009, every single country recorded a contraction in output; while the Eurozone as a whole, which had seen 2.16 per cent trend growth 1999–2006, suffered a

4.10 per cent contraction. Output growth in 2008 was virtually stagnant, with Ireland and Italy exhibiting a contraction one year before the rest of the Eurozone members. For default risk the most obvious indicator is the size of the government deficit and whether government revenue is growing or declining. The conditions for both indicators deteriorated markedly during the 2007–2010 period. Revenue has dropped for the Eurozone as a whole and markedly for certain countries such as Ireland, Portugal and Spain. Over approximately the same period, the total government deficit for the Eurozone has increased to around EUR0.5 trillion.

The impact on credit spreads of Eurozone sovereign debt has been noticeable. Figures 17.1 and 17.2 present the time evolution of the daily credit spreads for a selection of countries in our sample. Plots are in equivalent basis points. The top plot presents the spread for 5-year bonds and the lower plot for 10-year bonds. It is important to note that there has been a homogeneous rise in the yield for each country over the German benchmark as the heightened level of default risk discounts the par value of sovereign debt.

Simultaneously, we can see some radical shifts in the liquidity spread of the two traded instruments (also see Figure 17.2). The bid-ask spread for the bond and CDS fluctuates considerably during the crisis period and it is the information transmission between the credit and liquidity spreads for the two markets that forms the primary focus of this chapter.

One approach is to interpret a CDS simply as a short position in a defaultable bond. This interpretation is intuitive because once protection equivalent to the par value of the underlying bond has been purchased, then the portfolio of underlying and derivative should replicate the risk free rate (it is indeed a synthetic risk free rate). Therefore, the spread on the yield of the defaultable bond over the risk free rate should in effect be replicated by the cost of holding the protection (that is, there is a risk premia in holding bonds and under arbitrage free pricing the cost of protection should fully offset this premia). However, recent studies[7] suggest that trading strategies in corporate CDS generate far higher returns than the equivalent cost of the premia.

Manipulation of market liquidity is often the primary mechanism through which speculative attacks are channelled and in this case the object of interest is the bilateral liquidity structure of the sovereign debt

---

[7] See, for instance, Calice, Chen and Williams, 'Are there benefits to being naked: the returns and diversification impact of capital structure arbitrage?' (2012) European Journal of Finance, forthcoming. http://www.tandfonline.com/doi/abs/10.1080/1351847X.2011.637115 (last accessed 25 September 2012).

Table 17.2 *Eight sets of fundamental statistics of the ten typical Eurozone countries and the entire Eurozone*

Country	GDP Growth						
	1999–2006	2007	2008	2009	2010	1999–2006	2007
Austria	2.31	3.70	2.20	−3.90	2.00	65.45	59.30
Belgium	2.23	2.90	1.00	−2.80	2.00	100.58	84.20
France	2.23	2.40	0.20	−2.60	1.60	61.23	63.80
Greece	4.08	4.30	1.30	−2.30	−4.20	100.61	105.00
Germany	1.45	2.70	1.00	−4.70	3.70	63.14	64.90
Ireland	6.64	5.60	−3.50	−7.60	−0.20	33.38	25.00
Italy	1.46	1.50	−1.30	−5.00	1.10	107.25	103.60
Netherland	2.31	3.90	1.90	−3.90	1.70	52.46	45.30
Portugal	1.70	2.40	0.00	−2.50	1.30	56.64	62.70
Spain	3.75	3.60	0.90	−3.70	−0.20	50.89	36.10
Eurozone	2.16	2.80	0.40	−4.10	1.70	69.29	66.20

Country	Overall Employment Rate						
	1999–2006	2007	2008	2009	2010	1999–2006	2007
Austria	68.73	71.40	72.10	71.60	71.70	51.69	48.50
Belgium	60.20	62.00	62.40	61.60	62.00	49.96	48.40
France	63.00	64.30	64.90	64.20	64.00	52.63	52.30
Greece	58.18	61.40	61.90	61.20	59.60	45.11	46.50
Germany	65.69	69.40	70.70	70.90	71.10	47.08	43.60
Ireland	65.99	69.20	67.60	61.80	60.00	33.39	36.80
Italy	55.80	58.70	58.70	57.50	56.90	47.84	47.90
Netherland	73.41	76.00	77.20	77.00	74.70	45.66	45.30
Portugal	68.11	67.80	68.20	66.30	65.60	43.21	43.80
Spain	59.43	65.60	64.30	59.80	58.60	38.83	39.20
Eurozone	62.53	65.60	66.00	64.70	64.20	47.31	46.00

Country	Gov. Deficit						
	1999–2006	2007	2008	2009	2010	1999–2006	2007
Austria	−3845.58	−1159.90	−1328.20	−9607.50	−13 169.40	1.70	2.20
Belgium	−1199.73	−1105.00	−4622.30	−20 351.40	−14 355.30	2.00	1.80
France	−41 679.25	−51 433.00	−64 677.00	−143 834.00	−136 525.00	1.80	1.60
Greece	−9279.23	−14 465.00	−22 363.00	−36 150	−24 193.00	3.23	3.00
Germany	−52 707.50	6550.00	2820.00	−72 910.00	−81 630.00	1.48	2.30
Ireland	2313.63	46.50	−13 148.80	−22 957.90	−49 903.40	3.46	2.90
Italy	−38 954.63	−23 517.00	−42 694.00	−80 863.00	−71 211.00	2.34	2.00
Netherland	−2857.88	1048.00	3389.00	−30 915.00	−31 979.00	2.51	1.60
Portugal	−5061.71	−4671.20	−5037.70	−15 700.90	−15 783.00	3.00	2.40
Spain	254.25	20 066.00	−45 189.00	−117 306.00	−98 227.00	3.16	2.80
Eurozone	−149 421.94	−58 518.60	−186 009.50	−563 418.90	−550 480.70	2.10	2.10

Note: This table reports eight sets of fundamental statistics of the ten typical Eurozone countries and the entire Eurozone. The statistics reported are, by row, % real GDP growth, government debt (% of GDP), the government revenue (% of GDP), employment rate (% of eligible workforce), total government expenditure (% GDP), government fixed investment (annual millions of EUR chained, Eurostat measure), government deficit (annual millions of EUR chained, Eurostat measure) and % inflation rate. The average of each of the statistical

Gov. Debt % of GDP			Total Gov. Revenue				
2008	2009	2010	1999–2006	2007	2008	2009	2010
62.50	67.50	72.30	49.84	47.90	48.20	48.80	48.30
89.60	96.20	96.80	49.49	48.10	48.80	48.10	48.90
67.50	78.10	81.70	50.01	49.60	49.50	48.40	49.40
110.30	126.80	142.80	40.04	39.80	39.70	37.80	39.10
66.30	73.40	83.20	44.64	43.80	43.90	44.50	43.30
44.30	65.50	96.20	35.19	36.80	35.40	34.50	34.60
106.30	116.00	119.00	44.90	46.40	46.20	46.60	45.90
58.20	60.80	62.70	45.06	45.40	46.60	46.00	45.90
65.30	83.00	93.00	39.56	40.90	40.60	38.80	41.50
39.80	53.20	60.10	38.68	41.10	37.10	34.70	35.70
69.80	79.20	85.10	45.34	45.30	44.90	44.50	44.00

Gov. Total Expenditure			Gov. Total Investment				
2008	2009	2010	1999–2006	2007	2008	2009	2010
48.80	52.30	53.00	2822.31	2778.60	3032.00	3088.40	3296.20
50.20	54.20	53.10	4775.61	5446.00	5902.00	6346.00	5853.00
52.80	56.00	56.20	48789.88	62223.00	63412.00	63873.00	59182.00
49.20	53.20	49.50	5878.39	7731.00	7710.00	7938.00	6367.00
43.80	47.50	46.60	34400.00	34310.00	36740.00	39300.00	38940.00
42.70	48.90	67.00	4999.49	8869.80	9306.80	7545.90	5973.60
48.80	51.90	50.30	30173.25	35796.00	34602.00	37040.00	31879.00
46.00	51.40	51.20	15402.50	18986.00	20775.00	22092.00	21689.00
43.60	48.20	50.70	4513.88	4103.40	3965.50	4048.50	5653.00
41.30	45.80	45.00	26631.00	42587.00	42724.00	46068.00	39178.00
46.90	50.80	50.40	185156.08	231602.70	237609.90	247397.10	229125.90

Inflation Rate (Core CPI)		
2008	2009	2010
3.20	0.40	1.70
4.50	0.00	2.30
3.20	0.10	1.70
4.20	1.30	4.70
2.80	0.20	1.20
3.10	−1.70	−1.60
3.50	0.80	1.60
2.20	1.00	0.90
2.70	−0.90	1.40
4.10	−0.20	2.00
3.30	0.30	1.60

variable are taken for each sample country and the Eurozone during the 1999–2006 period, by contrast, the annual statistics of these variables are collected and outlined since 2007 to 2010. Note, that Eurostat has not published the annualised inflation rate for 2010, as of July 2011.

Source: Eurostat

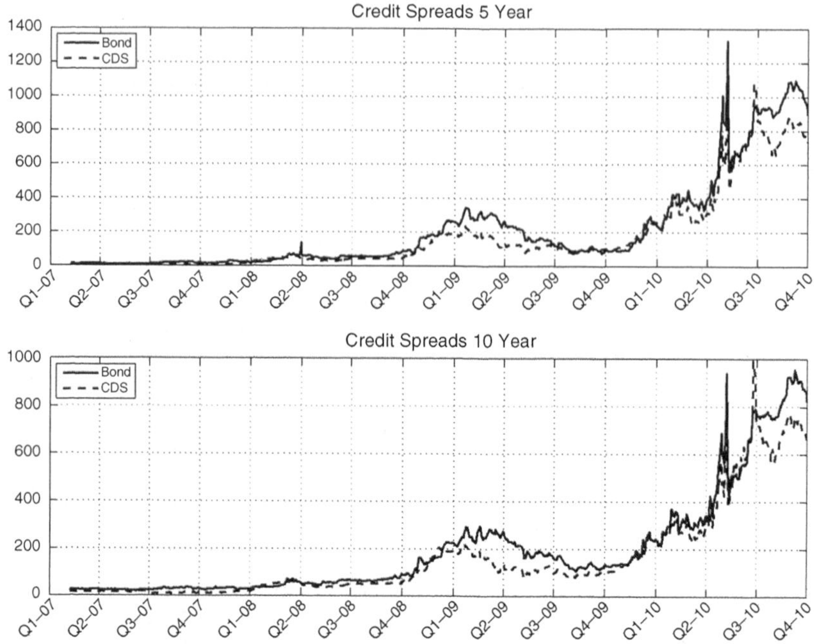

Note: For the bond market this is the basis point spread of quoted sovereign debt yields above the equivalent maturity German sovereign debt. For the CDS it is the difference in the quoted spreads on 5 and 10 year CDS. The y-axis is presented in basis points.

Figure 17.1 Credit spreads for 5 and 10 year maturity sovereign debt issued by the Greek government

market and the sovereign CDS market. A comprehensive survey of the speculative attack literature is beyond the scope of this study and, at present, there is no direct evidence from regulatory investigations to suggest that this type of strategy has been implemented by certain market participants. Therefore, we touch upon a few contributions that underpin the prevailing academic perspective on the effects of liquidity, asset prices and credit instruments.

An important question at this juncture is: does the basis point difference in the yield (spread) bid-asked capture the true liquidity of the bond (CDS) market? The bid-ask spread is one of a suite of liquidity proxies commonly used in the academic literature. Unfortunately for bond and CDS markets volume information is not as readily available as it is in the equity market. Therefore, robustness checks with alternative measures are not easily implementable.

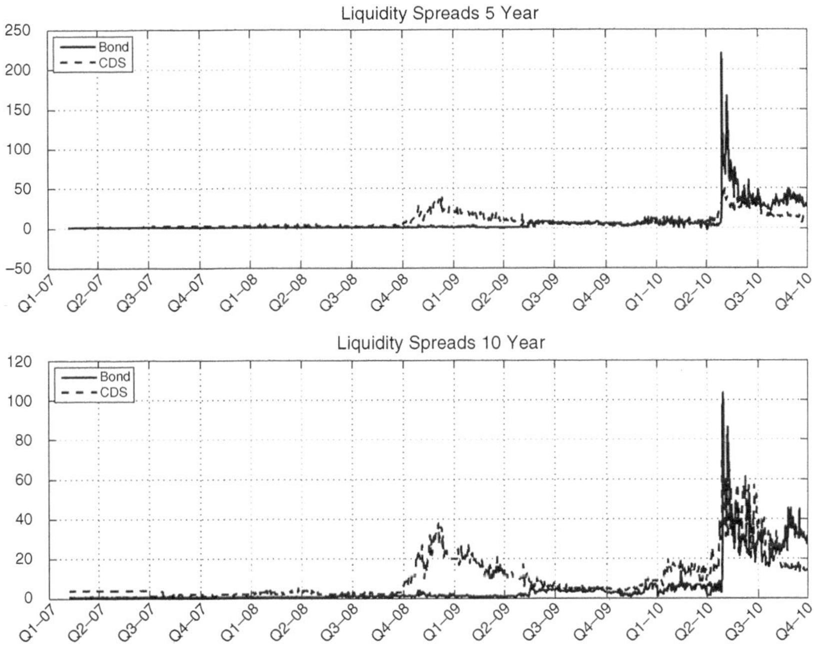

Note: The credit spreads for the bond market are quoted in basis points and are computed from the difference between the bid and offered yield. For the bond market this is computed by taking the daily transaction history and finding the median of the pairwise bid offered rates. For the CDS market the transaction history is incomplete, we have therefore collected and manually combined the Tick History, DataStream, CMA and Thomson-Reuters OTC sources to create the series, see notes to Figure 17.3 for more details.

Figure 17.2 Liquidity spreads for 5 and 10 year Greek sovereign debt, quoted in basis points

There are a few studies which use CDS spreads as a benchmark to control for credit risk in order to study liquidity effects in bond markets. Longstaff et al.[8] use the price of CDS contracts as information to measure the default and non-default risk components in corporate spreads and find that default risk is the main determinant of bond credit spreads. They find the non-default component is time varying and has a strong relationship with the evaluation of bond-specific illiquidity. Moreover, changes in the

[8] F.A. Longstaff, S. Mithal and E. Neis, 'Corporate yield spreads: default risk or liquidity? New evidence from credit-default swap market' (2005) 60(5) Journal of Finance 2213–53.

non-default component are related to measures of Treasury yield spreads as well as to measures of the overall liquidity of fixed income markets.[9]

The market liquidity effects and liquidity spillovers between the CDS, corporate bond and equity markets are examined in Jacoby.[10] Results from vector auto-regressions illustrate the presence of a common component between the stock and both the CDS and the corporate bond market whilst no common component is found specifically between the CDS and the bond market. Moreover, the evidence of a liquidity spillover is found only from the equity to the CDS market. Finally, it documents a time lag in liquidity shocks from the CDS to both corporate bond and stock markets.

A number of recent studies have addressed the co-movement of CDS markets, bond markets and equity markets. Bystrom,[11] for instance, finds a linkage between stock indices return volatilities and CDS spreads for a set of sub-indices of the European iTraxx index. The empirical results show that CDS spreads have a negative relation with stock prices whereas they are positively related to stock price volatility. The European CDS market and its relationship with the stock market has been investigated by Norden and Weber,[12] who find that the CDS market is sensitive to equity market movements. Furthermore, CDS spreads are found to be negatively related to stock returns.

II. NON-TECHNICAL OVERVIEW OF OUR METHODOLOGY

Most studies have used a two equation setting to look at the relationship between bond credit spreads and those implied by CDS contracts. We, in this study, have improved the methodology by including a market depth component in bid-ask spreads to illustrate liquidity dynamics. The second

---

[9] This study is the primary source of inspiration of our framework, delineating credit spreads as the yield spread over the appropriate benchmark and the liquidity spread as the daily average of the yield bid to yield ask.

[10] G. Jacoby, G.J. Jiang and G. Theocharides, 'Cross-market liquidity schocks: evidence from CDS, corporate bond, and equity markets', working paper (2009).

[11] H.N.E. Bystrom, 'Credit default swaps and equity prices: the iTraxx CDs index market', Technical Report 2005:24, Lund University working paper.

[12] L. Norden and M. Weber, 'The co-movement of credit default swap, bond and stock markets: an empirical analysis' (2004) 15(3) European Financial Management 529–62.

innovation is the specification of a time varying (TV) model to demonstrate the evolution of such a relationship.

In a TV-VAR, the matrix of coefficients themselves are treated as being a variable that changes through time. This allows the model to capture sudden changes in the information structure of the vector process. During a crisis the relative information flows from the bond and CDS markets would be expected to change radically; therefore, a time varying set-up would be the only method properly capturing these changes. A static model (that has been previously favoured) would average these changes over the sample period.

There are two types of estimation methods to capture these time variation features: a random coefficients model or a recursive (smoothing) coefficients model. We have selected the recursive type model and adjusted them to adapt to changes in information structure that could occur in this type of markets. A specific challenge is that it appears quite likely that the transmission mechanism of information shocks (both to credit and liquidity spreads) between the sovereign CDS and bond markets has multiple semi-stable equilibria, something that our estimator captures very effectively.

A serious issue of interest rate related data is that they are commonly found to be near integrated to unity, or I(1). However, empirical evidence suggests that structural breaks play a role in rejection of the null of a unit root. The nature of potential structural breaks in bond yields data is unclear. For instance, crash breaks are typically found to be changes in intercept. Yet, a fundamental change in the liquidity dynamics of a country's bond markets (particularly, during a financial crisis) may reveal itself in a different manner. To capture this potentially time varying effect, we propose and implement a recursive and iterated coefficients model.

The obvious alternative to this least squares approach would be the adoption of a state space model to generate a fully random stochastic vector that describes the evolution of the coefficients. However, experimentation with such models has yielded mixed results. For instance, we have found in preliminary data analysis that operating at the daily frequency reduces our sample and results in critical issues such as computing correct standard errors and general over fitting.

The use of a higher frequency data set is difficult as the CDS market is plagued, in its early phases, by intra-day stale prices and high levels of microstructure contaminants and broken transaction information (missing bid-ask and transaction information). Consequently, we estimate our model over daily aggregate data and explicitly attempt to capture heteroskedasticity, autocorrelation and in particular variance break points. The estimator has a single simple bandwidth (nuisance) parameter that dictates the degree of discounting or 'memory' of the model and this parameter is easily optimised using maximum likelihood or some other penalty function approach (for example, the Diebold and Mariano approach[13] or the rolling versus recursive Giacomini and Rossi forecast breakdown[14]). For the specific mathematical formulation of the estimator please refer to Calice, Chen and Williams.[15]

For this research we developed a least squares based alternative to the Kalman filter that is robust to structural changes, whilst being able to capture local stability in the coefficients. We call this approach recursive and iteratively weighted least squares (RI-WLS), which can be regarded as a specific class of the extended least squares approach. More specifically, the model is a multivariate extension of the single equation autoregressive model of Arvastson,[16] which is a standard autoregressive model with time varying coefficients estimated with exponential forgetting. In addition to the increase in dimension to the multivariate context, we also add a robustness component to deal with the potential outliers caused by the sudden appearance of a structural break.

III. DATA

For the complete description of the dataset please see Calice, Chen and Williams (2012). [17] The reporting of single and multi name CDS data has been a source of recent controversy. The data set is primarily sourced from *Thomson Reuters* via the *Tick History* and *DataStream* systems. Sovereign bond data is collected using the 'Super RICs' or Reuters Information Codes described in Figure 17.3.

The super-RICs pull trades reported by various data vendors on instruments in the tag range set by the code, that is, AT5YT=RR means all yields on traded bonds with a 5-year maturity from the daily collection date for Austrian government bonds. In practice the retrieved maturities

---

13 F.X. Diebold and R.S. Mariano, 'Comparing predictive accuracy', (1995) 13(3) Journal of Business and Economic Statistics 253–63.

14 R. Giacomini and B. Rossi 'Forecast comparisons in unstable environments', (2010) 25(4) Journal of Applied Econometrics 595–620.

15 Calice, Chen and Williams, 'Liquidity spillovers in credit markets: an analysis of the eurozone sovereign debt crisis', (2012) Journal of Economic Behavior and Organisation, forthcoming.

16 L. Arvastson, H. Olsson and J. Holst, 'Asymptotic bias in parameter estimation of ar-processes using recursive least squares with exponential forgetting', (2000) 27(1) Scandinavian Journal of Statistics 177–92.

17 Calice, Chen and Williams, above, n. 15.

are for sovereign bonds in the forward benchmark range.[18] The 5-year yields for the bid, ask and mid-quote are then interpolated.

We use the same approach for the CDS market. However, aggregation is much more complex. Multiple data vendors provide an array of intraday and end-of-day information. To compute the daily credit and liquidity spread indices, we utilize arithmetic means, medians and standard deviations of the spread-bid spread-asked and the mid-quotes for each end-of-day sample. Only traded CDS are used in the study.

Note also that the super-RICs automatically reject any inferred spreads taken from the bond market. Thus, our CDS credit and liquidity spread indices differ slightly from those available from CMA through *DataStream*.[19]

IV. RESULTS REPORTED IN CALICE, CHEN AND WILLIAMS[20]

For completeness, we have estimated the models for 5- and 10-year maturity benchmark sovereign bonds for each country under a large variety of specifications. The complete set of results for the TV-VAR models are catalogued in the Internet Appendix, available at www.abdn.ac.uk/~acc138.[21]

For the discussion in this chapter, the following plots are selected: the time evolution of the 5- and 10-year credit and liquidity spreads for Greece, Ireland, Netherlands and France; the time varying roots of the TV-VAR model for the 5-year TV-VAR for Greece and Portugal; and the time varying coefficients for the 5-year models for all four equations for Greece and Ireland. These may be compared to the plots of the time varying coefficients for the first equation for Spain and France for both the 5- and 10-year models.

---

18 These are bonds that mature relative to the month. For instance, the earliest maturity of trade for AT5YT=RR would be 4 years 11 months and the latest would be 5 years 1 month.

19 Unfortunately, Thomson Reuters and CMA ceased to provide CDS data through DataScope, DataStream and Tick History after 1 October 2010. Thus, this date identifies the end of our sample period.

20 Calice, Chen and Williams, above, n. 15.

21 This consists of 16 data plots for the group of nine countries in the sample, and a set of 144 individual plots, for the evolution of the various coefficients. This number increases to 288 when including the robustness check by imposing the restrictions on the intercept terms in the system.

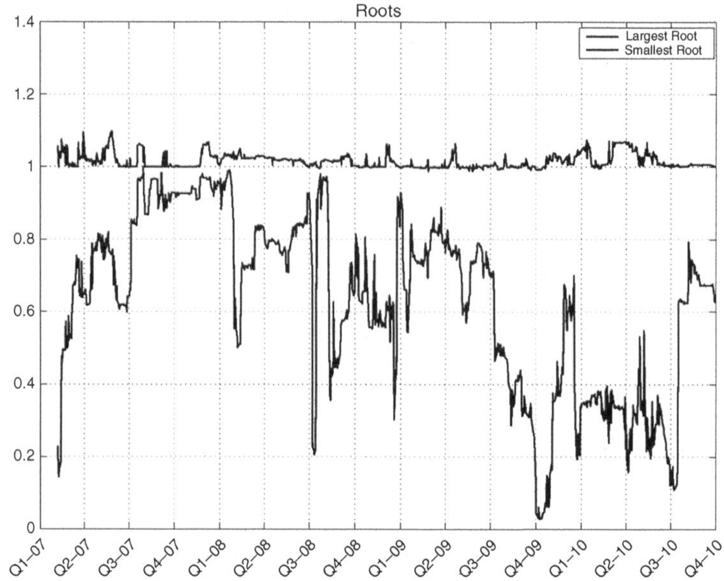

Note: The time varying roots are computed from the eigenvalues of the time varying matrix $\tilde{B}_t$. For each time iteration there are four roots; we plot the largest and smallest roots (upper and lower plot lines).

Figure 17.3 The time varying roots of the first order TV-VAR process for the 5 year model for Greece

A. Explosive Trends for Greece

The largest and smallest time varying roots of the slope coefficient matrix for the Greek model are presented in Figure 17.3. Several caveats need to be acknowledged when interpreting the roots. In a standard static coefficients set-up, the value of the largest root is indicative of the fundamental nature of the vector stochastic process. For instance, roots inside the unit circle indicate a covariance stationary process (that is, there is a long run mean value). Roots equal to one suggest the presence of at least one random walk in the vector process and as such the vector process is non-stationary. Roots greater than one suggest an explosive process which approaches infinity at a rate faster than a unit root process.[22]

[22] See for a discussion J.D. Hamilton *Time Series Analysis* (Princeton University Press, Princeton, NJ: 1994).

Given the nature of the interventions by the ECB and IMF in the Eurozone sovereign debt crisis, it would be expected that corrective actions would be implemented to prevent that explosive roots cause such extreme discounting that the par value of the sovereign debt would effectively fall toward zero (that is, infinite yield). Hence, a root above one for a given length of time indicates that the market has now completely priced in a substantial credit event as if it had already occurred.[23]

In contrast to the largest root, if the smallest root is close to zero, there is rank deficiency in the slope coefficients matrix. This indicates that certain variables are now redundant (that is, non-stochastic functions of each other). A negative root (less than negative one) indicates that one or more of the equations have a sinusoidal component that cycle the system either towards the stationary equilibria or, if the largest root is one, back to the stochastic trend driven by the one or more random walks in the system.

Figure 17.3 presents the evolution of the largest and smallest root for the slope coefficients for the 5-year model for Greece. The largest root is almost always above unity indicating the presence of an explosive trend. In particular, during the period from quarter 1 to 2, 2010 the roots are substantially above one. Its smallest root rises towards unity indicating that more than one root is at or above unity and the system is except explosive, that is, shocks are reinforced in the trend and drive it upwards (unlike a unit root or I(1) process), whether this is indicative of a genuine I(2) common explosive trend or a short lived quadratic deterministic trend is unclear. However, the result points to a failure in the price discovery mechanism as neither of these processes allows for standard arbitrage free pricing to exist in the market.

B. Information Transmission[24]

Figures 17.4 to 17.7 present the time evolution of the four equations of the Greek 5-year model. The four plots in Figure 17.4 present the coefficients for: (1) the credit spread from the bond market as a function of the lags

---

[23] In the context of substantial structural breaks in the slope coefficients of the VAR model, interpretation of the roots is less clear. A largest time varying root greater than one at time t indicates that if the process continues with this matrix of slope coefficients then the vector process will explode and rapidly approach infinity.

[24] In Calice, Chen and Williams, above, n. 15. Here we proceed to analyse in depth the models for Ireland, Portugal, France and Spain and we use a similar time variation in the information transmission between the CDS and bond markets.

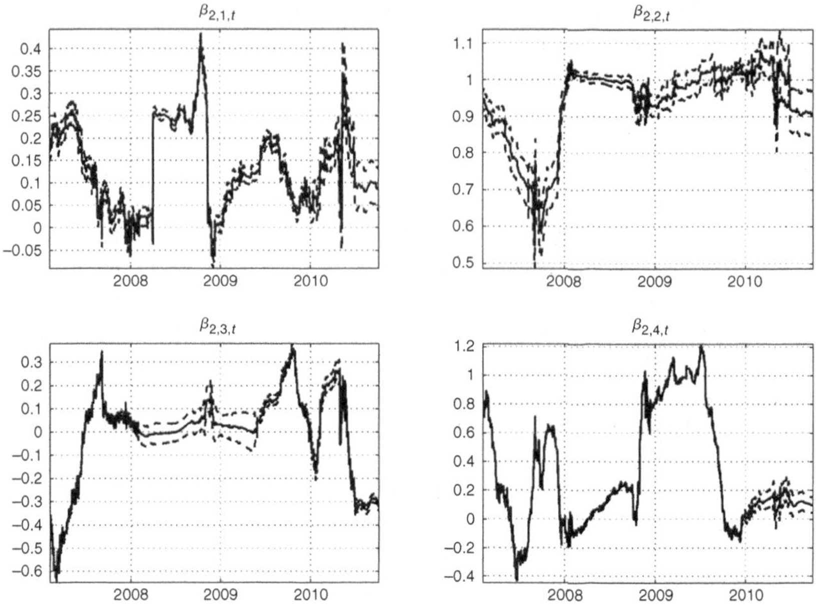

Note: Intercept coefficients are not plotted.

Figures 17.4–17.7 Time varying coefficients for the first equation for the co-evolution of credit and liquidity spreads for 5 year sovereign debt for Greece

of itself (the first coefficient of the first equation); (2) the lag of the credit spread from the CDS market (the second coefficient); (3) the lag of the liquidity spread of the bond market (the third coefficient); and (4) the lag of the liquidity spread of the CDS market, (the fourth coefficient).

The time evolution of the first coefficient illustrates the effectiveness of the RI-WLS in capturing the substantial and sudden changes in the coefficients over time, with periods of relative stability. For instance there is a gradual climb in the magnitude of the first coefficient from around 0.8 to 1 over 2007. In March 2008, when Bear Stearns was rescued, the coefficient plummets to around 0.6–0.7. At this point the TV-VAR loses traction in explaining the yield, the second, third and fourth coefficients are indistinguishable from zero. The first coefficient returns to a level just below unity before the end of 2008. The persistent explosive roots observed during 2010 are primarily a consequence of the fourth coefficient rising sharply from −0.4 to 0.4 and the third coefficient rising slightly less dramatically from −0.2 to around 0.3. This suggests that the liquidity of the CDS market is an important factor in explaining the explosive growth of the credit spreads for Greece (see Figure 17.4).

Figure 17.5 plots the time evolution of the coefficients for the credit spread from the sovereign CDS market of the 5-year Greek model. Note the opposite pattern for the lagged coefficient on the credit spread from the sovereign bond market. Our results clearly show a sharp rise around 2008 as the CDS market came under pressure following the demise of Bear Stearns, and banking credit spreads dispersed into the CDS markets.[25] The coefficient drops back to around 0.1 after the end of 2008, but is still quite volatile. The primary driver in the CDS equation is its own lag and the lag of its own liquidity spread; other than for a short period during early 2007.

Figure 17.6 plots the time varying coefficients for the liquidity spread on the bond market of the Greek 5-year model, as a function of the lags of itself and other variables. The first plot is the coefficient on the lag of the credit spread of the bond market. After March 2008 it rises substantially then falls just after quarter 3 of the same year.

The lag of the credit spread of the CDS market is found to be effectively insignificant for the entire sample period, except for a short period between March 2008 and the start of 2009, when it was marginally positive. The coefficient on the lag value of the liquidity spread of the bond market is high with an average of around 0.6. The most striking feature is the changing impact of the lag of the liquidity spread in the CDS market. The coefficient substantially changes, from between 1.5 and −2.5 over the whole of the 2008–09 period. As the explosive roots appear in late 2010, the coefficient settles to zero.

This finding is important for policy-makers. The liquidity and depth of the sovereign credit markets are critically important for the smooth and efficient functioning of international money markets. The evidence here suggests that the sovereign CDS market can have a substantial impact on the liquidity and transaction costs of the sovereign debt market. Furthermore, it is important to note that this effect can appear and vanish in a rapid manner. Thus, this compelling evidence lends support to the illiquidity spillover hypothesis, that is, that illiquidity in financial markets is contagious.[26]

---

25 See Calice, Chen and Williams, 'Are There Benefits To Being Naked: The Returns and Diversification Impact of Capital Structure Arbitrage' above, n. 7 for an analysis of this effect.

26 See, for instance, D.Y. Tang and H. Yan, 'Liquidity, liquidity spillover, and credit default swap spreads', Technical report, Kennesaw State University and University of South Carolina (2006).

The key conclusion is that without external intervention in the Greek sovereign debt market (that is, the effective 'imposition' of another structural break, through the stability mechanism) the explosive trend would continue until credit spreads rose to a critical level, at which point a default event would be triggered. Note also that recently haircuts on Greek sovereign debt have been reported to amount to up to 40 per cent. It is reasonable to assume that an efficiently functioning, deep and liquid market cannot operate in the presence of expected credit events of this magnitude. Furthermore, a reasonable question is 'has the sovereign CDS market destabilized the sovereign bond market?'

CONCLUSIONS AND DIRECTIONS FOR FUTURE WORK

In Calice, Chen and Williams,[27] we outlined an empirical model of cross liquidity and price discovery in parallel markets using a TV-VAR. We have used this model to elucidate the impact of cross liquidity effects on the Eurozone sovereign debt and CDS spreads during the Eurozone sovereign debt crisis.

We have documented three noteworthy findings. First, we have shown that explosive trends appeared during the sovereign crisis and that the CDS market does appear to have been a driver in most cases. Second, we have found a positive and significant lagged transmission from the liquidity spread of the CDS market (proxied by the bid-ask spread) to the credit spread in the bond market. Finally, we observe several variance breaks in the time varying models indicating that the noise structure inundating the VAR model changed markedly over the 2007–2010 period.

These findings indicate that: (a) static models would be uninformative and indeed biased when estimated over such a dataset; and (b) that the information structure of the sovereign credit market has undergone substantial and dramatic adjustments throughout the crisis period.

Future research could productively focus on analyzing potential spillover effects between countries, rather than simply the CDS versus the bond market for individual countries. We believe that the commonality in the time evolution of the coefficients for the various countries in the sample points towards this inter-country contagion.

27 Calice, Chen and Williams, above, n. 15.

Index